THE
NAZI
PARTY
COURTS

THE
NAZI
PARTY
COURTS

Hitler's Management of Conflict in His Movement, 1921-1945

by
DONALD M. McKALE

THE UNIVERSITY PRESS OF KANSAS
Lawrence/Manhattan/Wichita

Library of Congress Cataloging in Publication Data

McKale, Donald M., 1943-
  The Nazi party courts.

    1. Nationalsozialistische Deutsche Arbeiter-Partei. Oberstes Partei-
gericht. 2. Buch, Walter, 1883–. 3. Hitler, Adolf, 1889–1945. I. Title.
DD253.3.02M3   329.9'43   73-21906
ISBN 0-7006-0122-8

For my wife,
JANNA

Preface

SINCE THE CLOSE of the Second World War, scholars have meticulously examined the instruments of terror and coercion that characterized Hitler's brutal totalitarianism. The Gestapo, the SS, the concentration camps, and the "Special Courts" and "People's Courts" have received the greatest attention. But added to this awesome machinery of terror "justice" was a far less known—yet equally destructive—element within the National Socialist party organization: the party's internal judicial system, composed of *Parteigerichte* ("party courts"). The tasks of the Parteigerichte were chiefly constitutional. They were to protect the Nazi party by disciplining or expelling disobedient party members, by mediating dissension in the movement, and by banning from entrance into the party its sworn enemies such as Jews, Communists, and "liberals."

It is my objective in the pages that follow to portray the story of these perverted party tribunals. I especially hope to show how and why they developed from insignificant judicial committees established by Hitler in 1921 into institutions that became in the Third Reich bureaucratic mechanisms for intimidating and controlling party members. The courts, by purging from the movement members who disobeyed the orders of the party leadership, condemned such persons to the cruelties of social banishment, joblessness, and even prison.

Before 1933 the courts' expulsion of a party member meant little; however, following Hitler's appointment as German Chancellor, expulsion suddenly became a catastrophe for anyone ejected from the party. Contrary to the opinion of some scholars (for example, Martin Broszat, *Der Staat Hitlers: Grundlegung und Entwicklung seiner inneren Verfassung*, [Munich, 1969], p. 263), the Parteigerichte did possess "penal authority over freedom and life" of members of the Nazi party, and they frequently utilized that immense power.

All corporate institutions—whether social, political, economic, military, or religious in nature—possess certain methods for settling or suppressing internal conflict. The Nazi party was no exception. One of Hitler's preferred means for handling disagreements and strife in his movement was the Parteigerichte. During the *Kampfzeit* ("period of struggle," as the years 1919–1933 were called in the party), the courts were known as *Untersuchungs-* und *Schlichtungsausshüsse* ("investigation and conciliation committees"), shortened to *Uschla*.

Beginning in 1926 with Hitler's refounding of the party after the Munich Putsch and his imprisonment, one such Uschla was established at every administrative level of the movement. The entire system was supervised closely by Hitler and a *Reichs-Uschla* ("Supreme Court") headquartered in Munich. In November 1927 Hitler named as chairman of the Reichs-Uschla and the Uschlas an industrious and fanatical disciple from Baden, Walter Buch. Buch remained the party's nominal chief justice (subordinate to Hitler, of course) until the collapse of the Third Reich in 1945.

Above all, Buch masterfully built the Uschlas into a well-organized party judiciary that aided Hitler in a variety of ways. The Reichs-Uschla and its lower courts enabled the party chief both to encourage and to stifle conflict within the party, to pursue more effectively his clever intraparty tactic of "divide and rule," to control his subleaders by humiliating them (thereby increasing his own personal image among his followers), and finally, to govern the party by the powerful threat of expelling disobedient members. Prior to 1933 the Uschlas were involved in settling several major

viii

party feuds (for example, Goebbels versus Strasser, Kaufmann versus Pfeffer, and Dinter versus Sauckel), and were utilized in purging and disciplining the rebellious SA elements who followed Walter Stennes in 1931. Once in power, Hitler transformed the Uschlas into bona-fide "party courts," which were established as official legal institutions in the German state by the "Law for the Securing of the Unity of Party and State," decreed by the Reich government in December 1933. Under Buch's careful guidance, the tribunals rapidly became the "iron clamp" of the Nazi party, and their chief job was to ensure the organization's racial and political "unity." Any Nazi who refused to follow the orders of Hitler or the party leadership faced a grueling trial before the courts that could easily lead to his destruction—either in a concentration camp or as a rejected National Socialist existing in a totally Nazi-dominated society.

To guard the movement's racial "purity," for example, the party's Supreme Court in 1938 specifically ordered severe prison terms for party members found guilty of raping Jewish women and plundering Jewish property during the insane night of November 9–10. At the same time, however, the Court revealed its perverted sense of justice by excusing and acquitting members who had murdered Jews during the pogrom. Indeed, the Court's antiliberal and totalitarian philosophy dictated such decisions: the Nazi "community" was to come before the individual, and all that served the party (or Hitler) was to be promoted, while that which did not was to be ruthlessly destroyed. Throughout World War II, the Parteigerichte applied this philosophy more brutally than ever before to form their judgments and to ensure that all party members gave their bodies and souls to the war effort.

Few people could have guessed that the apparently insignificant Uschlas would mushroom after 1933 into a judicial system whose power was at times greater than that of the state, or public, judiciary. Yet, at the same time, the authority of the Parteigerichte was limited by the whims and orders of Hitler and his deputies, Rudolf Hess and Martin Bormann. Furthermore, the study of the courts offers an unusual look at the "two Germanies" under Hitler. First, the Parteigerichte records reveal that (despite Nazi propaganda) not every German and not every National Socialist was a fanatical follower of Hitler. Second, the same records show that the party possessed judges who were just as ruthless as members of the Gestapo and of the SS. Nowhere is the "good" and "bad" of Nazi Germany so vivid and shockingly distinct as in the documents of the Parteigerichte's proceedings.

I have also given considerable attention to the life and career of the party's chief justice, Buch. In many respects he was a typical National Socialist; he was an intense political activist, and his crude anti-Semitic ideology was what attracted him to Hitler and the Nazi party in 1921. Although his power as head of the party's judiciary was curtailed noticeably during World War II by Bormann, his son-in-law and leader of Hitler's party Chancellery, Buch nevertheless played a significant role in the party throughout the Third Reich. A special American mission sent to Germany in June 1945 to interrogate captured German leaders noted the following about Buch and his position in the movement: "Buch is therefore, in the last analysis, personally responsible for disciplinary measures taken within the Nazi Party. . . . Although he has not received the publicity that other Nazis holding comparable titles and posts have received, he is nevertheless one of the key men in the Party leadership because of his functions as the highest disciplinary authority after Hitler" (see the National Archives, Washington, D.C., Microcopy M-679, Roll 1/Frame 0216).

A few problems in studying such a limited aspect of the party's organization inevitably arose in the writing of the book, and these may need a brief explanation. The tendency was to treat the subject in a rather isolated and self-contained manner, without integrating it fully into its broader setting. Wherever possible, I have attempted to weave the history of the courts into the general framework of the party and to show how they were influenced by other party developments, and vice versa. I have also sought to organize the book so as to avoid a problem that was basically inherent in the subject: because of the nature of the courts, the cases that they handled, and the difficulties that they faced, the danger was present of producing a work that was somewhat static and repetitive. By structuring the study chronologically and by carefully choosing the cases that the courts dealt with, I hope I have successfully surmounted this obstacle and have spared the reader an undeserved agony.

The citations in the book that involve the party's official newspaper, the *Völkischer Beobachter*, should be clarified. For the Kampfzeit, the Munich edition of the paper was utilized; for the years after 1933, both the Munich and Berlin editions were consulted. Moreover, I have purposely cited full titles of some newspaper articles where I felt such citations would be useful evidence in themselves. The same inconsistency is present in the citing of original documents (for example, letters, orders, and other correspondence of the Supreme Court and the *Reichsleitung*, or party leadership). Some valuable documents stated briefly the subject of their contents, and in such instances I have given the original statements of subject as they appeared in the letters or official commands. Finally, the documentary collections that I used at the Bundesarchiv, Koblenz, which are cited as NS 22 and NS 26, are available on microfilm from the National Archives (T-580 collection) and the Hoover Institution at Stanford University (*NSDAP Hauptarchiv* collection), respectively.

This book could not have been written without the kind help and generous assistance of others. The idea for the study was first suggested to me in a graduate seminar on Nazi Germany conducted by an excellent teacher and scholar, Professor William S. Allen, now at the State University of New York, Buffalo. I sincerely thank him for his advice and suggestions. The research was made possible by grants from the Kent State University Graduate School and the Georgia College Faculty Research Committee, and several friends in the Federal Republic of West Germany helped me a great deal with their generosity.

For their helpful cooperation in locating and putting at my disposal the available source materials on Walter Buch and the Nazi party courts, I especially wish to thank Wheaton Byers and Mrs. Grohmann at the Berlin Document Center; Dr. Thilo Vogelsang of the Institut für Zeitgeschichte in Munich; the expert librarians at the Stadtbibliothek in Munich; and Miss Kinder and Mr. Schwartz of the Bundesarchiv in Koblenz. In addition, I would like to thank Robert Wolfe at the National Archives, Washington, D.C.; Gayle Peters, Archivist at the Federal Records Center, Atlanta, Georgia; and Charles Beard and the staff at the Georgia College Library.

I particularly wish to express gratitude to my former doctoral adviser and mentor at Kent State University, Professor Kenneth R. Calkins. Without his welcome encouragement and willingness to offer specific criticisms on style and organization, this study might well not exist at all. Further revisions of contents and stylistic comments were suggested by Professors Samuel M. Osgood, Henry N. Whitney, John Dreifort, Martin L. Abbott, and David Mead. Another colleague, Professor Everette N. Hong, encouraged me to study the concept of conflict management in business and political organizations. Whatever I may owe to these scholars for their help and advice, all errors of fact and judgment in the work are my responsibility.

I am also grateful to the editors of *Research Studies* (Washington State University) and *Jewish Social Studies* (Conference on Jewish Social Studies, New York) for permitting me to reprint portions of articles that I wrote initially for their publications.

Finally, a very special word of thanks to my wife, Janna, who labored infinitely harder than I during the past several years to help me carry the study to completion.

DONALD M. MCKALE

Milledgeville, Georgia
April 1973

Contents

Abbreviations

AO	Auslands-Organisation
BA	Bundesarchiv, Koblenz
BAZ	*Berliner Arbeiterzeitung*
BDC	Berlin Document Center, Berlin
DAF	Deutsche Arbeitsfront
DAP	Deutsche Arbeiterpartei
DNVP	Deutschnationale Volkspartei
DSP	Deutsch-Sozialistische Partei
DV	*Deutsche Volkszeitung*
DVO	Deutscher Vaterländischer Orden
DVP	Deutsche Volkspartei
FT	*Fränkische Tageszeitung*
GDVG	Grossdeutsche Volksgemeinschaft
Gestapo	Geheime Staatspolizei
GL	Gauleiter, Gauleitung
GRUSA	Grundsätzliche Anordnungen der SA
HJ	Hitler-Jugend
IfZ	Institut für Zeitgeschichte, Munich
IMT	International Military Tribunal, *Trial of Major War Criminals* (Nuremberg, 1947–1949)
KPD	Kommunistische Partei Deutschlands
MP	*Münchener Post*
NA	National Archives, Washington, D.C.
NS	Nationalsozialistische
NSAG	Nationalsozialistische Arbeitsgemeinschaft

NSBO	Nationalsozialistische Betriebszellenorganisation
NSDAP	Nationalsozialistische Deutsche Arbeiterpartei
NSDStB	Nationalsozialistischer Deutscher Studentenbund
NSKK	Nationalsozialistische Kraftfahrer-Korps
NSKOV	Nationalsozialistische Kriegsopferversorgung
NSV	Nationalsozialistische Volkswohlfahrt
O.Gr.	Ortsgruppe
Ogrl.	Ortsgruppenleiter, Ortsgruppenleitung
OPG	Oberstes Parteigericht, or Supreme Court of the NSDAP, 1933–1945
Osaf	Oberster SA-Führer
OSAF	Oberste SA-Führung
PK	Parteikorrespondenz
RDB	Reichsbund der Deutschen Beamten
Reichs-Uschla	Uschla at the Reichsleitung level, or the Supreme Court of the NSDAP, 1925–1933
RFSS	Reichsführer SS
RG	Record Group
RGBl	*Reichsgesetzblatt*
RL	Reichsleitung
SA	Sturmabteilung
SABE	SA-Befehl
SD	Sicherheitsdienst
Sipo	Sicherheitspolizei
Slg. Schu.	*Sammlung Schumacher*
SPD	Sozialdemokratische Partei Deutschlands
SS	Schutzstaffeln
Uschla	Untersuchungs- und Schlichtungsausschuss, Investigation and Conciliation Committee
VB	*Völkischer Beobachter*
VOBl	*Verordnungsblatt der Reichsleitung der Nationalsozialistischen Deutschen Arbeiter-Partei*

1

Introduction: Hitler and the Settlement of Conflict in His Party

MANAGING OR RESOLVING CONFLICT has been crucial to organizations and institutions throughout history. Rarely have institutions failed to handle their internal problems, and yet survived and achieved their goals. As random examples of "political" organizations that became (to a greater or lesser degree) casualties of conflict and strife, one could note Marx's International Workingmen's Association, the Chartist movement in England, the Communist party and National People's party in Weimar Germany, the American Populist party, and the recent Students for a Democratic Society.

Today, most major organizations (whether political in nature or otherwise) possess specific methods for managing internal conflict. The following, for example, have judicial systems designed to handle disagreements among employees or members: the Roman Catholic Church, large American corporations and unions, and agencies of the American federal government (including the army and navy). In addition, the Central Committee of the Soviet Communist Party organizes a "Party Control Committee," which "calls to account Communists guilty of violating the Party Program and Statutes or Party and state discipline, as well as violators of Party ethics."[1]

The National Socialist German Workers' Party (Na-

1

tionalsozialistische Deutsche Arbeiterpartei, or NSDAP) was a mass political organization that possessed its share of conflict and disruption, especially during the party's stormy rise to power in the Weimar Republic. The party's unchallenged leader *(Führer)* and dictator, Adolf Hitler, employed a variety of techniques for handling strife in the movement. Some of Hitler's tactics for controlling his organization have been studied in detail by scholars, particularly his personal and "unofficial" methods of resolving quarrels among his subleaders and suppressing opposition to his absolute authority.

Far less known and studied has been the NSDAP's "official" mechanism for dealing with its internal strife—the party's judiciary, which was composed of the so-called party courts *(Parteigerichte)* that were initially created by Hitler in July 1921.[2] Although the Nazi party has been represented by most historians and political scientists as the modern world's classic example of a totalitarian movement, the party was surprisingly democratic and liberal in the elaborate system it established to offer its members a reasonable opportunity to defend themselves against accusations by fellow members and a means for recourse against unjust actions by party leaders.

Above all, the Parteigerichte provided due process and appeal opportunities for all National Socialists, and the tribunals (particularly after 1929) operated according to strict investigation and trial procedures. However, the presence of good procedures did not guarantee that the courts would rule fairly or equitably. They were mainly bureaucratic instruments of control that were designed to manage (or suppress where necessary) conflict to the advantage of Hitler and the party's leaders.

Reflecting his passionate disdain for the functions of law and the operation of courts in general, Hitler never hesitated to ignore the rulings of his Parteigerichte if they disagreed with him. Unfortunately, such behavior was hardly confined to party law. After January 1933 and Hitler's being commissioned German Chancellor, the same Nazi contempt for law and liberalism spread to become the basis

2

for the creation of the frightening People's Courts *(Volksgerichte)* and the "protective custody" *(Schutzhaft)* employed by the police to overturn the decisions of the regular civil courts. It was in this manner that the major philosophical principles that first served as the foundation for the Parteigerichte eventually became fundamental to all of Germany in the Third Reich.

The party courts, of course, offered definite advantages to the personal image of Hitler, the man worshiped fanatically by Nazi party members as Germany's national hero and savior. With his official party commands of 25 April 1928 and 18 March 1933, the Parteigerichte were supposedly to stand above individual Nazis and even Hitler himself. However, the tribunals and their judges were in no way autonomous organizations; they were instead dominated completely by Hitler and his top lieutenants.

Thus, under the authority of prestigious judicial bodies, the Nazi leader was particularly able to enforce numerous decisions that were unpopular in the NSDAP while simultaneously maintaining a remarkable anonymity. The Parteigerichte enabled Hitler, in short, to avoid involving himself personally when he resolved differences among his subleaders or between party organizations. Furthermore, these courts permitted him to transform his own wishes into binding party policy under the signature of institutions that appeared to transcend individual persons. This carefully veiled power prevented his unpopular rulings from affecting adversely his greatest personal asset—his image as the unchallenged, "superman" Führer-figure of the Nazi party and, later, Germany.[3]

As has been noted often, this was a myth not without considerable importance in explaining Hitler's success in the NSDAP. When it came to handling strife in the party, he possessed an innate talent for utilizing several clever techniques to assert his authority and dominate his lieutenants. He employed such tactics from the beginning of his political career until his defeat and death in 1945. At every opportunity the Führer utilized his magnetic and dynamic personality to overpower his subleaders or to get people to believe in him; above all, he believed fanatically in himself. In his view, it was his mission to rebuild Germany from the chaos of World War I and the Versailles *Diktat* and to save her from total destruction by communism, liberalism, and the world Jewish "conspiracy." Relying on this mythical image (which, however, was very real to his followers), he made himself the focal point of unity in the NSDAP and made his favor the prize for which all party leaders competed vigorously. Factions in the movement strove not to overthrow him but to capture his support for their views; consequently, he could never be challenged, only claimed. Nazi party members, lacking a solid ideology or dogma such as Marxism to rally around, always found themselves gravitating helplessly toward the man who had succeeded in identifying the "idea" of National Socialism with his own charismatic person.[4]

Few of Hitler's party leaders agreed with Hermann Rauschning that the Führer was a timid and dependent individual.[5] The party's long-time office manager and most lackluster bureaucrat, Philip Bouhler, described Hitler as a "born organizer with the greatest of style" who produced a "strong central power" for Germany.[6] Otto Dietrich—Hitler's loyal press chief, who often fought with Joseph Goebbels and the Nazi newspaper czar, Max Amann, over propaganda—was convinced of his leader's powerful personality: "Over this new Germany of discipline and authority rules no emperor or king, no despot or tyrant: the Third Reich will be governed by the power of [Hitler's] personality."[7] The same repetitive adulation and fanatical worship of the man came from every party leader—Goebbels, Hermann Göring, and Walter Buch (the head of the Parteigerichte), to mention several.[8]

Another factor that contributed to Hitler's mythical image among his followers was his obvious aloofness from everyday party affairs. As early as 1928 he was rarely seen by his national party leaders, and he was completely inaccessible to the average Nazi.[9] The only persons assured of being able to spend lengthy periods alone with him were his pri-

4

vate secretaries (or deputies), Rudolf Hess and Martin Bormann. Administration and systematic work bored Hitler, and he consequently left as much as he could to his trusted lieutenants and their bureaucratic empires. The situation naturally worsened with his success. After 1933 his party leaders in Munich saw him as infrequently as did his government leaders in Berlin. Once in power, he flitted restlessly between Munich, Berlin, and his beloved Berchtesgaden, and he never stayed in one place too long. Thus, he became a sort of "phantom" administrator whose presence and handshake meant nearly as much as life itself to his subordinates.

Added to his personal charisma, his power over the NSDAP rested on a firm legal and constitutional foundation. The party's official statutes *(Satzung)* of July 1921 and May 1926 (drafted by Hitler and accepted by the Munich members) gave him dictatorial control and made him the party's "first chairman." The latter set of guidelines was not abandoned until 1936. The statutes solidly established the famous leadership principle *(Führerprinzip)* as the party's central organizational feature. The chain of command under the Führerprinzip was strictly authoritarian in nature: theoretically, Hitler's word was law, and the law was to be dispensed downward through the various subleaders and then returned upward, with each leader and his organization faithfully executing the Führer's order. In practice, Hitler's power was limited by a number of factors, not the least of which was the ability, thoroughness, and loyalty of those who carried out his commands. On the other hand, it was partly to offset the limits on his authority and to ensure the development of the Führerprinzip that the Nazi party established the Parteigerichte.[10]

As has often been noted, a habit in Hitler's decision-making as German Chancellor was his endless hesitation and seeming unwillingness (whether deliberate or otherwise) to make crucial decisions until the last moment. Such hesitation was just as frequently discernible in his managing of intraparty conflict. Where it best suited his own tactical or personal interests, he was prone to let a quarrel between his

5

subleaders drag on for months. Goebbels's hassle with the Strasser brothers was allowed to continue for three years (1927–1930), and the discontent that began to form in 1930 around Walter Stennes and the Berlin storm troopers (*Sturmabteilung*, or SA) remained uninvestigated and unsettled until a mutiny in the SA actually broke in April 1931. The same procrastination by the Führer was what spared the life of Ernst Röhm for a few extra months in 1934.

Some have seen in Hitler's vacillation a deliberate attempt to apply the tactic of "divide and rule" in managing party conflict and manipulating his followers. By refusing to make quick and firm decisions, it is argued, he purposely encouraged strife in the party and set himself up as the unchallenged *arbiter supremus* for his quibbling subordinates.[11] While this is certainly not implausible, it is also probable that Hitler's leadership corps would have been beset with petty conflict whether the Führer encouraged it or not.

Functionaries at all levels of the Nazi party were aggressive and egotistical personalities who had given their souls to a movement that demanded their absolute conformity. Most of them stemmed from a petty German bourgeoisie whose "collective consciousness" (if one may use that nebulous phrase) revolved mainly around a deep socioeconomic insecurity and a frustrated sense of self-importance. Totally banished from decision-making in major party policy, these "little men with big ideas" tended to quibble over irrelevant and frivolous matters in order to compensate for their lack of authority. To satisfy their need or desire to feel important, in other words, ranking Nazi officials argued or disagreed with one another, but rarely did they attack their mythical leader-figure, Hitler.

Another explanation for the personal strife that characterized the NSDAP was the sharp socioeconomic and political heterogeneity of the movement. In addition, the early development of the party organization was complicated by the challenge from its radical military arm, the SA. Within the party's leadership hierarchy, persons from nearly every walk of life could be found: farmers (Heinrich Himmler,

Walter Darre, Bormann), retired military officers (Göring, Röhm, Buch, Bruno Heinemann, Franz von Pfeffer, Franz von Epp), teachers (Julius Streicher, Bernhard Rust, Arthur Dinter, Wilhelm Kube, Josef Wagner), engineers (Gottfried Feder), architects (Alfred Rosenberg, Albert Speer), lawyers (Hans Frank, Helmut Nicolai), civil servants (Wilhelm Frick), labor-union officials (Albert Krebs), factory owners (Martin Mutschmann), pharmacists (Gregor Strasser), journalists (Otto Strasser, Dietrich, Walter Funk), authors (Hitler, Goebbels), chemists (Robert Ley), and commercial employees (Hess, Amann, Franz Xavier Schwarz, Karl Kaufmann, Hinrich Lohse), to name a few.

When it came to political philosophy, the leadership spanned a vast spectrum, from the extreme authoritarian and racial conservatism of many middle-class Germans to the socialism and liberalism of the urban workers in the larger cities. Such striking differences were similarly reflected in the rank and file. In general, the NSDAP appealed to the middle classes—namely, small-scale farmers, small-town shopkeepers, white-collar employees, and professional people. However, with Hitler claiming to represent the will of all Germans and to act as their long-awaited messiah, the movement attempted (in opportunistic fashion) to attract urban workers, industrial barons, and well-to-do farmers.[12]

Thus, a major problem for Hitler became one of harnessing together and uniting this mass conglomeration of subleaders and members, thereby molding an effective organization that could help him seize and retain what he coveted most—political power. Among his secrets in this respect were his charismatic personality and the mythical aura surrounding his person that he was able to create among his followers. Another weapon upon which he relied heavily (particularly after 1925) was the Parteigerichte. Where his law could not be enforced on his disciples through the mesmerizing effect of his captivating personality, these courts became his bureaucratic trump card. Once a party leader or member refused to accept Hitler as a myth-person or to follow party orders, he was quickly and ruthlessly expelled from the movement.

Beyond hesitating to settle conflicts, Hitler possessed an uncanny ability to convince his subordinates that they should "unite" for the "common good" of the NSDAP, forgetting their own personal interests. Unless a quarrel (either personal or organizational in nature) involved a clear case of party policy, he rarely decreed an unequivocal judgment in the matter, and he attempted to give some satisfaction to everyone concerned. Like a master administrator, he frequently played quarreling antagonists against one another by telling each what he wanted to hear.[13] He hardly confined the tactic to mediating party discord, however; the same principle dominated his propaganda addresses to the German people.[14]

Hitler was also not above purposely humiliating his subordinates to retain their loyalty and to punish or discipline them. If a favored party leader erred by bringing disgrace to the NSDAP through his personal behavior, the Führer merely slapped the sinner's hands and ordered him to beg his lord and master's forgiveness.[15] Yet, simultaneously, the chief could be terrifyingly cold and ruthless with quarrelers who threatened the smooth functioning of the party by feuding. In most instances, he called the antagonists together and "commanded" them to solve their differences immediately (if not sooner).[16] In February 1926 he decisively moved to crush a group of northern party leaders (led by Gregor Strasser and Goebbels) that he believed was endangering his position as party dictator. However, since only a small percentage of the strife was significant enough to threaten the party or its leader, such cases were rare.

Far more typical was Hitler's practice of settling conflicts through other party leaders and agencies. During the *Kampfzeit* ("period of struggle," or the years preceding 1933), he preferred to rely on the Parteigerichte or on special emissaries sent from the national party leadership *(Reichsleitung)* in Munich to handle dissension. On various occasions, celebrities like Strasser, Hermann Esser, and Feder were dispatched to a local group *(Ortsgruppe)* or district organization *(Gau)* that was experiencing difficulties. Similarly, the chairmen of the Parteigerichte—Buch and his predecessor, Bruno Heinemann—were utilized as troubleshooters; and during the Stennes revolt of 1931 and the party-sponsored anti-Jewish riots in 1938, Hitler gave Göring (his heir apparent until the Second World War) the unenviable task of working with the Parteigerichte to restore order in the movement.[17] By "using" others (whom he controlled like puppets) to settle conflict, Hitler was able both to keep himself further removed from petty bickering and quarreling and to draw dissatisfaction with unpopular decisions away from himself.

To implement his personal techniques for managing subleaders and to relieve himself of the administrative drudgery associated with settling conflicts, Hitler created in July 1921 two subcommittees in the NSDAP that were later to become the Parteigerichte. Having just wrested complete control over the movement away from its cofounder, Anton Drexler, the power-hungry Bohemian began quickly to consolidate his authority as party chairman and to build the party into an instrument through which he might someday overthrow the democratic Weimar regime that he passionately detested.

Hitler's wildest ambition, of course, was to capture political power in Germany for himself. Since the autumn of 1919 he had helped to transform Drexler's old German Workers' Party (Deutsche Arbeiterpartei, or DAP) from a tiny political club that met in musty Munich beer halls into the moderately large NSDAP, which had local affiliates outside the Bavarian capital and utilized such tactics as noisy propaganda rallies to attract new members. Yet, his real dream for the organization involved something much larger. He later noted that "through just such a little movement," he had always believed that "the rise of the nation could some day be organized."[18]

The subcommittees that Hitler established to tighten his grip over the NSDAP were the Investigation Committee

(Untersuchungs-Ausschuss) and the Conciliation Committee *(Schlichtungs-Ausschuss)*, whose specific organizational functions were outlined by the party statutes of 29 July 1921. According to the guidelines, the Investigation Committee was to consist of a chairman and two assistants. Obviously intended by Hitler to be an intraparty "policing instrument," its functions were to examine all applications for party membership, issue orders for the expulsion of rebellious members and locals, and form an "Information Service" in the movement. As an example of the significance that Hitler personally attached to the committee, the statutes granted him complete authority to appoint or remove its members as he wished. To underscore its importance even further, he modestly named himself chairman of the committee.[19]

The Conciliation Committee was the chairman's board of mediation for handling cases of personal strife or dissension. Somewhat less prominent than the Investigation Committee, the Conciliation Committee nevertheless had as its head the cofounder of the movement, Drexler. Hitler's idea for both committees came from his tour of duty in the army in World War I, and he established them to operate as judicial (that is, appeal) institutions and to perform the same basic functions as the "courts of honor" of the old officer corps in the army.[20]

Above all, the historical significance of the committees was their eventual consolidation by Hitler at the beginning of 1926 to form the system of party courts (that is, *Untersuchungs- und Schlichtungsausschuss*, or the *Uschla*). Their immediate value to the party, however, was limited by Hitler's general disdain for organizational and administrative work, and particularly for work done by committees or other bureaucratic groups. For him such groups were a "necessary evil." He was convinced that the only thing that was absolutely necessary for a successful political movement was a charismatic leader-figure who was responsible only to the masses (and not to committees or other organizational groups). To be sure, Hitler never discouraged his party followers from becoming actively involved in the daily work of the movement. He was merely suspicious of committees, and he believed that such institutions produced organizational paralysis and that they infringed on his authority.[21] It was hardly surprising, therefore, that the most functional of the two committees was the Investigation Committee, headed by Hitler himself. Its work centered primarily around purging disobedient Nazis and developing the party's Information Service. Although the committee was supposedly bound to operate according to the party statutes, it acted solely at Hitler's pleasure. Each expulsion or ruling was decreed as a "unanimous decision of the party" *(einstimmigen Parteibeschluss)*, and the committee's authority extended to the Munich leadership and the party's increasing number of Ortsgruppen outside the Bavarian capital. For example, when Otto Dickel, a leading member of the Augsburg Ortsgruppe, published a book in late 1921 "contradicting" the "tendencies" of the NSDAP, the committee expelled him.[22]

The Investigation Committee also busied itself with creating a department for collecting party information and memorabilia. Hitler, as he was to do on a greater scale during the Third Reich, ordered the establishment in September 1921 of a party archive. The archive was organized by the committee; and from members of the Munich and surrounding Ortsgruppen it gathered copies of party placards, pamphlets, propaganda brochures, press releases for party meetings, photographs, and membership certificates.[23]

To tighten his control further, Hitler made numerous changes in the NSDAP's leadership by moving his own human instruments into key administrative posts. There is little question that he possessed a special knack for elevating to positions of leadership men who would remain his loyal and obedient disciples and would identify themselves completely with his views. Dietrich Eckart, his "intellectual father" and one who suffered from too much eating and especially drinking, took full command of the party's propaganda organ, the *Völkischer Beobachter*. To be head of the

11

party's propaganda department (which Hitler had formerly led), Hitler named the vulgar and immoral Jew-baiter Esser. Until his Munich Putsch in 1923, he carefully expanded the organization of the party and intensified the role of propaganda in order to recruit new members and locals throughout Bavaria and western Germany.

Other cronies who landed vital offices were Amann (the party's new secretary), Bouhler (publications salesman for the *Völkischer Beobachter*), and Schwarz (treasurer). Finally, Hitler counted among his devoted followers several noted political figures in Munich: Röhm, a homosexual *Reichswehr* ("army") officer who had introduced Hitler to numerous influential military and political leaders in Bavaria; Rosenberg, an anti-Semitic and *völkisch* philosopher from the Baltic; and Feder, a self-proclaimed economic expert who wanted to do away with "big money" and high "Jewish finance."[24]

Apart from Hitler's creeping dictatorship, this was also the crucial formative period of the SA, an institution that was eventually to come into direct conflict with the party organization, particularly with the Parteigerichte. Organized along military lines and encouraged strongly by Hitler, the Brown Shirts became a virtual party army by 1922; they carried rubber truncheons and often pistols to protect Nazi meetings, and they brawled in the streets with Socialists and other opponents of the NSDAP. The SA frequently participated in joint military maneuvers with other paramilitary and "free corps" groups in the völkisch movement, and it even received the cooperation of officials of the Bavarian Reichswehr and of the Munich police. By encouraging such a party army (and later the *Schutzstaffeln* ["Protection Squads," whose members wore black shirts], or SS, which remained subordinate to the SA until July 1934), Hitler was already beginning to make force and terror equally as important as propaganda and mass meetings in his strategy to conquer Germany.[25]

Along with solidifying his dictatorship, founding new locals, and creating a quasi-military shock troop, Hitler moved increasingly during 1922 and 1923 to persuade other radical völkisch organizations to join his movement. The NSDAP was only one of many predominantly middle-class, anti-Semitic, and extreme nationalist groups on the far right (especially in Bavaria) that shared not only a similar political ideology but a common hostile attitude toward the political situation in Germany.[26] To most, the Weimar Republic was an illegitimate government, which was controlled by Jews, Bolsheviks, and other "German" enemies who sought to keep the nation weak and divided and thus to perpetuate the humiliation it had suffered at the hands of the Western democracies in World War I.

Hitler's attempt to woo his völkisch partners into the Nazi fold was only moderately successful. He was unable to convince the large Deutschvölkischer Schutz- und Trutzbund ("German Racist League for Defense and Attack") and free corps units like the Bund Bayern und Reich ("League for Bavaria and the Reich"), the Bund Oberland ("The Highland's League") and the Reichskriegsflagge ("War Flag of the Reich") to join his party; but in December 1922 he did succeed in attracting the formal support of the less significant German Socialist Party (Deutsch-Sozialistische Partei, or DSP). A month later the first national congress *(Reichsparteitag)* of the NSDAP was held in Munich,[27] and in the spring of 1923 Hitler was chosen to head a new far-right organization in Bavaria known as the Kampfbund ("Militant Association"). The Kampfbund was composed of a number of völkisch and free-corps groups (for example, the Bayern und Reich, the Reichskriegsflagge, and the NSDAP), which had formed a loose political coalition with the hope of hastening the overthrow of the Republic and then establishing a strong authoritarian rightist government in its place.[28]

By the autumn of 1923 Hitler had succeeded in convincing himself that the destruction of the Republic and the seizure of power by the extreme right could no longer be achieved solely through his own abilities and the organizational strength of his Bavarian-centered party (whose membership had grown to fifty-five thousand).[29] Instead, he now believed the Weimar system could be toppled only by illegal means—that is, by a daring, armed insurrection carried out by his SA and other rightist groups in Bavaria (for example, the Kampfbund) and promoted by sympathetic Reichswehr and Bavarian government officials. By the late summer, in fact, a joint conspiracy began to unfold among the far-right elements in Bavaria to smash by violence the *Reich* ("national") government in Berlin and replace it with a völkisch-military dictatorship.

Helping to fan the flames of the conspiracy and Hitler's own plans for a bold uprising was the slowly developing political and economic crisis in the nation. Inflation, the old economic bugaboo inherited by Germany from World War I, was assuming ruinous proportions at the beginning of 1923. The French military occupation of the Ruhr in January also presented the Republic with a serious danger. Yet this was only the beginning; in October, attempted Communist revolutions shook the states of Saxony and Thuringia, and the Bavarian government openly demanded the resignation of the Reich government.

Thus, to the impatient Hitler, it appeared that the time was ripe for a daring "march on Berlin" (as some Nazis termed it, with reference to Mussolini's successful "march on Rome" a year earlier) to rid Germany of the democratic regime that he and his fellow travelers on the far right so vigorously denounced. Furthermore, he was driven toward violence by restless SA members in his own movement. He feared that if he failed to act quickly, he might lose considerable support from such elements and be forced to watch a golden opportunity for power slip from his grasp.

Such was the background to his famed Putsch of 8–9 November 1923 in Munich. In an emotional speech to his followers on the evening of the eighth in the Bürgerbräukeller beer hall, he launched the coup by declaring a national revolution. Together with his coconspirators, he planned to win the support of the Bavarian authorities and the Reichswehr, capture Munich, and then move northward to Berlin with an armed force of SA, Kampfbund, and other rightist units. However, as most students of history know, the Putsch failed. Instead of capturing the German government, Hitler quickly found himself slapped with a prison term. At the last moment the army and the Bavarian authorities decided against supporting the insurrection, thereby ensuring its total collapse. On November 9 the planned march on Berlin and national revolution were abruptly halted by the hail of gunfire that fatally wounded sixteen SA men before the Feldherrnhalle in Munich. Hitler, who had decided to proceed on his own despite the loss of support from his allies in the Bavarian government, was forced to flee for his life when the shooting began, only to be captured a few days later, tried in a Munich court, and sentenced to prison at the fortress at Landsberg.[30]

There is little doubt that the Putsch had the effect of gaining for Hitler more adherents in the völkisch movement and greater publicity on a national scale.[31] In addition, its failure provided him with a valuable learning experience politically and a crucial lesson for the future organizational growth of his party. Above all, Hitler discovered that the road to power was not through the SA and armed illegality but through the development of a highly bureaucratized and loyal party that could work legally to propagandize his message and undermine the authority of the Weimar government. Moreover, the Putsch taught Hitler to trust only himself and his own party; in the future, he would refuse to ally with his völkisch sympathizers and would avoid placing himself in a position that was dependent on others.

In this respect the Putsch and its aftermath formed the background for the growth of Hitler's organizational and administrative abilities—talents that he had thus far failed to exploit effectively. It also set the stage from which the party's court system was to emerge and blossom into a ruthless judiciary bent on cementing together the diverging groups in the NSDAP, fostering a new law for Nazis, and contributing toward Hitler's political resurrection. With varying degrees of success the system was to achieve each goal.

15

2

Reconstructing
the Party, 1925-1927

WHEN HITLER RETURNED from prison to pick up the pieces of his shattered movement, one of his starting points was to create several new administrative institutions such as the Parteigerichte. He was well aware that the NSDAP had to be rebuilt and refashioned into a totally disciplined and devoted political machine. The courts, or the Uschlas, were in part the offspring of the massive chaos that engulfed the party in 1924 and 1925.

After the Putsch the party was swiftly banned in Bavaria and the rest of the Reich (except Thuringia); and with its hero, incarcerated at Landsberg, deliberately renouncing any affiliation with the organization, it collapsed and dissolved itself in petty factionalism. Thus, when he was granted an early parole and was released in December 1924, Hitler faced the apparently impossible task of reconstructing the party from scratch and bringing it once again under his authoritarian thumb.

In addition to the ban, the party was riddled with personal conflicts and divisions arising from the unexpected failure of the Putsch and from Hitler's own careful encouragement of such disunity while in his prison cell. During his sojourn at Landsberg, he cleverly inspired dissension among his highest lieutenants by officially renouncing his leadership of the party in July 1924 and by refusing to have any open contact with its members. Much to his satisfaction, his refusal to involve himself in the quarrels of his successors only increased their rivalries and yet kept him the focal point of unity among the different factions that emerged from the ruins of the old party.

One faction, which labeled itself the Greater German People's Community (Grossdeutsche Volksgemeinschaft, or GDVG), centered around Hitler's cronies from Munich and the surrounding areas of Bavaria: Esser, Rosenberg, Bouhler, Schwarz, and Julius Streicher. Streicher, who had joined Hitler in October 1922, was head of the Nazi Ortsgruppe in Nuremberg and was the publisher of an incredibly crude anti-Semitic paper called *Der Stürmer*.[1] The other major group was a more parliamentary-oriented organization established in northern Germany, the Freiheitsbewegung ("Freedom Party"), led by Röhm and the talented *Reichstag* ("German national legislature") deputy and Hitler sympathizer Gregor Strasser. Both factions claimed to have Hitler's unqualified blessing, but neither in fact possessed this cherished prize.[2]

To complicate matters even more, the official propaganda organ of the NSDAP, the *Völkischer Beobachter*, was banned in much of the country. Moreover, if membership figures meant anything, the record of the party was hardly impressive. Since the Putsch and the party's dissolution, its rolls had dropped over 50 percent, and its greatest attraction—Hitler himself—was officially barred from speaking in most states, including Bavaria and Prussia.[3] In the north and west, Hitler found on his release that he had lost considerable influence among members. Many living in the more industrialized areas of the north took the "socialism" part of National Socialism seriously, and they looked particularly to Gregor Strasser for leadership in the party. The situation facing Hitler after the Putsch was described thus by Röhm: "The entire völkisch movement lay in a deep crisis, disunited, split, group against group, defense league against party, leader against leader, a picture of disaffection and disruption."[4]

Adding to the party's troubles was the improved political and economic picture of the nation. By the beginning of 1925 the political situation of the Republic had stabilized considerably. After the presidential elections in the spring, the Reich government sported a president who was a nationally respected military figure and war hero, Field Marshal von Hindenburg. Unfortunately for the Nazis, Hindenburg's leadership tended to create a political climate unfriendly to a party that had always depended on political resentment and had worked for the destruction of the Republic in order to attract members. Economically the picture had turned against extremist parties; the rampant inflation of several years earlier had been halted, unemployment was leveling off, and wages and salaries were slowly increasing. Testifying to the sad fortunes of the NSDAP, the presidential candidate supported by the party in March, General Ludendorff, received barely one-half of one percent of all the votes cast.[5]

It was obvious, therefore, that if Hitler was ever to counter this dismal situation and transform the NSDAP into a significant power factor nationally, he would have to reconstruct and improve the party's organization. Without question, he still saw in the party a means to win power for himself. Yet he realized that if he was to instill in the movement what he had learned from his recent failures, he had to recapture and reconsolidate his own authority and that of the Munich Ortsgruppe over the entire party. Only then could he reestablish Munich's supremacy and develop an effective bureaucratic organization that could extend his power over all party leaders, employees, and members.

His first step toward the realization of his plans was a hard-fisted appeal for unity published at the end of February in the newly liberated *Völkischer Beobachter*. Appearing in the edition were new *Richtlinien* ("directives") for "refounding" the movement, and these also emphasized that the immediate task of the party leadership was to achieve the stability of unity. The paper also proudly announced that the ban on the party had been temporarily lifted in Bavaria

19

and that on the evening of February 27 in Munich, Hitler would speak publicly for the first time since the Putsch.[6] The address, attended by four thousand captivated listeners (among them the leaders of the now defunct GDVG and the Freedom Party), was held in the Bürgerbräukeller, the scene of Hitler's speech on the night of 8 November 1923. Appearing to his strife-torn disciples as the "resurrected messiah," come to unify and lead them to the "promised land," Hitler ceremoniously used the assembly to "refound" the NSDAP. Lecturing on the theme "Germany's Future and Our Movement," he left little doubt about his own role in the "new" party. Never given to possession of the vices of moderation and democratic compromise, he informed those present that he alone would command the movement and that "no one" would tell him how to do the job.[7]

To aid in rebuilding the movement, Hitler needed human "tools" in the party's national leadership in Munich and in the Gau organizations. As *Amtsleiter* ("department chiefs") in the Munich office, he quickly named several long-time lackeys who could be trusted completely to execute his orders like machines: Bouhler as office manager, Rosenberg and Amann to be in charge of the *Völkischer Beobachter* and the party's central publishing firm in Munich (Eher Verlag), and Schwarz as treasurer. To increase his authority, particularly in the north, Hitler commissioned as *Gauleiters* ("Gau leaders") several other trusted underlings—Robert Ley (Rhineland-South), Hinrich Lohse (Schleswig-Holstein), Ernst Schlange (Berlin), Martin Mutschmann (Saxony), Joseph Klant (Hamburg), Franz von Pfeffer (Westphalia), and Arthur Dinter (Thuringia). Above all, the Gau and its Gauleiter were to be the bureaucratic pillars of Hitler's new organization, tying together Munich and the party's Ortsgruppen and serving as Hitler's personal agents in centralizing the NSDAP's power structure. The Gauleiter was to win his Gau for the party through relentless propaganda and the creation of new Ortsgruppen, and it was his task to supervise all work in his Gau according to the program and aims of the NSDAP and according to orders of the Reichs-leitung.[8]

Hitler's appointment of totally loyal creatures to serve him was only the first step in his effort to centralize the movement and firmly reestablish his dictatorship over the party. To further these ends, he reactivated in August 1925 the Investigation and Conciliation committees (Untersuch-ungs-Ausschuss, Schlichtungs-Ausschuss), which had first been created in 1921 to aid him in controlling and policing the party. Now, four years later, both committees were re-vived and consolidated by the Führer into one larger unit called the Committee for Investigation and Conciliation *(Untersuchungs- und Schlichtungsausschuss,* which was short-ened to *Uschla).*[9]

It was Hitler's hope that the new Uschla would even-tually become the basis for a highly developed system of intraparty courts. The system was to help institutionalize Hitler's leader-figure image, and it was to ensure that his wishes would become party law and that his totalitarian philosophy would saturate the NSDAP. In short, the Uschlas were to aid the Nazi leader in recapturing and firmly rees-tablishing his absolute control over the party and its divided and disillusioned subleaders. More important, however, the Uschlas were to mushroom into the later Parteigerichte of the Third Reich. The Parteigerichte were given immense powers, which included depriving disobedient members of the right to make a decent living for their families and con-demning some to suffer in concentration camps. Conse-quently, the Uschlas were to become instruments of terror-ism and coercion; beginning with 1933 they coldly and brutally linked hands with the *Geheime Staatspolizei* ("Secret State Police," or the Gestapo) and the SS to form the foundations of National Socialist totalitarianism.

The first Uschla committee was established in Munich in January 1926. It started with a chairman appointed by Hitler and two *Beisitzer* ("assistants") chosen by the com-mittee chairman. Hitler intended the committee to be a kind of Supreme Court *(Reichs-Uschla)* in the NSDAP, heading similar courts, or Uschlas, in each party Ortsgruppe and Gau. In other words, it was the aim of Hitler and the party leadership to create an Investigation and Conciliation Committee at the national level (Reichs-Uschla) and in each district and local organization (namely, *Gau-Uschla* and *Orts-Uschla*), thereby forming a network of party courts throughout the NSDAP's administrative hierarchy. Following the model of the Reichs-Uschla, all Gaus and Ortsgruppen, beginning in the summer of 1926, established such tribunals, so that by October 1930 the network was nearly completed.[10]

THE USCHLA SYSTEM, 1926–1933

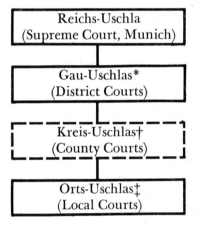

* In October 1930 there were thirty-five Gau-Uschlas, or district courts.
† In 1931 Kreis-Uschlas, or county courts, were established, to function between the Gau-Uschlas and the Orts-Uschlas.
‡ Gau-Uschlas frequently controlled one hundred or more Orts-Uschlas.

The Uschlas had bureaucratic and constitutional functions that were broadly defined in the party statutes presented by Hitler to a general meeting of the NSDAP in Munich on 22 May 1926. It was the task of each Uschla to mediate strife or dissension among party members, examine closely all applications for membership, and expel from the movement any organization or member unwilling to follow Hitler's orders and the goals of the NSDAP. Until 1929 the Uschlas lacked a detailed directive for their procedures, and they based their investigations and rulings mainly on affidavits and other written testimony; few personal interrogations or formal trials were held.

Nevertheless, members could be removed by an Uschla for a variety of vague and "catchall" reasons—"disgraceful actions" *(ehrenrührige Handlungen)*, violating the "endeavors" *(Bestrebungen)* of the party, and any "moral conduct" that might cause "general offense and therefore injure the party." Furthermore, one could be expelled for "causing repeated conflict and dissension," for being delinquent by three months in payment of party dues, or for general "disinterest" *(Interesselosigkeit)* in the movement. In the event that an Ortsgruppe or Gau failed financially, Hitler, in agreement with the Reichs-Uschla, was granted the authority to expel the organization. All possessions of the organization (such as membership books, records, party badges, or insignia) would then become the property of the Reichsleitung.[11]

Together with the purely legalistic task of purging rebellious elements, each Uschla was to be a court of conciliation and "honor" *(Ehre)*. Although the Uschlas were not specifically designated as tribunals of honor *(Ehrengerichte)* until 1933, one of their major functions was to absolve party members of "unjustified suspicions of their honesty" leveled by a comrade.[12] In this respect the Uschlas were patterned after the military courts of honor of the old German Army. The most valued possession of a National Socialist (or so he claimed) was his honor. This strong emphasis on honor came from the völkisch-military origins of the NSDAP, and it was to reach its greatest expression in the motto of the SS, Honor for Us Means Loyalty *(Ehre heisst Treue)*.

Basically, the Nazi code of honor was that of the "little man with big ideas"—the little man who normally found himself in the lower middle class, faced with a precarious socioeconomic existence. He deeply resented his situation and felt himself cheated of his rightful influence in society as an "honorable" and blue-blooded German. Vigorously denouncing Jews and other "German" enemies for his unhappy state of affairs, he decried what he called the materialistic "Jewish spirit" of the day and appealed for the country to return to a society based on the "old" Germanic concept of honor. "German honor," as one Nazi member described it, "is not tied to money, possessions, title, class, and rank. German honor is the honor of soldiers and therefore is bound to the love of one's fatherland, loyalty, manliness, comradeship, and honesty."[13]

Thus, for the pride-conscious and völkisch-minded National Socialist, the Uschlas were to function as courts of honor. Yet, while the Uschlas claimed to act as tribunals of honor, their judicial track record was something entirely different. The concept of Germanic honor abruptly became insignificant when the needs of the party were at stake. Dishonorable and scandalous actions of party leaders (for example, Streicher, Ley, Kaufmann, and the SA elements involved in the Stennes mutiny and the anti-Jewish riots of 1938) were tolerated and even suppressed by the Uschlas when it seemed that this would best serve the reputation and interests of the party.

In several respects, Hitler sought through the Uschlas to erect a new morality for Nazi members—a morality that would later become the watchword of Germany in the Third Reich. Under the guise of operating as courts of honor, the Uschlas (and later, the Parteigerichte) stifled and concealed dissent within the party. Above all, the actions of the Uschlas revealed that Hitler would stop at nothing to ensure that there would be rigid discipline at all levels and that the demands of the Nazi "community" would triumph over those of the individual member. Consequently, the grossest displays of immorality were frequently ignored if the member involved was the least bit valuable to the movement. The philosophy followed by the Supreme Court was simple:

"If a youth finds pleasure, he is thankful and silent." The Court's pat answer to party members who questioned the ethics of party leaders was to remind the critics that the NSDAP's sole concern was "political power," and this could only be won and retained by "fighters, not by nuns or mendicant friars" *(nicht durch Betschwestern oder Bettel-mönche).*[14]

The Uschlas also had the specific task of mediating disputes and feuds between members or organizations in the party. According to Hitler's wish, all quarrels were to be settled within the National Socialist community. Obviously, any political movement claiming (as the NSDAP did) to represent the collective will of the German people could ill afford any public display of internal discord. Quarrels between members involving such scandalous matters as adultery, homosexuality, excessive drinking, or the embezzlement of party funds, therefore, were not to be handled in a public court for all to witness, but before a party tribunal whose judges were sworn to silence in every trial. Above all, the poisoning taint of scandal had to be avoided, and the NSDAP's image as a unified and respectable enemy of the Weimar system had to be preserved.

Finally, it was the job of the Uschlas to examine the validity of applications by prospective party members for admission to the NSDAP. According to the party's statutes of May 1926, any "irreproachable member" *(unbescholtene Angehörige)* of the German people who was nineteen years of age and of "pure Aryan descent" *(rein arischer Abkunft),* was eligible for membership. Such a broad definition, particularly insofar as it raised the problem of deciding who was an "irreproachable" person, allowed the Uschlas plenty of room to interpret the law to the party's advantage and to the discriminatory exclusion of Jews and others considered "unworthy" of belonging to the movement.[15] Particularly during 1932 and after the seizure of power by the Nazis, this function of the Parteigerichte greatly increased in significance as the party sought at all costs to avoid race "pollution" by Jews and other "inferior" peoples.

Hitler's foremost consideration in choosing the first members of the Reichs-Uschla was that it should be an elite "court of honor," patterned after the tribunals of the officer corps of the old army. Acting on the theory that blood was thicker than water, he commissioned to sit on the Reichs-Uschla three party members who had been in the NSDAP since its earliest years and had served in the army under Kaiser Wilhelm II. Here, the Führer set a definite precedent for the Reichs-Uschla and its subordinate Uschlas.

To be the first chairman of the Reichs-Uschla and the chief justice of the party, Hitler named a retired major general, the sixty-eight-year-old Bruno Heinemann. Moreover, emphasizing the immediate role of the Uschlas in the party's organizational affairs, he appointed Heinemann head of the party's National Committee for Organization (*Organisationsausschuss*). First established in 1921 and revived in 1925, the Organisationsausschuss was to supervise the organizational development of Gaus and Ortsgruppen according to Hitler's orders.[16] As assistant judges on the Reichs-Uschla, Hitler named two close friends and long-time Munich members, Karl Ostberg and Ulrich Graf. Beginning in January 1926 these loyal Hitler vassals formed the Nazi Reichs-Uschla until the end of 1927, when Heinemann and Ostberg retired from their posts.

Considering Hitler's idea of what the Reichs-Uschla should be, Heinemann appeared especially suited to assume the prestigious office of chairman of the NSDAP's highest "court of honor." Born on 13 December 1858 in Naumberg near Leipzig, he had entered the army in 1877 and had served proudly until Germany's defeat in World War I. In the early months of 1919, while a deputy commander of the military fortress in Ingolstadt, Heinemann actively participated with other reactionary forces in northern Bavaria in destroying the Bolshevik-inspired Soviet Republic proclaimed in Munich by the successors of the Bavarian leader of the German Independent Social Democratic Party (Unabhängige Sozialdemokratische Partei Deutschlands), Kurt Eisner.

Following his retirement from the army a year later, he continued his support of the far right in Bavaria by joining the NSDAP in February 1922. With Hitler's Putsch and the resulting collapse of the party, he was forced to leave the movement, but he reentered it late in March 1925. It was at this point, while he was living in Munich, that his outstanding record as a member of the old officer corps was brought to Hitler's attention. A few months later he was named chairman of the Reichs-Uschla, with his office in Munich at the party's national headquarters on the Schellingstrasse.[17]

Undoubtedly, Hitler felt that Heinemann would bring to his new job a mentality whose chief characteristics would be stone-blind devotion and loyalty to the goals of the NSDAP and its Führer. In addition, Hitler probably believed that Heinemann's former rank in the army and the fact that he was the first officer holding the rank of general to join the party would enhance the prestige of the office of Reichs-Uschla chairman. But unquestionably, the old man fell far short of Hitler's expectations. As the latter soon discovered, Heinemann was neither blindly obedient to the wishes of his Führer nor was he able to command the respect of other ranking party leaders. Beyond a flair for strictly bureaucratic and organizational matters, he was staid, boorish, and hardly the type needed to fulfill the endless task of the Reichs-Uschla in conciliating the petty quarrels and conflicts that arose throughout the party. Probably the most accurate assessment of Heinemann by a fellow member came from the master propagandist and Gauleiter of Berlin after November 1926, Joseph Goebbels. Goebbels, obviously unimpressed, observed: "His Excellency, Heinemann: retired general, correct, asks dumb questions, totally incapable of complex thoughts. Imbued with a code of honor: the judge of honor."[18]

One of Heinemann's assistants on the Reichs-Uschla was Karl Ostberg. Ostberg was born in Munich on 4 March 1890. A policeman by profession, he had served in the army during World War I. After the end of the war he joined the viciously anti-Semitic Deutschvölkischer Schutz- und Trutzbund and the Munich-based Bund der Beobachter- freunde ("League of Friends of the *Beobachter*," a group founded by Franz Eher, editor of the *Völkischer Beobachter* prior to its purchase by the Nazis, to save the paper from bankruptcy). In March 1920 Ostberg entered the NSDAP "to fight against the other parties of lies." He participated in the Putsch and then joined the GDVG, which was led by Esser, Rosenberg, and Streicher. On 1 July 1925 he reentered the "new" party and was soon appointed to its Reichs-Uschla.[19]

Another popular Munich member named to the Reichs-Uschla was Ulrich Graf, since the earliest days of the DAP one of Hitler's strong-arm henchmen, who followed his master everywhere with the obedience of a trained watchdog. Born on 6 July 1878 near Munich, Graf served for eight years in a Bavarian regiment before leaving it in 1904. Professionally, he was a "cheap meat butcher" *(Freibank-Metzger)* and amateur pugilist (who occasionally brawled in the streets), and he was active for many years in Munich city politics until his death in 1945.

In the Nazi party he joined the small select group that formed around Hitler in the DAP at the beginning of 1920 (a group, it will be recalled, that included Eckart, Röhm, Esser, and Feder). He also became one of the first SS men, belonging to the elite *Stosstruppe Hitler*, which arose in the spring of 1923.[20] His most notable feat in the party came during the Putsch, when, acting heroically as Hitler's bodyguard, he personally shielded his Führer from the hail of gunfire in front of the Feldherrnhalle. Testifying later at Hitler's trial, he boasted to the court that "it was clear to me at this moment, that these hours would perhaps be the greatest in Germany's history."[21] Above all, Graf represented the blindly loyal and dedicated servant that Hitler was seeking at the beginning of 1926 to execute the difficult work of the Reichs-Uschla.

These were the "old fighters" from the Munich local whom Hitler first chose to lead the party's Uschlas. Each one—Heinemann, Ostberg, and Graf—was a tested disciple who was well known to members in and around Munich. Naturally, these were important qualifications for the unpleasant duties of the Uschlas, such as expelling disobedient comrades who refused to submit to party discipline and to Hitler's absolute authority. The Reichs-Uschla began to function in January, and from the outset it proved to be an invaluable instrument to Hitler for centralizing his power and for controlling the NSDAP.

In its first months in operation, the Reichs-Uschla was given the task of handling several conflicts that arose in the badly disorganized northern Gaus. There Hitler and Munich were especially concerned with recapturing total control over the party organizations and with suppressing the fight for independence among a number of Gaus and Ortsgruppen. Hitler's strongest rival in the north was Gregor Strasser, the popular Nazi Reichstag deputy and leader of the former NSDAP splinter group the Freiheitsbewegung. While in prison, Hitler had lost considerable power to Strasser in the north and west in terms of appointing or confirming *Ortsgruppenleiters* ("local leaders") and Gauleiters. In some instances, in fact, locals were even choosing their own Ortsgruppenleiter in democratic elections—a process that enraged the authoritarian Hitler.[22]

Strasser, who took the "Socialist" principles in the NSDAP's program of February 1920 far more seriously than Hitler, had organized in September 1925 the National Socialist Working Association (Nationalsozialistische Arbeitsgemeinschaft, or NSAG), which published a political journal, the *NS-Briefe* (National Socialist Letters). The NSAG was composed of party leaders from eleven northern Gaus (including the young and fiery editor of the *NS-Briefe*, Joseph Goebbels; Strasser's publisher-brother Otto; Karl Kaufmann, Gauleiter in the Ruhr; Franz von Pfeffer, Gauleiter of Westphalia; Joseph Terboven, Ortsgruppenleiter in Essen; and Bernhard Rust, Gauleiter of Hanover-South). Above all, the NSAG was an attempt by its leaders to organize the more industrialized and proletarian north for Hitler and to woo him away from the narrow conservative and nationalist influence of his Bavarian cronies (namely, Esser, Bouhler, Streicher, and Rosenberg).[23]

For his part, however, Hitler viewed the northern group as a threat to himself personally and to the NSDAP's Munich-centered leadership. He finally called a meeting of top northern and southern leaders for February 14 at Bamberg in northern Bavaria; his objectives were to suppress the NSAG and to lay to rest any idea that "socialism" was being emphasized in the NSDAP and that the party was moving to the left. At the conference, he harangued the socialism-oriented "unbelievers" for four long hours, raising his voice level more than the intelligence of his listeners and attempting to persuade them to submit totally to his more conservative and nationalistic leadership. Hitler categorically refused to revise in any way the party's program of 1920, which Strasser proposed to do, and he succeeded in forcing a compromise from Strasser. After this the NSAG collapsed completely, and with it the northern threat to Hitler's leadership (if in fact it ever really existed).[24]

Strasser and his organization, of course, were far too important to be handled by a mere bureaucratic institution in the party, such as the Uschla. Yet, while Hitler was brilliantly relying on his own charisma and Führer-image to whip the northerners into line, he was cleverly utilizing Heinemann and the Reichs-Uschla to assert Munich's supremacy by settling several lesser disorders in the Saxon, Berlin, and Halle-Merseburg Gaus. In January, dissension flared in Saxony between Gauleiter Martin Mutschmann and the Ortsgruppe in Dresden. The bone of contention was two-sided in nature. First, it involved Mutschmann's attempt to impose his iron authority on the Ortsgruppe as its Gauleiter. The issue on which the Gauleiter sought to do this, however, concerned a matter of strategic political policy in the NSDAP: the party's relations to the paramilitary defense leagues (Wehrverbänden).

During 1925 two defense leagues—the Tannenberg-Bund ("Tannenberg Association"), headed by General Ludendorff, and the Frontbann ("Front Union"), organized by Röhm—had become active in Dresden and counted a number of local Nazis as members. Moreover, because of the Hitler Putsch, the Nazi SA had been banned in Saxony, and both the Frontbann and Tannenberg-Bund had attached themselves to the NSDAP to fill the role of the banned SA. Yet during the autumn of 1925 Hitler and Esser had visited Saxony and spoken in Dresden and Chemnitz, generally criticizing this policy and the membership of Nazis in other völkisch groups. According to Hitler, the NSDAP should have nothing to do with defense leagues except where they benefited the SA and subordinated themselves to the party's political leadership. His attitude was thus rather vague, and it led, in Saxony at least, to a wide variety of interpretations. In addition, the decision criticizing "double membership" was quite unpopular, and many party members in Dresden by the end of 1925 were undecided between the defense leagues and the NSDAP.[25]

Mutschmann, hoping to develop his Gau by strengthening the Dresden Ortsgruppe and other Ortsgruppen and by keeping Gau members as content as possible, decided to permit the defense leagues to continue associating with the NSDAP. The Ortsgruppenleiter in Dresden, Anton Goss, disagreed with the *Gauleitung* ("Gau leadership") and broke with the Frontbann and Tannenberg-Bund. In January 1926 he organized an SS for older members in his group and a special Deutsche Wander-Abteilung ("German Hiking Section") for the younger ones. Consequently an ugly quarrel ensued at a Gau meeting in Dresden between Mutschmann and the Ortsgruppe, and Goss ordered the newly organized SS to escort the angry Gauleiter from the meeting hall. The next day Mutschmann retaliated by announcing that he was dissolving the Dresden Ortsgruppe and the entire party organization in east Saxony.

As was often typical in such confrontations, the immediate reaction of both antagonists was to plead for the support of their lord and master in Munich. Goss telegraphed Hitler his "unswerving loyalty and devotion," and Mutschmann denounced Goss to the Führer and requested that notice of his dissolution of the party organization in east Saxony be printed in the *Völkischer Beobachter*.[26] With both subordinates at his mercy, Hitler commissioned the Reichs-Uschla to investigate and then determine whether the Dresden local had acted correctly in breaking off relations with the defense leagues.

By gathering written affidavits and testimony from various party leaders in Dresden who also belonged to the leagues, the Reichs-Uschla discovered that the Frontbann and Tannenberg-Bund were far more interested in following the war hero Ludendorff than in following Hitler. Furthermore, recognizing with Goss that connections to either league might lead to a ban of the entire NSDAP in Saxony, the Reichs-Uschla decided in favor of Goss and voted to revoke Mutschmann's dissolution of the party in east Saxony. Heinemann then advised Hitler of the Reichs-Uschla's decision, and in a concluding note to Goss, he emphasized the urgency of resolving the personal differences between himself and Mutschmann.[27]

The episode in Saxony illuminated several fundamental policies that were being pursued by Hitler and the Reichsleitung in 1926 and 1927. In matters involving disagreements between leaders over party strategy (that is, defense league–party relations), Hitler used the Reichs-Uschla to issue a definitive (and doubtless unpopular) ruling. The evidence uncovered by the Reichs-Uschla, which showed the intention of the Saxon defense leagues to follow Ludendorff instead of Hitler, probably had the effect of heightening the Führer's suspicion of other völkisch groups. Since the Putsch he had acquired a negative attitude toward alliances with such organizations, and this suspicion was quickly becoming a cornerstone of his strategy to achieve political power. After hesitating to act on the issue of "double membership" for National Socialists, he ultimately decreed a formal judgment in February 1927 that absolutely forbade the policy.[28] Finally, the affair in Dresden illustrated how Hitler was able to use the Reichs-Uschla to overrule Mutschmann (one of his prominent financial supporters), while retaining the Gauleiter's confidence.

Hitler's employing of the Uschla to curtail the power of Gauleiters and Ortsgruppenleiters was hardly unusual. Throughout 1926 the Reichs-Uschla intervened repeatedly in Gaus to settle factional disorders and to increase the authority of the Reichsleitung. In the spring the Reichs-Uschla mediated a bitter quarrel between the Berlin and Potsdam locals that involved petty accusations arising from a "German Evening" sponsored by the Potsdam group on the night of March 13. The "Evening" was marred by several unpleasant incidents, and it resulted in considerable tension between the host Ortsgruppe and the more proletarian and lower-middle-class Berlin group. After sorting out the maze of accusations from both sides, the Reichs-Uschla suggested to Hitler that he reprimand the Gauleiters of each Ortsgruppe for failing to prevent the squabble. Consequently, Hitler informed Ernst Schlange (Berlin Gauleiter) and Wilhelm Klaunig (Brandenburg Gauleiter) that "the whole mess . . . could have been avoided by a decisive and energetic leadership."[29]

A few months later, angry locals in the Halle-Merseburg Gau organized a meeting to oust their Gauleiter, Walter Ernst. To combat this effort by the Ortsgruppen to free themselves from the Gauleitung, Hitler quickly sent Heinemann (as his "personal representative") to the conference in Halle on July 25 to ensure that the will of the Reichsleitung would be followed in the matter. Ernst was subsequently expelled from the party and replaced as Gauleiter by Paul Hinkler, a teacher and popular party member from Halle.[30] During the autumn, Heinemann and the Reichs-Uschla continued to police the Gaus and to intervene wherever necessary to restore some semblance of order in their organizations.[31]

If Hitler employed his Reichs-Uschla as a bureaucratic watchdog over Gau organizations, he did the same with it in regard to rebellious Ortsgruppen that refused to meet their financial obligations to Munich. Outside the major cities, many Nazi branches were extremely small (less than ten members), representing sleepy villages in the country-side that were scarcely in contact with the mainstream of national political life. They were rarely visited, for example, by party celebrities from Munich—least of all by Hitler, who was banned from speaking in much of the Reich until the end of 1927. Moreover, each Ortsgruppe, whether large or small, existed solely as a means of propaganda and financial support for Hitler and the Reichsleitung. The financial ex-penses of most groups included paying fees to join the NSDAP *(Aufnahmegebühren)*, SA assessments, and any extra expenditures required by Munich. But to complicate mat-ters, many needed money to pay local election debts, to sup-port formation of an SA, or to deal with greedy Ortsgrup-penleiters who were hardly above pilfering their treasury.

Naturally enough, these and other problems tended to dampen enthusiasm, and they often led to apathy. The Reichsleitung, nevertheless, refused to compromise or to allow locals to backslide in paying their members' dues to the national party organization. Beginning in the summer of 1926, Hitler ordered the national treasurer of the NSDAP, Schwarz, and the Reichs-Uschla to audit carefully the ac-counts of all party organizations to ensure that each was paying its dues regularly. The result was embarrassing, to say the least—a number of groups were found to be three months in arrears, and still others had compiled a far worse record. Hitler, calling such organizations "worthless,"[32] ordered the Reichs-Uschla to expel them from the move-ment and to announce their removal in the *Völkischer Beobachter.* Consequently, a mass purge of delinquent Orts-gruppen and members in party organizations in Munich occurred throughout late 1926 and into the summer of 1927.[33]

Such housecleaning tactics left little doubt in the minds of members of the NSDAP that Hitler meant business when he emphasized the need to reconstruct and reorganize the party. The purges obviously reflected his efforts to improve his former habits in organizational affairs. His goal was to replace administrative inefficiency that had characterized the pre-Putsch party with some degree of rationality and order. A large following at any price was now taboo—without strict discipline and solid organization, mass support could mean very little (as the Putsch had shown) in the party's quest for political power. Moreover, the party's need for money was greater than its need for an enormous train of pseudosupporters who felt no financial responsibility to the movement. Paying reliable employees and developing an effective propaganda machine were expensive, and until the NSDAP could attract wealthy contributors from industry and big business (as it was able to do in 1932 and 1933), the bulk of its funding had to come from its predominantly middle-class membership.

In addition to helping Hitler restore order in the lower levels of the party in 1926 and 1927, the Reichs-Uschla was often ordered by the Führer to mediate personal feuds that involved prominent Gauleiters and members of the Reichsleitung. Personal conflict was indeed a striking feature of the NSDAP throughout its history. Generally, such rivalries had three principal causes: the deep split in the party arising from the failure of the Putsch, the dogmatic and intolerant mentality of many of its leaders, and Hitler's own encouragement of a certain amount of discord. By encouraging factions and individuals to compete for his favor, Hitler was able to keep himself the focal point of unity in the movement and successfully apply his notorious policy of "divide and rule" among his lieutenants.

Settling personal strife was a most difficult task for the Parteigerichte. Most national and district Nazi leaders were aggressive and egotistical personalities who had sworn allegiance to a totalitarian movement that demanded their absolute conformity. Completely excluded from decision-making in regard to major party policy, they tended to quarrel over irrelevant and inconsequential matters in order to compensate for their lack of authority. Through such frivolous haggling and squabbling, many attempted to satisfy their need or desire to feel important. Furthermore, they were extremely insecure individuals, which helps in part to explain their vigorous competition for the hallowed favor of their hero and Führer, Hitler, and of the Reichsleitung. Consequently, such leaders were not easily swayed either toward admitting guilt or toward retracting the most petty and unfounded accusations against one another.

Hitler especially discovered the value of the Reichs-Uschla as a mechanism both for encouraging and controlling dissension during 1927. Before the year was out, it had aided him in handling feuds involving Goebbels, Otto Strasser, Bouhler, Pfeffer, Karl Kaufmann, and the NSDAP's crudest anti-Semites, Streicher and Arthur Dinter. Dealing with such notables, however, proved to be more than the aged Chief Justice Heinemann could manage. As Hitler slowly found him lacking (that is to say, disagreeing with the Führer), the old man was finally forced to retire in November. His Reichs-Uschla, nevertheless, served Hitler well if for nothing else than providing party leaders with a private forum through which to register their petty grievances and enhance their sense of importance at being listened to by the party's highest "court of honor." Moreover, while attacking one another before the Reichs-Uschla, they most assuredly could never pose a challenge to Hitler's authority.

In most instances, the Reichs-Uschla was helpless (without Hitler's firm support) to discipline those leaders who tangled before its benches. Such was the case with Dinter, the independent Thuringian Gauleiter and repulsive anti-Semite who had been a member of the NSDAP since 1921. Together with a young and ambitious deputy, Fritz Sauckel, Dinter had slowly developed his Gau (traditionally a stronghold of the Communists and Socialists) into a fairly flourishing Nazi organization. In the Reichstag elections of May 1924, for example, völkisch sympathizers of the NSDAP in Thuringia had helped to give the far-right candidates almost 10 percent of the votes cast.[34]

After Hitler's reconfirmation of him as Gauleiter in April 1925, Dinter began to grow increasingly independent of the Munich leadership. In March 1927 he became embroiled in a dispute over money that he owed to a party local in Baden, Mannheim; and despite the orders of the Reichs-Uschla that he repay the Ortsgruppe, he flatly refused and labeled the Court "onesided" and "superficial."[35] A few months later, Dinter was again the center of attention before the Reichs-Uschla. This time, however, he was involved in a bitter quarrel with his long-time deputy, Sauckel, and his Gau Propaganda Leader, H. S. Ziegler.

The conflict represented, in fact, the beginning of a power struggle in the Gau, and it marked the curtain raiser for Dinter's subsequent fall as Gauleiter and for his removal from the NSDAP in October. Dinter, it seems, accused Ziegler of irresponsibility in managing the Gau's newspaper and publishing firm, the Verlag Nationalsozialist.[36] Because of his earlier collision with the Reichs-Uschla, however, the Gauleiter refused to settle the matter through the Reichs-Uschla. Nevertheless, at the insistence of Ziegler and Sauckel, a Reichs-Uschla inquiry was opened (but a formal decision never rendered), and they made the best of it. They attacked Dinter for his absenteeism in the Gau, his preoccupation with "parliamentarism" (he was a deputy in the Thuringian *Landtag*, or state legislature), and his religious-mystical interests. (Dinter was the leader of an extreme völkisch-oriented religious group, the Geistchristlichen Religionsgemeinschaft, or Christian-Spiritual Religious Community.) Finally, they charged that the Gauleiter refused to speak to small locals in Thuringia and, consequently, that he no longer had "personal contact with individual local and regional leaders."[37]

Fully aware of Munich's concern over Dinter's carefree autonomy, Sauckel secretly recommended to Hitler that he appoint someone with more "personal restraint" (namely, himself) as Gauleiter, arguing to the Führer that the "best solution for the district of Thuringia would be if Dr. Dinter resigned his office in the near future."[38] Heinemann, obviously impressed with Sauckel's ambition and his organizational talents and irritated at Dinter's lack of respect for the

Reichs-Uschla, immediately suggested to Hitler that the Gauleiter be removed from his post and replaced by Sauckel.[39] The Reichs-Uschla chairman's advice to Hitler revealed that Sauckel and Ziegler were slowly winning the struggle for power in the Gau. It also meant that by mid 1927 some in the Reichsleitung were up in arms over Dinter's apparent disregard for the orders of the party's leadership. Yet the Reichs-Uschla—the usual instrument employed by Munich to handle rebellious Gauleiters—was helpless (without Hitler's approval) to remove or even discipline him. The Reichs-Uschla did not issue an official ruling, but writing as head of the Reich Organization Committee, Heinemann attempted to soothe Sauckel by hinting that a change in the Gauleitung might be forthcoming soon.[40] Finally, the Reichsleitung decided to purchase the Gau's publishing house, hoping thereby to remove a major bone of contention in the dissension.[41]

This was wishful thinking, however. The backbiting and quarreling continued unabated, as did Dinter's alienation from Munich. Barely half a year later, Hitler was personally forced to intervene and remove Dinter as Gauleiter, naming Sauckel to succeed him.[42] The man of "personal restraint" (as Sauckel had earlier described himself to Hitler) had overthrown one of the NSDAP's pioneers. Such intraparty intrigue, "backdoor" maneuvering, and power struggles were common in the party; they were the means through which many offices were won and lost. Finally, the removal of Dinter, a man who sought to establish himself as the leader of a new Germanic religion, illustrated Hitler's general problem of controlling the heterogeneous elements in his movement. Not only did he face the bringing together of varying socioeconomic and political groups, but the devout Lutheran had to be united with the serious Catholic and the extreme völkisch believer.

Many top-level personal clashes handled by the Reichs-Uschla dealt with money affairs and particularly with accusations of fraud or embezzlement of party funds against sticky-fingered leaders hoping to make a fast mark for themselves. Such was the case in the dissension that arose in Nuremberg against Streicher in September 1927 and in the triangular quarrel involving Bouhler, Pfeffer, and Kaufmann that raged throughout the year. In Nuremberg, a strong faction opposed to the local leadership *(Ortsgruppenleitung)*—Streicher and his deputy, Karl Holz—had begun forming a few days after the NSDAP's national congress in August. The faction included several section leaders in the party local and the Nazi representatives in the city council.

After the Reichsparteitag (which was designed in part to demonstrate the NSDAP's unity) the opposition informed the Reichsleitung that Streicher and Holz had used the occasion to defraud Munich of five hundred marks.[43] At the same time the local Uschla in Nuremberg (led by a member of the opposition) ordered the expulsion of Holz for having appropriated party funds to amuse himself for several days with a barmaid in nearby Bayreuth. But Streicher, believing firmly in his deputy and accusing the Uschla chairman of leading a palace revolt *(Palastrevolution)* against the Ortsgruppenleitung, immediately dissolved the Uschla and declared its decision invalid.[44] Responding to the situation, Hitler ordered the Reichs-Uschla to investigate the disorder. In addition, he called in the Reichsleitung's chief lawyer and legal adviser, Dr. Hans Frank, to help determine if a true case of embezzlement existed.

Upon exchanging a flood of letters and telephone calls with both sides, the Reichs-Uschla and Frank discovered that Munich had paid 450 marks to a Nuremberg member, Johannes Klegraefe, whose local shop had supplied flag materials and decorations for the Parteitag. Further investigations by Frank, however, produced a confession from Klegraefe that the work had never been done. Klegraefe maintained that he and Streicher's office manager, Georg Gradl, had wanted the extra money to provide music for the Nuremberg SA choral society. The opposition faction was furious over this contention, and it protested vigorously to Munich that Klegraefe and Gradl were merely "front men" for Streicher and Holz, who had actually received the money.[45]

The Reichs-Uschla, ignoring the written testimony of several ranking party officials in Nuremberg, soon met and decided to protect Streicher by expelling Klegraefe and Gradl for their "flagrant breach of confidence" *(grober Vertrauensbruch)* to the party. Only weeks later, however, Streicher refused to expel Gradl and promised Klegraefe that he could reenter the party in a short time. Nevertheless, Hitler himself intervened and supported the Reichs-Uschla's ruling by adamantly denying Klegraefe's application for readmission.[46] Having been removed from the party, Klegraefe refused to return the 450 marks to the Reichsleitung, and in May 1930 the Reichsleitung filed for damages against him in a Nuremberg civil court. Not surprisingly, the judge showed more than a casual interest in Streicher's role in the fraud.[47]

At the same time, the Reichs-Uschla and Munich never questioned Streicher's integrity nor that of his adjutant, Holz. The supreme "court of honor" accepted without reservation that Klegraefe and Gradl had acted alone. Any hopes that the opposition entertained of getting Streicher and Holz removed from the party (or even reprimanded) by appealing to Munich were useless at the outset. Streicher was never Hitler's close personal favorite, but he was exactly the kind of powerful autocrat and political demagogue that the Führer admired. Added to this, Streicher's vulgar anti-Semitic paper, *Der Stürmer*, offered the NSDAP a valuable propaganda organ. Consequently, the "Parteitag Affair" was mainly a tip-off of things to come; again in 1928 the Reichs-Uschla responded to the opposition against Streicher and attempted to discipline him, but it failed to receive Hitler's full support.

Accusations of fraud were also at the core of the feud in the Reichsleitung that was begun in March 1927 by the commander in chief of the SA *(Oberster SA-Führer,* or Osaf), von Pfeffer, with Bouhler and the Ruhr Gauleiter, Kaufmann. In 1925 Hitler had commissioned Pfeffer as district leader of Westphalia, but with the restructuring of the Gau the following year, he became chief of the SA—a post he was to hold until the first SA uprising in Berlin under Walter Stennes in September 1930. Pfeffer's personality, especially his tendency to give orders in a tone resembling that of a drill sergeant, irritated many leaders in the party's political organization, including Heinemann. Pfeffer's disagreements with Hitler over the role of the SA in the party are well known;[48] yet during most of 1927 he was embroiled in a verbal war with Kaufmann, Bouhler, and Heinemann himself.

The disagreements, which were taken before the Reichs-Uschla, presented the Court with a case so absurd as to defy being funny. The accusations and backbiting that occurred showed not only the pettiness and aimlessness that characterized much of the strife within the party, but they revealed how well Hitler's policy of "divide and rule" actually worked at the highest levels.

The fireworks began in March, when Pfeffer charged that the consolidation of the Westphalian and Ruhr Gaus in the preceding year had left the new Gau (the Ruhr, under Kaufmann's command) with substantial debts. Pfeffer's assertion implied that Kaufmann had conducted the financial part of the consolidation badly and that his only concern was to supervise a larger Gau. Calling this "personal slander," Kaufmann protested to the Reichs-Uschla, claiming that Pfeffer, Goebbels, and he had worked closely in merging the districts and that Pfeffer had mentioned nothing about debts from his former Gau in Westphalia. He also named Goebbels as a witness for his side. During the consolidation of the Gaus, the volatile young man from Elberfeld had been the office manager of Kaufmann's old Ruhr district and the editor of the *NS-Briefe*, the journal published by the NSAG.[49]

Responding to Kaufmann's protest, the Reichs-Uschla opened an investigation and quickly ruled Pfeffer's allegations unjustified and harshly recommended to Hitler that Pfeffer be expelled from the party. But the Führer rejected the Reichs-Uschla's decision and told Heinemann that he would personally settle things with Kaufmann at a party conference in Essen scheduled for mid May. Once at the meeting, Hitler did attempt to console the irate Gauleiter by expressing his own misgivings about Pfeffer and asking Kaufmann to let the matter rest "in consideration for the entire movement."[50]

Yet Heinemann, who was also on sour terms with Pfeffer, refused to let the affair drop, and he interrogated Goebbels later in the month while the latter was on one of his frequent pilgrimages from Berlin (where Hitler had appointed him Gauleiter in November 1926) to Munich. With his usual unpredictability, however, Goebbels testified against his old friend and former party boss (Kaufmann) and stated that Pfeffer's accusations were in fact true.[51] The hassle became even more complicated when Bouhler, supposedly writing for the Reichs-Uschla, informed Kaufmann of Goebbels's testimony and remarked that the Gaus in question had been merged "much too liberally." Any success Hitler may have had in calming Kaufmann in Essen, therefore, was now lost. The Gauleiter, more irritated than ever, now attacked Goebbels to Hitler and Heinemann, demanding nothing less than a final ruling.[52]

Bouhler's intervention was more than coincidence. Like Heinemann, he, too, was on unfriendly terms with Pfeffer. Bouhler's letter to Kaufmann concerning Goebbels's statements did not represent the views of either the Reichs-Uschla or Heinemann. On the same day, he had also dispatched a note to Pfeffer (again supposedly on behalf of the Reichs-Uschla), asking him for a comment on the Kaufmann matter and accusing Pfeffer of failing to repay a substantial amount of money to Hitler's official photographer, Heinrich Hoffman. Moreover, Bouhler charged Pfeffer with advertising the availability of low-interest loans through the SA in a Silesian newspaper (implying that the SA chief was trying to make money at the expense of the party).[53] In discovering the loan offers, Bouhler had opened some of Pfeffer's official mail while the latter was on vacation.[54] Considering Bouhler's hostility toward Pfeffer, it was obvious that his sole intention was to aggravate the Kaufmann-Pfeffer feud and to begin his own attack on Pfeffer.

To confuse the situation further (and make it even more ridiculous), Pfeffer suddenly ordered an investigation by the Reichs-Uschla for the protection of his "honor" as a National Socialist, and he threatened Bouhler that he might take the case to Hitler. Not to be outbluffed, Bouhler responded by ordering a Reichs-Uschla investigation of Pfeffer. Consequently, by mid June the Reichs-Uschla had a three-ring circus on its hands: Kaufmann wanted Pfeffer investigated, Bouhler wanted Pfeffer investigated, and Pfeffer wanted both Kaufmann and Bouhler investigated![55]

Obviously, the aged Heinemann and his Reichs-Uschla assistants had lost complete control of the situation. For his part, Heinemann had lost the objectivity that he sorely needed in order to render a rational judgment; his sympathy lay overwhelmingly with Kaufmann and Bouhler. Moreover, even before the squabble had begun, relations between himself and Pfeffer had been extremely tense. In the spring, the two had quarreled over several cases before the Reichs-Uschla involving SA men, and Heinemann had informed him then that to "avoid any future misunderstanding, I refuse further written or personal contact with you."[56] But when Pfeffer queried him about Bouhler's unauthorized opening of SA mail, Heinemann abruptly replied that "all letters . . . received by the business office will be duly opened and processed as the business manager feels necessary in the interest of service."[57]

Holding stubbornly to the initial decision that the Reichs-Uschla had made several months earlier, Heinemann again suggested to Hitler in July that Pfeffer be removed, arguing that the Court was "no longer in the position to cooperate with him."[58] In short, Heinemann made it clear to the Führer that he wanted no future responsibility in mediating between the three quarreling leaders. The burden, therefore, now fell entirely on the Führer, who disagreed with the Reichs-Uschla chairman on how to handle the conflict. What became most evident was Hitler's general contempt for law and the normal functions of law courts. Even when his own judicial creatures, the Parteigerichte, failed to agree with him, he simply set their rulings aside as though they had never been decreed. Instead of expelling Pfeffer, he employed a favorite tactic: delaying a judgment until the last possible moment and then attempting to satisfy all sides. After Heinemann's retirement in November, he finally called the antagonists together with the new Reichs-Uschla chairman, Buch, and settled the strife.[59]

By far the most publicized personal clash in the NSDAP's early history was that in northern Germany and Berlin between Goebbels and the Strasser brothers, Gregor and Otto. Because of the support that the Strassers received in the northern Gaus for their left-wing program and because of the opposition that they encountered from Hitler and the Munich leadership, the rivalry eventually touched most major organizations in the party, including the Reichs-Uschla. Until the spring of 1926, Goebbels was one of Gregor Strasser's ardent followers in the north, helping Strasser organize the NSAG and coediting its journal, the *NS-Briefe*. After Strasser had been defeated at the Bamberg conference in February and Hitler had invited Goebbels to Munich in April for a speaking engagement, however, Goebbels broke with the Strasser circle and transferred his allegiance to the south. Soon thereafter he was approached by Hitler about taking the job of Gauleiter in Berlin (replacing the dull and less active Ernst Schlange), a position that Goebbels accepted in November.[60] Hitler's wooing of Goebbels to his side was crucial to the NSDAP's future; it represented another major success for the Führer in his fight against the Strassers to gain complete control of the party in the north.

The first open confrontation between the brothers and Goebbels occurred in June 1927. It resulted in part from the increasingly tense political situation in the Berlin Gau and partly from Goebbels's apparent crisis of confidence as the new Gauleiter. On May Day, Hitler had spoken in the

44

capital before five thousand persons, but only four days later the police slapped a temporary ban on the NSDAP. The reason given was a particularly provocative Nazi meeting held by Goebbels immediately after Hitler's appearance. The liberal press in Berlin quickly began to speak of a rift between Hitler and his Gauleiter over the latter's political tactics. The *Berliner Tageblatt* spoke of "hostile brothers" *(feindliche Brüder)* in the NSDAP, and *Welt am Abend* said: "By the ban of the Berlin National Socialists . . . Adolf the Great sees his most hallowed leader [Goebbels] in danger and fears a new loss of his own freedom to speak. As we learn from reliable sources, Hitler has consequently undertaken to wash vigorously the head of his meritorious pupil."[61]

Obviously worried by such reports, Goebbels appears to have suddenly experienced a lack of confidence in himself. He wrote to Hitler at the beginning of June, accusing the Strassers of treacherously informing the press of disagreements between himself and the Führer and of publishing an article in their own *Kampfverlag* ("Combat Publications") newspapers aimed at defaming his character. The article, entitled "Folgen der Rassenmischung" ("Results of racial mixing"), had appeared already in April and was allegedly written by Erich Koch, a party leader in the Ruhr and a close friend of the Strassers'. Supposedly, the article implied that Goebbels's club foot was a sign of racial impurity. But it was Goebbels's firm contention to Hitler that Otto Strasser and another of Strasser's close associates, Karl Kern from Berlin, had actually written the article, using Koch as their "straw man" *(Strohmann)*. He further maintained that the Strassers' "sole objective" was to "destroy" him in the party. He closed his note to Hitler by threatening to resign as Gauleiter if the Reichsleitung failed to act on his protests.[62]

Several days later the harried Gauleiter called a secret meeting of sixteen prominent party functionaries in Berlin and demanded that they give him a vote of confidence. At the meeting he vigorously accused Otto Strasser of writing the article supposedly written by Koch and of informing the

Welt am Abend of disagreements between himself and Hitler. It probably added to his suspicions and insecurity when he discovered a few days later that Gregor Strasser had learned of the "secret" discussion and had even received a written report on it within hours after it had broken up.[63]

Now it was the Strassers' turn to complain to Munich. Gregor informed Hitler's private secretary, Rudolf Hess, that Goebbels had made "inexcusable assertions" *(unerhörte Behauptungen)* against himself and his brother. He also claimed that Goebbels's newspaper, *Der Angriff* ("The Attack"), was not a neutral and private undertaking, as Hitler believed, but a party project designed to replace the Strassers' own newspaper, the *Berliner Arbeiterzeitung (BAZ)*, as the official Nazi organ in Berlin. Strasser maintained that Goebbels had promised several members that Hitler would write the lead article in the first edition of *Der Angriff* scheduled for the beginning of July. Yet Strasser also pointed out to Hess that during a recent visit with Hitler in Munich, the latter had flatly denied any intention of writing such an article.[64] Thus, with these accusations, the heretofore personal clash between Hitler and the Strassers acquired a new dimension—the beginning of a virtual war in the Berlin party press that would continue for three long years and would eventually lead to Otto Strasser's resignation in June 1930.

The role of Heinemann and the Reichs-Uschla in the affair was minimal. Beyond collecting letters of complaint from both sides, the Court made no official ruling, and only Heinemann was permitted to take part in discussions held among Hitler, Hess, and the rivals. As with the Bamberg confrontation earlier, the feud involved personalities and issues that were much too important to be dealt with by a mere bureaucratic institution. Goebbels was Hitler's fair-haired protégé, and the Strassers (despite their defeat at Bamberg) still possessed considerable influence and a number of newspapers in northern Gaus. The question, therefore, was not the personal squabble between Goebbels and Otto Strasser over Koch's article in the Strasser papers. The key issue was Hitler's attempt to increase his control over the NSDAP in the north by maintaining Goebbels's loyalty and by supporting the Gauleiter's position in Berlin.

These were Hitler's concerns in a closed meeting held on June 20–21 with Goebbels, Hess, and Heinemann. The purpose of the huddle was not to decide whether Otto Strasser or Koch had written the infamous article. Hitler's foremost consideration was to silence the charges in the Berlin press of a rift between himself and his hallowed Gauleiter. During the discussion it was decided that the *Völkischer Beobachter* would quickly publish an article "denying the lies in the Marxist press." It was also agreed that Hitler would personally travel to Berlin to show his solid support of his protégé.[65] The article in the *Beobachter* appeared several days later:

> The *Berliner Tageblatt, Vossische Zeitung, Welt am Abend,* and other "German" papers have recently reported a "brotherly quarrel in the house of Hitler," of "hostile brothers"; that in the NSDAP a "disagreement between Hitler and Goebbels" has broken out; that I have vigorously "washed the head" of Dr. Goebbels; and that I have told a well-known leader of the nationalist movement that I "was not in agreement with the methods of agitation employed by Dr. Goebbels."
>
> I have this to declare: all of the above assertions have been freely invented by the Jewish press for obvious reasons. Nothing has changed in the least in my relationship to Dr. Goebbels, and just as before, he possesses my complete confidence.[66]

Hitler's motive for not attempting to settle the feud in a decisive fashion was simple—he stood to gain more from it than either of the adversaries. By allowing it to continue, he could destroy the threat of a possible Goebbels-Strasser front against him (like that of two years earlier), and eventually he could completely consolidate his own power in the north. Nowhere was his policy of "divide and rule" more apparent or successful; consequently, the conflict continued until 1930. Moreover, whether it was Hitler or the Reichs-Uschla who made the final ruling in party strife, justice and the welfare of the individuals involved meant little. Gregor Strasser's long list of complaints remained in the Reichs-Uschla's files, uninvestigated and condemned to collect dust. Neither of the Strassers was invited to attend Hitler's discussion with Goebbels in mid June. The only sympathy shown to the brothers came from Heinemann. He was unwilling to supply Goebbels and others with the names of the party members who had informed the Strassers about the secret meeting that was held in Berlin to give the Gauleiter a vote of confidence.[67]

The role of the Reichs-Uschla in assisting Hitler to handle the major personal rivalries that emerged in 1927 was something less than spectacular. The Court had proved far more valuable to the Führer as an instrument to stabilize Munich's relations with its subordinate organizations by carefully policing Ortsgruppen and Gaus, suppressing their attempts for autonomy, and mediating serious factionalism in some. In short, Hitler found the Reichs-Uschla quite useful in helping to centralize the NSDAP's administrative structure and bring it more firmly under his authoritarian thumb.

There is little doubt that his efforts to rebuild and reconstruct the struggling party were vital to its future. In 1926 and 1927, when the country was experiencing relative political calm and the economy was beginning to pick up, the movement urgently needed a strong and tight-knit centralized organization in order to survive. This was even more crucial when one considers that Hitler himself—the star attraction and focal point of party unity—was officially prohibited from speaking throughout much of the nation until the end of 1927. Above all, this meant that close ties with Ortsgruppen and Gaus and the increasing of party membership rolls depended heavily on the ability of the national bureaucracy to propagandize Hitler's message and establish a solid political structure made up of utterly devoted vassals whose fealty to the Führer was absolutely assured. In this respect, such efforts were noticeable; by the end of 1927, the NSDAP had succeeded in expanding its total membership to the level it had been in November 1923 (approximately fifty-five thousand).[68] But what was most significant was that these were loyal and dedicated followers of Hitler and just the type of National Socialists he demanded.

At the same time, however, the party's national congress in Nuremberg in August 1927 had signaled a definite change in the movement's emphasis on propaganda and organization to attract new members. With the bitter experience of the Putsch still fresh in his mind, Hitler now began to dedicate himself to transforming the party's image from that of a "pseudo-military shock troop"[69] bent on destroying by violence the Weimar regime into that of a respectable party participating in elections and working within the democratic process. Consequently, whereas the NSDAP had worked in the past to attract the proletarian masses from the larger urban centers in the north and in the Ruhr, it switched at the end of 1927 to aiming its anti-Semitic and nationalist propaganda at the small-town lower middle classes and at the young. Hitler and other party leaders, for example, began to speak more often in the agricultural south and in Bavaria, attacking Jewish-controlled chain stores, agricultural estates owned by Jews, agrarian groups dominated by wealthy farmers, and Germany's rapprochement with France. Since the party's new emphasis was on election triumphs in order to show its slowly growing political virility, the Reichsleitung was pointing for the Reichstag election scheduled for May 1928 (the first in four years).[70]

To execute the changes, Hitler clearly recognized the need for some major changes at all levels of the party's administrative bureaucracy. Several Gauleiters were either dropped or "retired," and those that remained were given the important power of choosing Ortsgruppenleiters in their Gaus (a power previously reserved for Munich). A massive organizational shake-up occurred in the Reichsleitung. A new Nazi group for women, the Rote Hakenkreuz ("Red Swastika"), was created under the leadership of Elsbeth Zander. Heinrich Himmler, secretary to Gregor Strasser since 1925, replaced his boss as leader of the Reich Propaganda-Abteilung ("Propaganda Department"), and Strasser moved over to head the Organisationsausschuss, succeeding Heinemann.[71]

Heinemann was also replaced as head of the Reichs-Uschla. During 1927 the weakness of the Court and its aging and undynamic chairman had become quite apparent. The Reichs-Uschla found it impossible to discipline ranking subleaders inasmuch as few of them respected the judgment of its chief justice. For the most part the party leadership was composed of relatively young and active persons who were scarcely impressed by a retired general who was almost twice as old as they were.[72] Moreover, Heinemann was not the rubber stamp Hitler was seeking as head of the Reichs-Uschla. Heinemann had disagreed with the Führer in demanding Pfeffer's removal and had been sympathetic to the Strassers in their feud with Goebbels. In fact, in some instances the old man had actually committed the cardinal sin of expressing his disagreement with Hitler in party correspondence,[73] and many leaders were skeptical about whether he actually represented the views of the Reichsleitung. In May, Hitler had found it necessary to issue a circular to all Gaus and Ortsgruppen confirming that in "official party correspondence," Heinemann was not expressing his own "private opinion," but that of the "party leadership."[74]

In late November, Hitler decided to make the changes in the Reichs-Uschla that were needed to assure him of its absolute loyalty. He replaced Karl Ostberg, an assistant judge, with Hans Frank, the NSDAP's leading lawyer and a human instrument who was totally captivated by Hitler. Although he had officially joined the party only in 1927, Frank had been closely associated with the movement since 1919, when he counseled the small DAP as a program adviser to the party's expert on "high finance" and "interest slavery," Feder. Following the Putsch, Frank asked Hitler for an opportunity to serve the party again.[75] Except for a minor disagreement with his Führer in 1926 over the party's attitude toward the Tyrol, he remained one of Hitler's closest advisers and legal counselors. His rise in the NSDAP, beginning with 1927, was phenomenal—from the post of Reichs-Uschla assistant (which he held until 1933), he became during the Third Reich the Bavarian minister of justice, Reich minister without portfolio, and governor general of German-occupied Poland in 1939.

The other personnel change that Hitler made in the Reichs-Uschla was to "retire" Heinemann. His age (he was seventy in 1927) and his frequent absences from office during the summer because of illness provided the chief with a convenient excuse to ease the old man out. When Heinemann's exit became official, Hitler publicly announced that Heinemann had "requested" to be removed, and the Führer expressed his "deepest personal thanks" to him for his work and described him heroically as "an example of one fulfilling his duty to the utmost."[76]

Although Heinemann had a rather brief and inglorious career as head of the Reichs-Uschla, he had nevertheless aided Hitler considerably in establishing the courts firmly in the party's political organization. Under his direction, the Reichs-Uschla had become one of the party's central control and coordination agencies through which Hitler's personal wishes were transformed into binding policy. It has been estimated, for example, that the Reichs-Uschla handled at least two hundred different cases between January 1926 and November 1927.[77]

In addition, the Court had helped to protect Hitler's personal image in the party by drawing the dissatisfaction and discontent with its rulings (some of which were in fact imposed on the Court by Hitler) to itself. This could not help but promote the romantic and mythical conception among Nazi members that Hitler was the man chosen by fate and history to lead the NSDAP to victory in Germany.[78] Thus Heinemann, with his flair for bureaucratic detail and efficiency, had served his leader well. Hitler's choice as the new chairman of the Reichs-Uschla was another retired army officer (but one much younger than Heinemann), Major Walter Buch—a man who possessed the qualities of fanatical dedication and loyalty to the ideals of National Socialism and to Hitler personally.

3

The Unhappy
Party Judge

THE COMMISSIONING OF BUCH as chairman of the Reichs-Uschla was a crucial event in the history of the Parteigerichte. The tireless energy that this tall, thin, and dark-haired Hitler disciple brought to his new post was a principal ingredient in the continued development of the Parteigerichte during the closing years of the NSDAP's stormy Kampfzeit to conquer the Weimar Republic. Moreover, he was to remain chief of the party judiciary until the collapse of the Third Reich in 1945.

The son of a highly respected senate president with the Baden State Court of Appeals *(Oberlandesgericht)* in Karlsruhe, Buch was born in Bruchsal on 24 October 1883. He chose not to follow in his father's steps; and after finishing the gymnasium, he entered an infantry regiment in Constance, where he became an officer candidate *(Fahnenjunker)* and eventually a first lieutenant. This was the beginning of a military career that spanned seventeen years of active infantry service and saw him hold twenty-six different posts.[1] In the first months of World War I he served as a regimental adjutant and later as a company and battalion commander. With Germany's defeat in November 1918 and the dissolution of the special Machine Gun Apprentice School in Döberitz, where he was then commanding a battalion, he resigned from the army. He explained his decision by saying that he "did not want to work in the new command under the flag of Ebert [Friedrich Ebert, the German Socialist who was the first president of the Weimar Republic]."[2]

Buch's long army career and the disastrous World War had profound effects on his political and philosophical views. His career seemed to confirm for him that life was a Social Darwinistic "struggle for existence" and that militarizing the nation was not only necessary for Germany's survival in the world but was a precondition for its future rebirth and greatness. In addition, the war and the resulting political revolution in November 1918 increased the anti-Semitic attitudes that he had learned as a young boy from his rigid Lutheran parents. Each of these characteristics—anti-Semitism, glorification of military life, and an intense nationalistic feeling—was a factor in his decision later to join the local branch of the Nazi party in Karlsruhe.

He felt especially strongly about the value of military education for German youth. Such an education, he maintained, taught the young the virtues of "loyalty, trust, obedience, courage, bravery, and comradeship." Buch firmly believed that without these, Germany could never survive in the future. Consequently, once he entered the NSDAP, he continually urged the party's Hitler Youth Association (Hitler-Jugend, or HJ) to adopt an educational program that would indoctrinate its members in such ideals. Only then would it be possible, he emphasized, "to make the young people immune to the Jewish poison in all areas of public life."[3]

Buch's principal reason for entering the NSDAP was his deep-rooted anti-Semitism. He had learned to hate Jews and other "foreign races" while a child at home. His father (whom the son admired and respected highly) had turned toward Hitler shortly before his death in July 1921 because of the Führer's strong emphasis on anti-Semitism. Regarding his father's conversion, Buch later remarked that the "belief of my aged father has been my own."[4] Upon resigning from the army at the end of 1918, he immediately joined the secret, anti-Semitic Deutschvölkischer Schutz- und Trutzbund. This was another important step in his development as a radical Jew-hater. The group's major objective was the "moral rebirth" of Germany, and it attributed the country's collapse in World War I to the "pernicious and destructive influence of Jewry." In addition to Buch, the organization produced several others who later became ranking Nazi officials: among them were Streicher, Sauckel, Reinhard Heydrich, and Wilhelm Murr.[5]

Buch's anti-Semitic philosophy represented a synthesis of German völkisch thought with the ideology of a new "revolutionary nationalism" that began to develop among far-right elements at the beginning of the 1920s.[6] Thus, he despised Jews not so much for religious or cultural reasons, but on biological and racial grounds. For Buch, whose anti-Semitism was typically Nazi, the Jew had been Germany's enemy throughout history. He once declared that the "Jew is not a human being, he is a manifestation of decay"; he saw this "decay" most clearly in the decline of the German family and of the Germanic concepts of "honor" and "justice."[7] Supposedly, the destructive characteristics of Jewish blood had been allowed to mix with pure Aryan blood during the nineteenth century, and this fateful development had led to Germany's collapse in World War I. The reason for this, Buch argued, had been the liberal Enlightenment and the French Revolution, whose sole aim was "the emancipation of Judaism."[8] The result was the defeat of a superior people (that is, the Germans), whose destiny in the world was unlike that of other peoples: "There is no race with an equal or even similar depth of soul to the German. . . . The assertion that the French Revolution was contrived as a conspiracy by the Jewish enemy for the destruction of Germanic-Nordic blood can be proven with little difficulty today."[9]

Buch contended that, above all, German family life had suffered from the Jewish "destruction." Recalling the words once spoken by Martin Luther, he declared that the family was "the source of every people's blessings and misfortunes." He argued that the Jews were "artists at transformation" *(Verwandlungskünstler)*, and he was convinced of their in-

55

fluence on the decline in the number of children produced in the average German family during the nineteenth century. The Jewish attitude toward marriage, he maintained, was different from the German; matrimony for the Jew was a means to an end and was entered into solely for social advancement and economic gain. But in sharp contrast (or so he asserted), the German married for the production of healthy children and a close family life.[10] The result of this decay in family life was that German children were no longer educated in the noble virtues of trust, obedience, honor, and loyalty to their country. In his view, it had been the "inferior" (*Minderwertigen*, referring to the youth) in World War I who had taken "the reins in hand and led the people into . . . misery."[11]

There were two other vital areas that Buch believed had been eroded because of Jewish influence penetrating the German family: the old Germanic concepts of "honor" and "justice." Particularly the honor and pride of the German in himself and his nation, he insisted, had been undermined by the Jews. He complained, for example, that telling lies, slandering another person, or breaking one's word were no longer considered dishonorable. Here, too, he saw the decline of the family and the sexual intermingling of Germans with Jews as most responsible. In his judgment, German "honor" was something *unconditional*: "There can be no vacillation such as an 'indeed—but'; only a clear-cut 'yes' or 'no' can help."[12] The destruction of the moral honor of the individual German through sexual association with Jews was also responsible for the loss of national and ethnic honor. In typical Nazi fashion, he believed that the Weimar regime was controlled by Jews and Communists, and he asserted that the Versailles "Diktat" and the later acceptances of the Dawes plan and the Young plan were only Jewish tricks to repurchase Germany's honor as a nation.

He further contended that the terms "honor" and "justice" were inseparable; for him these were things that the Jew felt could also be purchased. Believing the myth of his völkisch ancestors, he argued that "Jewish dominance over peoples rests on the power of their money."[13] As an example, he cited what the Weimar legal system considered as "justice" and necessary protection for one's "honor" in a case of slander: the penalty of a money fine. He theorized that in a state ruled by "pure" Germans (that is, National Socialists), however, this would never be allowed to occur, because the Aryan concepts of honor and justice meant something more than money: "To the German, honor is more than money and more than life itself. With justification, the German feels himself struck in his blood when his honor has been insulted. His spirit, which pulsates through his blood, he feels is insulted by slander."[14]

Reflecting a distinct medievalism and the effect of his military background, Buch insisted that "every German man must be obligated and justified to encounter with weapons any other German man who insults his honor."[15] He contended that there was no general and valid law for all humanity in this respect—least of all a Jewish law for German people. Like sexual intercourse between different animals or between Germans and Jews, the applying of Jewish morality and Jewish justice to Germans was a violation of the "divine world order" *(göttliche Weltordnung)*. Buch's argument against this transgression was simple: "The more impure the blood, the less the capability for deciding what is just and unjust."[16] His solution was even simpler: "Justice in Germany or German law can only be . . . what is useful to the German people and to Germany."[17] This iron maxim, he argued, would form the basis for the new law of the future National Socialist state: "All enemies of the German people have sworn that they are against [us], not just those who are in control of the present system within the German frontier. From an instinct of self-preservation they hate us, because they know: that after we seize power there will be nothing remaining for them!"[18]

Buch's perverted ideology reveals an individual who felt himself and his nation threatened by forces that could be controlled only by violence. He was a man obsessed by fear; in this respect he was characteristic of European fascism in the 1920s and 1930s.[19] At the same time, however, his philosophy of Social Darwinian struggle, primitive militarism, nationalism, and ugly anti-Semitism—all reflected the broader synthesis unique to German National Socialism. For Buch the essence of Nazism was the "preservation of the German species" *(Erhaltung deutscher Art)*, which was threatened with destruction by Marxism, liberalism, and, above all, Judaism.[20]

His fear and resentment helped to explain his intense political activism following his retirement from the army. Believing the legend that Germany had been "stabbed-in-the-back" by the Socialist "criminals" of November 1918, he immediately joined the enemies of the new Weimar regime. In addition to his membership in the Schutz- und Trutzbund in 1920 and 1921, he entered the Bund Oberland, the Deutscher Vaterländischer Orden ("German Fatherland Order"), and various other war veterans' clubs in Baden. Along with his father, he became an active member of the German National Peoples' Party (Deutschnationale Volkspartei, or DNVP), which was formed by "old guard" conservatives at the beginning of 1919.[21] He and his wife, Elsa (whom he had married in September 1908), and their four young children lived in Scheuern, a tiny village outside Karlsruhe. Sometime during this period, Buch was appointed coeditor of a small völkisch newspaper in Karlsruhe, the *Badische Wochenzeitung*. Originally, the paper served as the headquarters of the local Schutz- und Trutzbund; when Buch entered the NSDAP, he worked diligently to transform the *Wochenzeitung* into a mouthpiece of the party.[22]

The precise date that Buch left the DNVP and joined the Nazi party is unclear. His home Ortsgruppe, Karlsruhe, was officially founded in May 1922, but he first met Hitler and was active in developing the Ortsgruppe during the previous year.[23] Until October 1923 he labored especially hard to expand the local, and he used his influence with the *Wochenzeitung* to support the group's propaganda efforts. Together with a young and zealous comrade, Emil Danzeisen, he helped the local to organize meetings and establish relations with other far-right groups in the area. Much of Danzeisen's time was spent in speaking about Hitler and the NSDAP to students in fraternities and athletic groups in Karlsruhe.

Such efforts hardly produced a booming stronghold for the Nazis. In May 1923 Buch informed his friend and principal contact in the Munich NSDAP, Amann, that Baden was "hostile country" *(feindliches Ausland)* for the party. Revealing his own subversive activity against the local authorities, he reported to Amann the following month that it was necessary for him to keep away from the party office in Karlsruhe in the near future. The police, he said, and "indeed the [whole] community knows exactly what is happening when I am there." While he was away during the last week of June, the police searched his home in Scheuern and the office of the *Wochenzeitung.* Apparently, however, they found little that would interest them except a few documents from the old Schutz- und Trutzbund.[24]

Despite his busy political activity with the party Ortsgruppe, Buch's burning ambition was to return to his old profession of commanding troops and educating young officers. Yet his idea was not to return to the army; notifying the Munich NSDAP, he expressed his strong desire to return to a military form of life through the party. Using Amann as his contact, he applied in the summer of 1923 for a national position in the SA.[25] He busily collected several impressive reference letters from his former wartime commanders and sent them to the Reichsleitung.[26] To complete his application, he traveled to Munich in July for a personal interview with Hitler. His efforts were successful, and the following month Hitler commissioned him commander of the SA units in Franconia, with headquarters in Nuremberg. This was only three months before the Munich Putsch.[27]

Although he was called with Streicher from Nuremberg to Munich on November 8, Buch's role in the Putsch was not significant. Blaming the failure of the insurrection on a Jewish conspiracy, he immediately called for a pogrom in revenge against the Jews. More important was his effort after the uprising to regroup and camouflage the SA, which, along with the entire NSDAP, was quickly banned in most states. In addition, the leader of the SA, Hermann Göring, was badly wounded and had been smuggled into Austria to escape capture by the Weimar authorities.

On November 13 Buch was named leader of the entire SA by the newly appointed secret leadership of the NSDAP (namely, Amann, Drexler, and Rosenberg). He quickly recruited his old friend from Karlsruhe, Danzeisen, to become his adjutant, and the two began the task of disguising the different SA units in Bavaria and Franconia. They organized athletic groups, rifle clubs, and choral societies as cover organizations for the illegal SA. Buch, however, was unable to support his family of five through his clandestine activities; consequently, in the following year he was forced to resign his post.[28]

When Hitler declared his intention to "refound" the NSDAP in February 1925, Buch quickly reentered the party and was made an SA commander in Munich. His background of hard work and undying devotion to the movement had not been forgotten by Hitler and the Munich leadership, and these qualities undoubtedly contributed to Hitler's choosing him as chairman of the party's Reichs-Uschla in November 1927. At the end of the month Hitler called Buch to a party meeting in Weimar, where he formally introduced the new Reichs-Uschla chairman to the Gauleiters. Furthermore, Hitler talked privately and bluntly with his fledgling chief justice: he informed Buch that the job of Reichs-Uschla head was not easy and that it would tax Buch's patience and loyalty to the limit. In this respect, the Führer's words were to prove fatefully correct.[29]

Beyond his blind loyalty to Hitler, several facts made Buch appear especially suited to lead the Nazis' highest "court of honor." Not only had he served impressively for seventeen years in the officer corps of the army, but he had also presided over the Deutscher Vaterländischer Orden's district court of honor in Munich. Yet the decisive factor in his appointment was probably his willingness to subordinate himself completely—even though he once held the rank of major in the army—to the former corporal and younger man Hitler. He had always emphasized to the Reichsleitung that he knew "nothing of personal sensitivity in placing myself under the strong command of a younger person."[30] After Hitler's friction with Heinemann over the old man's refusal to submit to the Führer's wishes in several Reichs-Uschla cases, this quality must have particularly worked to Buch's advantage.

His assignment to head the Reichs-Uschla and the Parteigerichte can only support the view that Hitler possessed a special knack for elevating to positions of leadership men who would remain his loyal and obedient disciples and would identify themselves totally with the aims of the party. Also, the appointment offered Buch the opportunity to continue his active political career (one that typified the lives of many ranking Nazi functionaries). Prior to the party's seizure of power in 1933, he served (in addition to presiding over the Reichs-Uschla) as a Reichstag deputy, party speaker and writer, coeditor of the *Völkischer Beobachter*, and major general in the SS *(SS-Gruppenführer)*.[31] Such intense activity kept Buch away from home much of the time, and despite his emphasis on close family ties and the pride with which he always spoke of his wife and children,[32] he was something less than a model father. His oldest daughter, Gerda (who married in September 1929 the head of the SA's insurance system, Martin Bormann), remarked later that, as a young girl, she and the family had always regarded their father "as merely a visitor" who "never stayed with us for any length of time."[33]

Buch's attitude toward Hitler was a rather peculiar one. Unquestionably, he worshiped his leader with religious fanaticism and identified completely with the basic ideology of nazism. Like his predecessor, Heinemann, he did not always agree with Hitler on matters involving the Reichs-Uschla, but he was willing to subordinate his own ideas to those of the Führer and to carry through the latter's decisions at any cost. He was in close contact with Hitler on every matter of importance that came before the Reichs-Uschla, and the Führer apparently had an extraordinary talent for convincing Buch in private discussions. Yet at the same time, Buch recognized early a fateful trait in Hitler that was eventually to cost the world dearly. Aware of what he termed Hitler's "contempt for humanity" *(Menschenverachtung)*, he wrote to his boss in 1928:

> I have recently acquired an impression about a number of things and feel it is my difficult duty to tell you, Herr Hitler, that you have a contempt for humanity that fills me with grave uneasiness. I do not believe, Herr Hitler, that a person who is filled with human contempt from recent experiences can continue to fulfill a task that has burdened a people's fate for centuries. . . . It is quite clear to me that for some time you have believed yourself capable of building on the bitter disappointments of people and that during the past months you have received such a vote. I hope, however, these votes will be permanent.[34]

Unlike Hitler, Buch respected his fellow Germans enough to believe that the success of National Socialism could only be achieved by developing a movement that offered reputable leaders and a substantive ideology. Unfortunately, neither he nor anyone else could predict the coming of the Depression a year later, with its tragic economic and political consequences. Yet, he never seemed to learn that Hitler's last wish for the NSDAP was to employ intelligent and socially respectable leaders. In this respect, at least, the following observation of him by a contemporary was correct: "Major Buch was the unhappy supreme party judge. . . . I dealt with Buch often and always found him an honorable man with the best intentions. . . . His views on relations that were harmful to the party distinguished themselves only too often from those of Hitler and were not carried through."[35]

In several important respects, Buch was a member of the generation that was born and reared under the glorious flag of Bismarck's Second Reich but which found no difficulty in justifying the Nazi swastika or the cruel injustices of Hitler's Third Reich. His glorification of power and the military, his strong national feeling, his crude racism—all were widespread sentiments in the society of the Second Reich and far more so in Hitler's regime. His limited family environment and narrow religious training combined with seventeen years in the army to destroy any chance that he may have had to develop a balanced or rational political philosophy.

On the other hand, Buch was an "activist," and the Nazi party offered him a means for expressing his emotions of fear and hatred and his sense of superiority. His personality, moreover, presented certain internal contradictions. While he was vigorously anti-Semitic and preached a philosophy of justice that totally subordinated the individual to the Nazi movement, he was "uneasy" about what he termed Hitler's apparent "contempt for humanity." While he preached the virtues and morality of a close family life, his eldest daughter complained that she always regarded her father "merely as a visitor."

Nevertheless, insofar as the Nazi Parteigerichte were concerned, the real significance of Buch was not his enigmatic personality. His importance lay in his role as a member of the NSDAP and chairman of its Reichs-Uschla and in his contribution between 1927 and 1945 in aiding Hitler's rise to power and domination of Germany through a brutal totalitarianism.

4

The Road to Power, 1928-1933

THE NSDAP'S FINAL DRIVE to power in Germany was a stormy and rocky affair to say the least. Electoral disappointments were mixed with frustrations over Hitler's new "legality" course; factionalism and low morale were combined with brief intervals of unity and euphoric optimism; and organizational changes were continued amid a growing animosity between the party structure and the SA. The Uschlas, because of their peculiar nature as instruments of "investigation and conciliation," were closely involved in all of these.

Indeed, the development of the party's judiciary from 1928 to 1933 (as was the case with most of the party's bureaucratic organizations) both paralleled and reflected the growth and needs of the entire movement. Yet, at the same time, the Uschlas' functions remained basically constitutional: purging disobedient party members, mediating factionalism in Ortsgruppen and Gaus and dissension among leaders, and examining closely applications for membership, to ensure that only "irreproachable" persons of "pure Aryan descent" gained entry.

The year 1927 ended for the NSDAP on a rather unencouraging note. The nation's political and economic scene remained fairly stable while the party began the difficult work of pointing for the upcoming national election in May 1928. Even though its membership had jumped 55 percent during the year, to fifty-five thousand, the party could claim only four deputies in the Reichstag (Gregor Strasser, Feder, Wilhelm Frick, and Hans Dietrich) and fourteen members in the various state legislatures (predominantly in Bavaria and Thuringia).[1] Speaking in Essen in early December, Hitler set the tone for the party's future when he said: "The National Socialist idea will be carried to all circles of the German people. Intellectuals and manual laborers, miners and industrial leaders, wealthy businessmen and employees shall know what National Socialism means, what its goals are, what its struggle is, and they [all] will be won for the National Socialist philosophy."[2] In short, his objective was to build (through relentless propaganda and election triumphs) a mass movement of millions that could bring him political power.

Such a mass party, however, was not to be created without strong discipline, unity, and sacrifices by the party's leadership and its rank and file. Victory could only be won when all members were thoroughly indoctrinated in the party's most sacred principle, "the community comes before the individual" *(Gemeinnutz geht vor Eigennutz)*. In this respect the party attempted to introduce a new morality and a new code of ethics to members—a code that rewarded only actions that served the needs and the interests of the NSDAP. In the tiny red Nazi membership book (issued to each member beginning in 1927), Hitler's introductory lines called on every National Socialist to fulfill his obligations to the movement and to "consider that the greatest work can only be completed by people when they are willing to subordinate themselves to the greater common necessity and common good."[3]

This, in essence, was to be the future guideline for decision-making in all party organizations, particularly in the Uschlas, which were solidly established in all Gaus and most Ortsgruppen by the end of 1930. Through their directives and rulings, the Uschlas were to educate members in sacrificing their personal interests for those of Hitler and the entire Nazi "community." The Uschlas, therefore, became the primary agencies for developing the morality of total, individual selflessness and loyalty to the movement.

The "new" Reichs-Uschla, now headed by Major Buch and including Ulrich Graf and Dr. Frank, began its work at the close of 1927 by assisting Hitler in settling the quarrel between Bouhler, Kaufmann, and Pfeffer. The seemingly endless conflict had become well known in the Reichsleitung, the SA, and several Gaus, and Hitler believed it was time to end it. In a closed meeting at party headquarters on the Schellingstrasse, the Führer and Buch met with the quibbling leaders, who finally confessed that their disagreements were the result of "mutual misunderstandings." Under the Führer's watchful eye, the apologies flowed thick and heavy, and a few days later, a note was dispatched from Buch's office to members of the Reichsleitung and Ortsgruppen in Kaufmann's Gau, announcing that the dispute had been "settled."[4]

While Buch was helping to achieve this success, however, several new storms were brewing in the Württemberg, Silesian, and Rhenish Gaus, and in the Nuremberg Ortsgruppe. In each instance, the disorders involved rebellion by locals against their Gauleiter, and the Reichs-Uschla was called on to mediate between the warring factions. Except for the hassle in Württemberg (where the Gauleiter, Eugen Munder, was forced to resign for committing adultery with a fellow member's wife and for opposing Hitler's readmittance of an old opponent, Christian Mergenthaler, into the NSDAP), the Reichs-Uschla supported the leaders under attack and ruthlessly suppressed the rebels by expelling them.[5]

In Silesia, dissension arose at the beginning of 1928 between the Ortsgruppe in Breslau and the Gauleiter, Helmuth Brückner. Like Streicher and some other Gauleiters, Brückner was a boastful and outspoken personality who attempted to rule his Gau with an iron hand. The Breslau faction, forming an *Arbeitsgemeinschaft* ("Working Association") to fight the Gauleiter, flooded the Reichsleitung with protests demanding his removal. Munich's response was to send Buch and Gregor Strasser (Brückner's close friend) to the

Gau to remind the opposition that "justice is what serves the movement." When this failed, the Gau-Uschla (on orders from Brückner) expelled the troublemakers and requested that the Reichs-Uschla confirm its action. The Reichs-Uschla obliged immediately. Instead of using the mass of affidavits that it had collected (which were overwhelmingly hostile to Brückner) in order to investigate him, it utilized the records to protect him and to prove that the opposition was guilty of "continuous agitation" and of breaking party discipline. In addition, the Reichs-Uschla relied for its verdict on the hearsay evidence of an obviously prejudiced outsider in the case, Strasser.[6]

The Court accorded the same iron support to the leader of the Rhineland-South Gau, Robert Ley, when he became locked in a quarrel during the spring with the staff of his party paper in Cologne, the *Westdeutscher Beobachter*. Ley, who was famous for his excessive drinking, was involved in a drunken orgy with several party friends in a Cologne brothel, and the *Beobachter* published a story of the infamous event on its front page. A few months later the city's Socialist press printed (both in poetry and photographs) its version of the Gauleiter's activities, and soon the Reichsleitung began to receive denunciations of Ley from several locals and the Gau SA.[7] Hoping to minimize the importance of the incident, the Reichs-Uschla quickly advised one local: "The party is neither a bridal wreath nor an association for moral concerns. It is an alliance of fighters for the future of the German people. . . . Fighters are not to be compared with the narrow-minded."[8]

Further ignoring the uproar in the Gau, the Reichs-Uschla and Hitler totally accepted Ley's claim that he was innocent. In a secret discussion with Hitler and Buch in Munich, the humbled leader begged forgiveness and "guaranteed Herr Hitler on his word of honor that he never had been in the house of ill repute." Moreover, to counter the accusations, Ley assured Hitler that he would promptly file a legal suit against the house's pimp *(Zuhälter)* for blackmail *(Erpressung)*.[9] This represented the extent of the inquiry into Ley's blatant act of impropriety; he was a tested and loyal Hitler vassal and was far more valuable to the party than a few small Ortsgruppen. In addition, the party's Gauleiter corps was fairly well established by now, and Ley was a pillar in its structure.

Another stone column in the party's second-rank leadership was Streicher. At the beginning of 1928 serious opposition to Nuremberg's boss and autocrat began to gain momentum again. The decision made by Hitler and the Reichs-Uschla several months earlier not to investigate or reprimand Streicher for his role in the "Parteitag Fraud" had done little to blunt the mounting discontent with the powerful leader. Consequently, several section leaders and prominent members in the city notified Hitler that they had organized a new Nazi Ortsgruppe, the Middle Nuremberg NSDAP.

Enraged by this obvious act of disobedience and independence, Hitler immediately demanded that the group disband;[10] but its leaders continued to organize, and by late spring it appeared to be threatening the NSDAP's campaign effort in Franconia for the upcoming Reichstag and Bavarian Landtag elections in May. The opposition, which included ranking SA officers from the Franconia Gau, busily divided itself into "sections," issued circulars and invitations to anti-Streicher meetings, and held numerous *Werbeabend* ("recruiting evenings," a popular Nazi-style meeting that generally included entertainment—songs, comic skits, and so forth—and propaganda speeches). In addition, the rebels established their own newspaper, the *Deutsche Volkszeitung*, whose articles consisted of vicious attacks on Streicher (which accused him of stealing from the party local, labeling several local leaders "Jewish bastards," and favoring the SS over the SA) and on the Munich leadership for continuing to support him.[11]

Although the Reichsleitung received urgent letters from Ortsgruppen near Nuremberg expressing fear and panic over the situation,[12] the Reichsleitung responded with remarkable coolness. Using Buch, the Reichs-Uschla, and Propaganda Chairman Himmler to console the excited locals, it sought to encourage the impression that Streicher still had everything under control. Buch himself quarreled bitterly with Streicher and even expressed the hope that Hitler would intervene against him, but such was only wishful daydreaming.[13] Finally, in mid April, Hess made an emotional plea to the dissidents for unity, asking them to "take regard for the great common aim" of the NSDAP by dropping their attack until after the May elections. But in a response that did little to inspire the Reichsleitung's hopes, their leadership quickly replied that "in the struggle against Streicher, nothing more can be said about the great common aim over that of the individual person."[14]

Only the election results on May 20 could measure Munich's success in controlling the rebels. In the Reichstag election, the NSDAP experienced a bitter disappointment. Despite its new emphasis on winning political power at the polls, the party captured 100,000 fewer votes than in December 1924 and only 2.6 percent of the nation's vote (which gave it an unimpressive twelve seats in the national legislature). But unexpectedly, a pleasant surprise for the movement came from results in Nuremberg and the electoral districts of Franconia and Upper Bavaria–Swabia. The serious wrangling in Nuremberg notwithstanding, the Nazis received 100,761 votes (8.1 percent) in Franconia and 72,127 votes (6.2 percent) in Upper Bavaria–Swabia, and Streicher was reelected to the Bavarian Landtag. Interestingly enough, both districts gave the party its highest percentage of votes in 1928; the other districts where it managed relatively well were in the rural areas of Hanover-Brunswick (4.4 percent), Schleswig-Holstein (4.0 percent), and Weser-Ems (5.2 percent).[15] Insofar as the Nazis and German Nationalists (DNVP) lost significantly nationwide and insofar as the big winner was the German Social Democratic Party (Sozialdemokratische Partei Deutschlands, or SPD) and to a lesser extent the German Communist Party (Kommunistische Partei Deutschlands, or KPD), the whole electoral experience represented a major setback for the far right in German politics.

70

The victory of Streicher and the NSDAP at the polls in Franconia, however, destroyed any further threat to the party from the Middle Nuremberg opposition. Streicher, who was hardly even questioned by the Reichsleitung (except by Buch) about his behavior, immediately ordered his Orts-Uschla to expel the rebels, and the Reichs-Uschla agreed with him.[16] Instead of being fugitives from justice, the purged now found themselves the victims of injustice, dispensed mainly through the Parteigerichte. Obviously, the sole concern of the courts was to protect Hitler's name and image in Nuremberg and to support his loyal vassal Streicher at all costs. In this respect the Uschlas' decisions revealed clearly that unconditional obedience to Hitler was the only major qualification one needed to become either a member of the NSDAP or one of its political elite.

The sudden rash of disorders in the spring and the necessity of utilizing the Reichs-Uschla to handle them prompted Hitler in late April to issue an order aimed at increasing the authority of the Reichs-Uschla. The command, which stated that the rulings of the Reichs-Uschla were "to be obeyed by all party members and officers including the first chairman of the party,"[17] even subordinated Hitler to the Court. The phrase "including the first chairman," however, was clearly a gross fiction and was designed to deceive party members by making them believe that the Reichs-Uschla was an institution that supposedly stood above all party leaders (including Hitler).[18]

In theory the effect of the order was to strengthen the power and prestige of the Reichs-Uschla considerably, but in reality it meant almost nothing; the Führer could appoint and remove the members of the Court at his pleasure, and he could control or overrule it at any time. In short, Hitler was creating a tool that he could dominate entirely and one that could take full responsibility for his decisions that were unpopular in the NSDAP. Beyond these considerations the new command signaled the start of a sophisticated reorganization and updating of the Uschla system that was to follow in 1929 and 1930.

An indication of the extent to which Hitler controlled the Reichs-Uschla and his party's leadership came toward the end of 1928. In a rare occurrence indeed, when the Führer was accused of libel by Gottfried Feder, one of the NSDAP's theoreticians and a self-styled expert on the "destruction of interest slavery," the Reichs-Uschla convened and promptly acquitted Hitler. In a further effort to squash Feder and to show the party how utterly hopeless and ridiculous it was to attack its chief, Hitler asked for an opinion on the matter from the Gauleiters. They, too, exonerated him quickly; and Feder, faced with a phalanx of opposition, begged for a reconciliation.[19]

Naturally, the Reichs-Uschla's guiding principle was to protect the leaders favored by Hitler or the Reichsleitung. During the summer, Goebbels's rivalry with Otto Strasser heated up once again as the Berlin Gauleiter began to challenge the Strassers' *Berliner Arbeiterzeitung* by using the local SA to intimidate the paper's news agents and by declaring his own *Der Angriff* to be the party's "district organ" for the capital. In addition, the Strassers began to encounter similar competition from other leaders in northern districts with regard to the circulation and sale of their newspapers. In Essen, a movement was begun by the Ortsgruppenleiter, Joseph Terboven, and others in the Ruhr Gau to eliminate the Strassers' *Essener Arbeiterzeitung* and to establish a new party paper, the *Neue Front.*

To block his competitors, Otto Strasser filed charges against Terboven in a civil court in Essen, and he complained to the Reichsleitung.[20] The reply of the Reichsleitung was a noncommittal note from Buch, who informed the irate publisher that in "the event a complaint arises against another Party Comrade, it should either be buried in the common ground of philosophy or taken before the forum of the competent USA [Uschla]."[21] The fight for control of the party's press in Berlin and the north was thus allowed to continue, only to be settled by Strasser's resignation from the party in June 1930.

Strasser was rapidly becoming a condemned loser with

the Uschla. While complaining about Goebbels, he and Erich Koch attacked Kaufmann and accused the Ruhr Gauleiter of pocketing money from his Gau treasury. Kaufmann, who was found guilty of the charge (and of several other offenses) by the Reichs-Uschla and then lied to Hitler by denying everything, was nevertheless totally exonerated.[22] The only punishment he received came a year later, when he was being considered for the new position of Gauleiter of Hamburg. Hess, reminding him that the Reichsleitung had not forgotten about his breach of honor to Hitler, informed him that "Herr Hitler must make your [new] appointment as Gauleiter dependent on your request for a pardon in the appropriate manner from your Führer." Full of anxiety, Kaufmann swiftly and humbly asked for the pardon.[23]

Hitler's protection of dishonest leaders, such as Kaufmann, Streicher, Ley, and others, obviously made a shambles of the idea that the Reichs-Uschla should function as the party's supreme "court of honor." It also upset Chief Justice Buch, who disliked having characters hold high party offices and having Hitler turn a deaf ear to their shenanigans. Without much luck, Buch attempted to convince his boss that the NSDAP was now strong enough to rid itself of those "misfits" (Schädlinge) and "unprincipled weaklings" (charakterlose Schwächlinge) who could only damage the party's image and call forth accusations of "Marxist corruption."[24] Unfortunately, the head of the Reichs-Uschla took his job a bit too seriously at times, and his definitions of "misfits" and "weaklings" were hardly the same as those of his leader. To Hitler, they were persons who disagreed with him. On the other hand, Buch himself was not lily-white innocent in such matters; he thought nothing of hearing cases that involved close personal friends in the Reichsleitung (for example, Georg Hallermann, an SA adjutant; Dr. Frank; and Elsbeth Zander) and of showing them the same favoritism that Hitler accorded to others.[25]

Despite his differences with Hitler, Buch's career in the NSDAP began to blossom in 1928. The same was true for his Reichs-Uschla assistants, Graf (who was reelected to the Munich city council) and Frank (who became leader of the Nazi's new organization for lawyers and judges, the Bund nationalsozialistischer deutscher Juristen).[26] Buch was chosen by Hitler as a party candidate for the Reichstag, and in May he was elected. His work in the Reichstag mainly involved the study of youth questions and the problem of government compensation for disabled veterans. Moreover, his immunity before the law as a deputy (by Article 37 of the Weimar Constitution) was utilized by the party when he was appointed the responsible editor for the *Völkischer Beobachter*. The object was to use his immunity to prevent or delay civil suits brought against the paper or its editor for publishing articles that slandered or defamed opponents of the Nazis.[27] Buch himself wrote many of the articles, which finally prompted the Reichstag to open criminal proceedings against him.[28]

Buch also found himself in demand as a party speaker, addressing various party organizations and SA units. His speeches were usually canned affairs on the Uschla system, party "justice," or the Jewish influence on the "decay" of the German family. Similar to most Nazi leaders, he was one who had little to say intellectually but who always spoke his thoughts anyway. Because of his perverted *Weltanschauung* ("view of the world"), he hardly possessed the vice of being rational, and his speeches were labors of passion designed to play on the fears and emotions of his listeners.[29]

Party speakers had always been a feature of the NSDAP's propaganda efforts, but with the party's disappointing loss in the May elections, they became a particularly crucial factor. In October a course of instruction for speakers, under the guidance of Fritz Reinhardt (Gauleiter of Upper Bavaria–Swabia), was established (leading to the creation in June 1929 of his *Rednerschule,* or Speaker's Training School). At the end of the year the party proudly announced that some three hundred speakers had addressed over twenty thousand meetings and assemblies during 1928 (with Goebbels [188] and Gregor Strasser [139] leading the way).[30] Because of their importance, such speakers (who were usually paid for their services) were held strictly accountable for their work and were disciplined by the Uschla.

Most troubles involving Reich and Gau speakers centered around their failure to appear at a scheduled engagement sponsored by a local or district organization. Many were roving Ortsgruppenleiters or Gauleiters who were bitterly disliked outside their home organizations, and when they spoke to an unfriendly group, serious problems often arose. An example was the so-called Eckernförde Affair in April 1930. Streicher's deputy Gauleiter in Nuremberg, Karl Holz, was a guest speaker at an assembly of the party local in Eckernförde (Schleswig-Holstein Gau). Early in the meeting, Holz became embroiled in a vigorous argument with the Schleswig SA commander, Joachim Meyer-Quade.

The disagreement centered around who possessed disciplinary authority over the assembly hall when a band of Communists entered and began to heckle Holz and disrupt the program. The Communists were successful mainly because Holz and Meyer-Quade were longstanding enemies. The two began to quarrel loudly, with the results that order collapsed completely, brawling ensued, and the meeting was brought to an abrupt and inglorious end. The Schleswig SA complained bitterly about Holz to the Gau-Uschla and the Reichs-Uschla, but neither tribunal investigated the Franconian leader seriously.

As a consequence of such problems, some party speakers failed at the last moment to summon enough courage to show. When this happened, it was the job of the Reichs-Uschla to work closely with the Reich Propaganda Department to investigate the delinquent speaker and, if necessary, to punish him by withdrawing his speaking privileges (and thereby also that source of income). In November 1928 Wilhelm Kube (Nazi deputy in the Prussian Landtag and leader of the Ostmark Gau) failed to appear as a program speaker for several Ortsgruppen in the Baden Gau. The Baden Gauleiter, Robert Wagner, protested to the Reichs-Uschla and the Propaganda Department. However, both agencies exonerated Kube when it was discovered that he had given the Ortsgruppen the required two-weeks advance notice that he would not attend their meetings. Similarly, the Reichs-Uschla acquitted Dr. Hans Nieland, a Nazi Reichstag member and head of the party's Foreign Department *(Auslands-Abteilung)* in Hamburg, when he refused to address several rowdy and impolite locals in the Westphalia-South Gau.[31]

Because of the increasing use of the Uschla in policing and controlling such everyday party activities, it became apparent to Hitler that the entire judicial system required a major reorganizing and updating. Since their creation, the Reichs-Uschla and its lower courts had operated rather haphazardly and without an extensive set of guidelines to define their objectives, jurisdiction in the party, and technical procedures for investigations and trials. In most instances, for example, use of affidavits or other written testimony had been the courts' only method for securing evidence and rendering a decision; personal interrogations and formal trials were rarely used. But in the summer of 1929 Buch initiated discussions with the Gau-Uschla chairmen to lay plans for a detailed order that would guide the Uschlas' actions. A long session on the guidelines was held at the Nuremberg Reichsparteitag in early August, and the result was the first major directive for the Uschlas *(Richtlinien für die Untersuchungs- und Schlichtungsausschuss der Nationalsozialistischen Deutschen Arbeiterpartei)*, which was issued by the Reichsleitung two weeks later.[32]

Above all, the directive confirmed the constitutional nature of the Uschlas by giving a comprehensive description of their functions. Their chief aim was "to protect the common honor of the Party and [its] individual members" by absolving party members of "unjustified suspicions of their honesty" and by compromising "differences of opinion in the best possible manner." Any disciplinary action (such as expulsion) was to be pronounced according to the party statutes of May 1926, and all Uschla judges were sworn to absolute silence on every court procedure.[33] Interestingly enough, the order also provided possible "double jeopardy" for party members involved in cases before public or civil courts outside the NSDAP. Even though a member might be acquitted in a trial before a civil court, his competent Uschla could open proceedings against him "if it became known that the facts of the civil proceedings contained in themselves a breach of honor and injury to the NSDAP."[34]

In addition, the directive elaborately defined a set of new technical procedures for Uschla investigations and trials. Especially noteworthy in the procedures were the presence of the "leadership principle" and the fact that no Uschla was authorized to open an investigation or to discipline a party member by itself. As had generally been the case, the Uschlas were intended by the directive to be primarily advisory bodies and agencies to collect evidence for their respective political leaders (that is, the Ortsgruppenleiter for the Orts-Uschla, the Gauleiter for the Gau-Uschla, and Hitler for the Reichs-Uschla). The political leader was indeed given a large measure of control over his Uschla; he could appoint and remove its members, and he was responsible for ordering it into session, signing the Uschla's decree for any disciplinary action, and then carrying out the decree. Although such leaders were obligated to act according to these regulations, more often than not, many (like Streicher and Kaufmann) continued to assume that laws were made to be broken, and they either made their own decisions arbitrarily or bullied their Uschla into line by intimidating its judges, threatening it with dissolution, or removing its chairman.[35]

Finally, the directive made extensive arrangements for a preliminary inquiry (such as the collection of oral testimony and written affidavits) and for a trial (which included a closed meeting of the Uschla with the contending parties and their witnesses, an interrogation of the defendant and his witnesses by the judges, a questioning of the witnesses by both the plaintiff and the defendant, and a final ruling by the Uschla). It also outlined four judgments that an Uschla could render. First, it could declare itself incompetent to handle a particular case because it concerned "private and family affairs" that did not involve the NSDAP, because it related to a "higher party reason" *(höheren Parteiraison)*, or because another Uschla was competent. If an Uschla did decide to complete an investigation, however, it was authorized to issue one of three verdicts: acquittal of the accused, guilty with a warning, or guilty with expulsion from the party. Moreover, the order established new guidelines for appeals, by which expelled persons could appeal their cases upward to the Gau-Uschlas and the Reichs-Uschla.[36]

There is little question that the directive was a significant step in the development of the Parteigerichte. Where the Uschlas' primary objectives and their investigation and trial procedures were concerned, it remained the basic foundation for the Uschla system and for the later Parteigerichte of the Third Reich. On the other hand, the strong control given to political leaders over the Uschlas represented a serious limitation on their freedom and on their ability to issue equitable and fair decisions. Not only did it ensure that many Uschlas would continue to operate as merely bureaucratic "tools" for their leaders, but it meant that their use of evidence would rarely be discriminating or objective. As always, they would (if necessary to satisfy their political leader) function as kangaroo courts, depending heavily for their judgments on hearsay evidence and biased witnesses and generally dispensing with justice instead of administering it.

Another effect of the directive was to increase the centralized control of the Reichs-Uschla over its subordinate Uschlas. At the end of 1929 the Reichs-Uschla began requiring all Gaus to report the names, addresses, and professions of their Uschla chairmen. When some Gaus failed to reply, the Reichs-Uschla dispatched a circular that angrily snapped, "It is incomprehensible that these Gaus think of themselves as organizations when they give no attention to the orders of the R.L. [Reichsleitung]." The circular continued, "Such nonobservance of unified organization . . . runs strictly against the wishes of the Führer."[37] Attempting to tighten its control even more, the Reichs-Uschla even began to hound subordinate groups and Uschlas about failures of form in the transaction of party business. It made no secret, for example, of its disapproval of any disrespect shown to party leaders in official party correspondence.[38]

The Reichs-Uschla's efforts at bringing its subordinate benches into line in day-to-day party activities were fairly successful. Within a few months it possessed a comprehensive list of most Gau-Uschla chairmen and their professions, which revealed them to be well educated and predominantly from the middle class (see table 1). Although the largest

TABLE 1. GAU-USCHLA CHAIRMEN

Name	Gau	Profession
Konrad Backfish	Baden	Surveyor
V. Kratz	Bergisch-Land-Niederrhein/Bezirk	School Principal
Hans Jaene	Brandenburg	—
Erich Hildebrand	Danzig	—
Just Dillgardt	Essen/Bezirk	—
Hermann Kluge	Gross-Berlin	—
Walter Tiessler	Halle-Merseburg	Postal Inspector
Kurt Korn	Hamburg	Lawyer
Richard Herbert	Hessen-Darmstadt	Dentist
Otto Spiess	Hessen-Nassau-Nord	School Principal
Otto Wamboldt	Hessen-Nassau-Süd	Postal Inspector
Gustav Leidenroth	Magdeburg-Anhalt	Merchant
Wilhelm Klitzing	Mecklenburg	—
Christian Kühn	Mittelfranken	Lawyer
Bauer	München	Teacher
Ulrich Schön	Niederbayern	Customs Official
von Heimburg	Oberbayern	Police President

TABLE 1. CONTINUED

Name	Gau	Profession
Karl Götz	Oberfranken	Government Administrator
Ernst Tiefenböck	Oberpfalz	Medical Doctor
Mohr	Ost-Hannover	Lawyer
Georg Eschmann	Ostmark	Professor
Arno Nitschmann	Ostpreussen	Engineer
Graupner	Pommern	Blacksmith
Heinrich Mainz	Rheinland	—
Willi Schmelcher	Rheinpfalz	Architect
Robert Grill	Saargebiet	—
Kluge	Sachsen	Lawyer
Ferdinand v. Hiddessen	Schlesien	Cavalry Captain
Werner Schmalmack	Schleswig-Holstein	—
Ludwig Böhm II	Schwaben	Lawyer
Leister	Süd-Hannover-Braunschweig	Government Administrator
Heinrich Ehrlich	Unterfranken	—
Gustav Bertram	Weser-Ems	Railroad Administrator
Piclum	Westfalen	Lawyer
J. Kobold	Württemberg	Engineer

SOURCE: "Verzeichnis der Gau-Uschla-Vorsitzenden," October 1930, IfZ, F 28, pp. 40–41 (photocopy).

number (6) possessed law degrees, the NSDAP did not necessarily demand that its judges be lawyers. Inasmuch as the party and its leaders despised the Weimar legal system and law of any kind (except their own), the party's judiciary was to be the antithesis of the system that was then current. Above all, the Uschlas were to be tribunals of "honor" whose judges ideally would be "officers from the old army" with a "healthy German concept of honor."[39]

Despite the growing significance of the Uschlas and despite the directive of 1929, the task of most Uschla chairmen was not easy. Because of the negative nature of their work (namely, investigating fellow members and ordering punishments or expulsions) and because of their subordinate relationship to political leaders, they were often the most unpopular officials in the NSDAP. The average party member viewed the Uschla as a "necessary evil" (as did many political leaders), and such conditions did not pass unnoticed by the Reichs-Uschla. Chief Justice Buch, recognizing what he called the daredevilish temperament *(draufgängerische Temperament)* of some Gauleiters, attempted continually to console Gau-Uschla chairmen by telling them that it was their "eternal duty" to convince their leader that the "Uschla's activity does not weaken the authority of the Gauleiter, but strengthens it."[40]

A glaring weakness in the directive of 1929 was its complete lack of guidelines dealing with the Uschlas' relationship to the NSDAP's paramilitary wings, the SA and SS. The party's dual heritage as political organization and defense league affected not only its general development in the early years, but also the growth of the Parteigerichte. Since the Uschlas were a part of the movement's political organization, any encroachment by an Uschla into the quasi-military affairs of the SA (or SS, inasmuch as it was a part of the SA until July 1934) only added to the inherent ill will that existed between the political and military branches. A ticklish question facing the Reichsleitung, therefore, was that of defining the jurisdiction of the Uschlas in cases involving SA or SS men.

Solving the problem became particularly urgent during 1930, when the combined membership of the SA and SS passed the one hundred thousand mark and Hitler commissioned Röhm as his new SA chief of staff (Osaf), replacing Pfeffer. Hitler's general attitude toward the SA and his disagreements with Pfeffer and Röhm were well known in party circles.[41] Following the Putsch and the resulting dissolution and reconstruction of the NSDAP, Hitler clearly intended the future function of the SA to be "political," not military. He stated in *Mein Kampf* that it should be an auxiliary troop for "defense and education in the National Socialist movement."[42] With the memory of the Putsch fresh in his mind, he demanded that the SA subordinate itself completely to the party organization and that it adhere strictly to the latter's policy of "legality" to achieve power. This meant avoiding armed confrontations with the authorities or police, but winning in the streets by using brass knuckles and rubber truncheons on Socialists, Communists, and other opponents of the Nazis. In November 1926 the Führer had instructed Pfeffer that "it is not by dagger and poison or pistol that the road can be cleared for the movement, but by the conquest of the streets. We must teach the Marxists that the future master of the streets is National Socialism, just as it will some day be the master of the state."[43]

The antagonisms between party and SA and between Hitler and his staff chiefs were also reflected in the development of the Parteigerichte. Here, too, there was a dual conflict between institutions and personalities. It will be recalled that tempers flared between Pfeffer and Reichs-Uschla Chairman Heinemann over cases involving the national SA leadership (*Oberste SA-Führung*, or OSAF). Relations between the two eventually became so strained that Heinemann pushed for Pfeffer's removal from the party. Moreover, Pfeffer and Buch were hostile toward one another; when Hitler relieved Pfeffer of his command in September 1930, Buch fully agreed with the action.[44]

Such top-level backbiting and bickering (which also characterized Buch's relationship with Röhm) were hardly methods for solving the troublesome problem of the jurisdiction of the Uschlas over the SA and SS. The first orders in this direction came from the OSAF;[45] but from the standpoint of the Uschlas, nothing was forthcoming from the Reichsleitung until the beginning of 1930. In January, Buch was forced to assist in settling a feud between the Orts-Uschla and SA officers in the Plauen Ortsgruppe (Saxony Gau). According to the chief justice, Uschlas were not competent to handle "complaints between SA men in SA cases." He defined what the Reichs-Uschla considered to be "SA cases" as disobedience, violation of a given command, failure to obey military discipline, and attempts to seek revenge against a commanding officer. He explained that an SA man could "probably" turn to the Uschla as a party member if he felt himself "attacked in his honor by a superior" while performing SA duty. Yet he made it clear that in any Uschla proceeding involving an SA member (as a witness, plaintiff, or defendant), the presiding Uschla should contact the man's superior officer and request him "to command the concerned SA man to follow the orders of the Uschla."[46]

The first serious attempt at cooperation between the OSAF and the Reichs-Uschla in solving the questions at issue came in the spring. The consequence was a directive issued by the OSAF (GRUSA VIII, or *Grundsätzliche Anordnungen der SA*) in May. According to the new guidelines, expulsion from the SA remained an "SA affair" (which the order attempted to define by citing examples), and the Parteigerichte could handle cases of SA members only when they involved expulsion from the party. If, on the other hand, an Uschla member or a political leader discovered that an SA member had "injured the interests of the party by his performance of SA duty," he could demand an investigation by the man's commanding officer. The officer was authorized to expel the member from the SA or to order his expulsion (through the Uschla) from the party. The order also defined the competence of each Uschla (Orts-, Gau-, and Reichs-Uschla) regarding cases against ranking SA leaders, but it stipulated that such cases would automatically be referred to the next higher Uschla for confirmation. It further directed that any SA man involved in proceedings before an Uschla was obligated to notify his commanding officer im-

83

mediately and that the officer would then decide whether or not the Uschla's evidence warranted an investigation.[47]

Stated mildly, the GRUSA was a dismal failure in dealing with such moot points. Dissatisfaction on both sides was so great, in fact, that the Reichsleitung was forced to rescind the order seven months later.[48] Except for defining the competence of each Parteigericht in matters involving SA leaders, it offered nothing new or concrete. A noticeable weakness was its failure to define adequately what was meant by "SA affairs." Above all, instead of implementing Hitler's proclaimed policy of subordinating the SA to the party's political organization, the order tended to confirm the SA's autonomy. Only in cases where an SA member had clearly "injured the interests of the party" was the Uschla permitted to intervene, and then solely with the agreement of the man's commanding officer.

Despite the failure with regard to the SA, Hitler and the NSDAP began suddenly in the summer and autumn of 1930 to achieve some major successes on other fronts. One was the final resolution of the Goebbels–Otto Strasser rivalry in Berlin, which ended with Strasser's resignation from the party in June. Hitler, by refusing to condemn Goebbels and other northern leaders for competing with Strasser's newspapers and by luring Himmler (hitherto a Strasser sympathizer) to his side a year earlier,[49] was slowly winning his battle to crush completely the last remnants of the Strasser circle in the north. After an open disagreement with Strasser in April over a strike involving metal workers in Saxony, Hitler began his move to persuade the publisher to either capitulate or be forced out of the party.

At the beginning of May, he instructed the Reichs-Uschla to reject a demand by Strasser that Goebbels's business manager in Berlin, Wilke, be expelled for discriminating against the *Berliner Arbeiterzeitung (BAZ)* at Gau meetings. Hoping to reassure Goebbels, the Reichs-Uschla informed him that "negotiations" with Strasser were "still undecided," but that Hitler's decision would be made "with the greatest of certainty in the course of the following weeks."[50] The "negotiations" ended abruptly, however. Shortly thereafter, Hitler met Strasser in a Berlin hotel and the latter stubbornly refused to relinquish his left-wing beliefs about socialism in the NSDAP and to become Hitler's press chief. Consequently, the Führer's only alternative was to work for Strasser's removal, thus ending the personal strife in Berlin, the newspaper war in the north, and Strasser's irritating demand that the party pay more attention to Socialist principles in its program.[51]

Hitler accomplished Strasser's exit mainly through Goebbels. In a meeting of Berlin members at the end of May, Goebbels openly declared that the *BAZ* was injurious to the NSDAP and hinted that Strasser's expulsion could be expected in the near future. His continued attempts to push his *Angriff* and hurt the sale of the *BAZ* were working and were forcing Strasser to rely increasingly on a new daily paper, *Der Nationale Sozialist*.[52] During the following month, several Strasser sympathizers and co-workers on the *BAZ* were purged by Goebbels's hand-picked Gau-Uschla, and on June 23 Goebbels requested that the Reichs-Uschla confirm his expulsion of Strasser. When he refused, a week later, to permit Strasser and his banished friends to defend themselves before a Gau meeting, Strasser submitted his resignation and went into open opposition to the party.[53]

The victory in the seemingly endless feud was solidly Hitler's. By cleverly employing the Uschlas to apply his tactic of putting off until tomorrow what he had no intention of doing today, he had kept the conflict simmering for three long years. It is dangerous to speculate, but had he broken completely with the Strassers in 1927 or 1928 over the newspaper issue, the numerous northern leaders who once belonged to the NSAG (such as, for example, Terboven in Essen) might never have founded papers of their own and gradually shifted their allegiance to Munich for protection. Moreover, the "cowardly and cunning" tactic (in Otto Strasser's words) of letting Goebbels and his Gau-Uschla settle the affair helped considerably to preserve Hitler's magnetic image in the NSDAP (particularly with those members who remained sympathetic to Strasser's left-wing principles). Significant, too, was Strasser's own publication of his resignation[54]—a move that helped even more to shift responsibility for his exit away from Hitler.

A far more important success for the party's leader was the NSDAP's dramatic breakthrough on the national political scene in the Reichstag election in September. With the arrival of the Depression at the end of 1929 and because of the helplessness of the "Great Coalition" government of Hermann Müller, leader of the SPD, to meet the challenge of the catastrophe, Nazi support at the polls slowly began to increase. Unemployment rose rapidly and continued unabated. In Landtag elections in Baden, Lübeck, Thuringia, Saxony, and Braunschweig the NSDAP did extremely well, and in Thuringia the party captured its first major post in a state government when Frick was named minister of the interior.[55] As a symbol of the party's rapidly expanding membership and bureaucratic organization, the Reichsleitung in the summer vacated the old party headquarters on the Schellingstrasse and moved into the "Brown House," a much larger office building nearer downtown Munich.

Already in March, however, Müller had fallen as Chancellor and had been replaced by the leader of the Catholic Center Party (Zentrum Partei), Heinrich Brüning. Soon thereafter, President Hindenburg invoked his emergency powers through the famed Article 48 of the Weimar Constitution, and Germany began to be ruled by presidential decree. Then came the devastating Reichstag election on September 14. Stressing the overthrow of the Republic in their massive election campaign, the Nazis received almost six and one-half million votes (18.3 percent) and 107 seats in the Reichstag. The NSDAP now found itself with the second-largest (next below the SPD) fraction in the chamber. Along with the Communists (KPD), the party ate heavily into the support of the DNVP and the liberal German People's Party (Deutsche Volkspartei, or DVP), and it captured a majority of the four million new voters who had gone to the polls.[56]

86

The impact of the sudden victory was felt immediately within the party. Its membership ballooned to over three hundred thousand (compared to half that a year earlier),[57] and its administrative organizations such as the Uschlas were caught totally unprepared. Added to its normal everyday activities, the Reichs-Uschla now found itself with a "flood of paper work" in its attempt to answer mail from its lower tribunals and to examine the mass influx of new membership applications. Some cases of strife before the Reichs-Uschla were either postponed or transferred to the Gau-Uschlas for settlement,[58] and the Reichs-Uschla informed the rest of the party that such "unhappy circumstances" would continue until it could expand its staff. A first step in this direction came in December, when an SS leader from Bavaria, Wilhelm von Holzschuher, was named a deputy chairman to Buch; a major expansion of the Reichs-Uschla, however, was not to come until later.[59]

While the pleasant rise in the NSDAP's political fortunes brought the party increased administrative work and certain organizational changes, it by no means solved all of the movement's problems. As the party flourished with new members, so did the SA and SS, whose combined ranks went well over the one hundred thousand mark by mid 1930. But the recent election triumphs did very little to impress the party's soldiers, many of whom were unemployed and had families that were being victimized by the Depression. The mass increase, particularly in the SA, raised again the problems of the organization's relationship to the Uschlas and of the jurisdiction of the Uschlas over SA men. With GRUSA VIII a clear failure and with considerable dissatisfaction surfacing in September in restless SA units in Berlin and the northeast over Hitler's "legality" course, the necessity for discovering a compromise agreeable to both the Uschlas and the SA became urgent. It was little wonder, therefore, that lengthy discussions began soon among Hitler, Röhm (his new staff chief as of 1 January 1931),[60] and Buch, with the aim of drafting a directive that would be authoritative in all SA-Uschla affairs.

Röhm's presence was felt immediately in the meetings. Differences of opinion between himself and Buch over questions of authority helped to delay serious progress on issues that were much more vital. Röhm insisted that any future changes in SA-Uschla orders (such as the rescinding of GRUSA VIII) must be countersigned by him to become valid. On this point, at least, Buch finally relented;[61] but before other questions could be answered and the directive fully completed, the Stennes rebellion shook the party during the first week of April 1931. Before it ran its course, the uprising was to test the unity of the party, and it was to illustrate vividly Hitler's basic problem of successfully harnessing together the varied and dissatisfied elements in the NSDAP. The Uschlas, when called on by Hitler to discipline the SA, emerged to help destroy the revolt and to keep it contained mainly within the confines of the movement.

The insurrection of the SA in Berlin and the surrounding Gaus in the northeast was mainly the result of growing morale problems and unrest among certain violence-prone social-revolutionary elements in the NSDAP. The principal sources of discontent were the deepening of the Depression (almost five million Germans unemployed in January)[62] and Hitler's increasing emphasis in public on "legality" to achieve power—a strategy that many in the SA believed to be futile. Most SA commanders in the eastern districts viewed the policy as a blow to their organization's proud "fighting tradition," which stemmed from the bloody days of November 1923.

Unemployed workers' and peasants' sons, who formed the SA's rank and file in the east, felt that legality was a "dead-end" course that would never bring the drastic social and economic changes necessary to rescue them (and their families) from hunger and even starvation. They wanted, in short, an immediate and total political revolution—a violent upheaval from below to relieve their sufferings. In a quarterly report to the OSAF at the beginning of 1931, an SA officer from the Ostmark Gau reflected this deep dissatisfaction: "Possible new elections will scarcely bring anything good for us. . . . Has Munich lost all touch with us SA men? All commands that come from there bring new insignia or new orders to reorganize. And all of this at a time when the SA man has nothing to eat!"[63]

Greater discontent was provoked by Hitler's proclamation to the SA in late February, ordering it not to engage in brawling and street fighting.[64] This was especially true in Berlin, where an open conflict between Hitler's prize Gauleiter, Goebbels, and the local SA commander, Stennes, had erupted already in September 1930. Stennes, whose command extended into several eastern Gaus outside Berlin (mainly Silesia, Brandenburg, Mecklenburg, Pomerania, and Ostmark), felt that Goebbels was deliberately disregarding the SA in favor of the local SS.

Hitler's personal visit to the capital in September to restore order and his dismissal of Pfeffer as Osaf did little to remove the resentment. In the following months, the Reichs-Uschla received a rash of complaints from SS leaders against Stennes and his lieutenants.[65] Reflecting the friction developing between the two organizations, a close associate of Stennes's grumbled: "The establishment of the SS was undertaken because the SA was no longer reliable, etc.! Can the SA let itself fall so far as to be degraded to second-class soldiers?! Where in all of the District Co. BR [District Company Brandenburg] region does the SS have a fighting tradition? Nowhere! All tradition belongs only to the SA."[66]

By the end of March the situation had deteriorated so much that Röhm was forced to travel to Berlin in order to demand unconditional obedience from Stennes. But the latter absolutely refused to pay such homage, whereupon Röhm removed him from his post and recommended to Hitler that Stennes and his followers be thrown out of the party. For his part, Stennes quickly met with Goebbels and then held a conference with his subordinate leaders in which he vigorously denounced the Munich leadership.[67] As rumors began to fly that Hitler had ordered his expulsion, Stennes telegraphed Hitler (who was meeting in Weimar with SA leaders outside Stennes's command) on April 1, asking if he, Stennes, was still a member of the NSDAP. Hitler's reply was blunt: "Your role is not to question, but to execute my command."[68]

The order might well have been a tip-off of things to come for Stennes. Obviously by-passing the Reichs-Uschla, Hitler officially expelled the rebellious leader the following day and announced to the party that under "no circumstances" would he "tolerate deliberate disobedience or unlawfulness to be introduced into the movement."[69] Stennes's answer was to issue a proclamation calling on the SA in the east to revolt against the treasonous leadership in Munich, which (in his words) had stifled the "revolutionary momentum of the SA" with "bourgeois-liberal tendencies." Accompanied by several SA units, he occupied Berlin party headquarters and the office of *Der Angriff*. Apparently wishing to avoid a clash with the police, however, he ignored Otto Strasser's advice and quickly evacuated the buildings late in the afternoon of April second.[70] Insofar as Stennes was concerned, the rebellion had ended after only two days.

Considering the evidence compiled by the Reichs-Uschla, indicating that there was substantial support for Stennes in several northeastern districts, the sudden collapse of his uprising was both surprising and mystifying. One might have explained it by arguing that the Nazi membership in mid 1931 was essentially nonviolent and that it was committed to Hitler's policy of "legality." But a far more plausible explanation centered around the psychology utilized by Hitler and the Reichsleitung in dealing with Stennes. Hitler, committing himself personally to defeat of the insurrection and following the principle that "criminals must be punished before they commit their crime," acted quickly to purge Stennes and to demand that the SA make declarations of its loyalty only to himself.

Added to this, since Stennes's call for the SA to rebel came after his expulsion, he appeared to be seeking revenge rather than to be opposing Hitler on basic issues of party policy. Such suspicions were confirmed when Stennes suddenly abandoned the Berlin buildings on April 2 and failed to continue his struggle. At that point it would have been interesting had he chosen to fight on. Hitler's alternatives (none very pleasant) would have been limited: to compromise with Stennes, to call in the police, or to command the SS to remove the SA from the premises physically. As Otto Strasser prophetically warned Stennes, a "half revolt is a total defeat."[71]

Another explanation for the collapse of the rebellion was the manner in which the NSDAP's entire political organization reacted to the threat. Considering the haziness that had always characterized SA-party relations, it was noteworthy that the stifling of the revolt and the purge of the SA leaders behind Stennes were not handled by Röhm and the OSAF, but by the party's political apparatus—mainly Hermann Göring (appointed by Hitler as a special Political Commissar for the East to help restore order) and the Uschla system. Because of the many complaints received by the Reichs-Uschla in the previous months, the Reichsleitung was well aware of the unrest crystallizing around Stennes. Consequently, the Court was seriously investigating the grievances.[72]

Once the revolt began, what was most impressive was the cooperation the Reichsleitung received from those Gauleiters in the northeast whose organizations were the most vulnerable. Within hours after Stennes was removed, the leaders of Brandenburg (Schlange), Silesia (Brückner), Mecklenburg (Friedrich Hildebrandt), Pomerania (Wilhelm Karpenstein), and Ostmark (Wilhelm Kube) informed Göring of the names of SA officers in their district who were sympathetic to the Berlin rebel. Göring immediately notified Munich, and the Reichs-Uschla officially expelled the officers.[73] The system continued to operate in the following weeks as a large number of Stennes's adherents were uncovered and purged.[74]

The Gaus hardest hit were Berlin and Brandenburg. In Berlin, Goebbels was given a "blank check" to deal with the rebels as he saw fit.[75] Not only did he face resistance from the SA, but he was surprised to find that Stennes had several associates on the staff of Goebbels's pride and joy, *Der Angriff*. On April 3 Goebbels ordered the expulsion of eight employees of the paper, including its manager and a member of the editorial staff. Refusing to believe that Hitler had empowered Goebbels with such extensive authority, several of the banished group protested to the Reichs-Uschla, but without success. By May, Goebbels had succeeded in removing most of the dissident elements and in restoring order in the capital.[76]

The situation in Brandenburg remained extremely tense for some months. Considerable friction continued to exist between the political leadership of the Gau and its SA counterpart. By the middle of April, forty SA leaders in the Gau had been expelled;[77] the air was filled with recriminations, charges, and countercharges. On the one hand, the SA complained about the corruption of the political leaders and about their attempts to "intervene in the SA power of command." The politicos, on the other hand, accused ranking SA officers of embezzling money from the party, of continuing to associate with Stennes, and of consciously undermining the position of the Gauleiter, Schlange.[78] To complicate matters, Schlange was involved in a personal squabble with his district commander, Otto Süss. Buch, in a moment of exasperation over the situation, informed Schlange: "Cooperation between the SA and the political leadership is now working smoothly as a model in the national leadership, and it is working in all districts with fewer exceptions each day; why shouldn't it be the same with you and your troubles?"[79]

A major source of the trouble was the difficulty that Schlange and his Gau-Uschla were having in understanding the formal procedure for expulsions. Part of the reason for the confusion was a new Uschla directive issued by Munich in mid April (which will be discussed in more detail later). Throughout the summer, the Reichs-Uschla communicated regularly with both Schlange and his Gau-Uschla in an attempt to enlighten them on the "entire essence of Uschla."

Nevertheless, such efforts proved futile, and Buch finally proposed to Schlange and Süss that the three of them meet personally instead of perpetuating their "time-consuming war of paper" *(zeitraubenden Papierkriegs)* through the Parteigerichte.[80] Negotiations for the meeting moved slowly; and much to Buch's frustration, cooperation between the SA and the Gauleitung threatened to collapse entirely. By the end of October, proceedings against ten ranking SA officers were still pending before the Gau-Uschla. In addition, numerous other appeals and proceedings had been transferred to Göring's office in Berlin for settlement. There was a strong feeling in the Gau that most of the officers would be expelled without a fair trial. Complaining to the OSAF, a Brandenburg SA leader expressed the fears and suspicions of his people: "The SA of the Brandenburg District Company must have the feeling that only one side will be taken. . . . The leadership has told me that it is powerless in the whole affair and that it has the feeling that the district political leadership has the upper hand in all cases against SA leaders."[81]

To calm the SA and, hopefully, to achieve a final settlement of the "continued misunderstandings" *(schwebenden Unzuträglichkeiten)*, Buch and the OSAF ordered the adversaries to attend a joint investigation scheduled for early November in Berlin.[82] Present at the meeting (which lasted for two full days) were Buch, Schlange, Süss, a representative sent by Röhm, and several other SA and party functionaries from the Gau. Each case pending against SA leaders was carefully reviewed, and special attention was given to discussing the points of disagreement on both sides. The meeting, according to Buch, was successful, and he noted later that "a platform was found which all participants will now concern themselves with carrying forward."[83] Thus, after seven months of incessant bickering and quarreling, order was finally restored to the last bastion of unrest arising from the Stennes action.

The full strength and extent of Stennes's following was

difficult for the Reichsleitung to assess accurately. On the surface, at least, the sudden collapse of the revolt appeared to indicate that his support was almost nonexistent. Yet the mass expulsions in April and the following months suggested otherwise. Apparently, Stennes's adherents in the north and east numbered into the thousands; the first edition of his opposition newspaper *(Arbeiter, Bauern, Soldaten)*, which he published on the heels of his defeat, sold between twenty and thirty thousand copies. In Berlin, roughly 30 percent of the local SA and 20 percent of the city's Hitler Youth were sympathetic to the rebel. Consequently, many leaders in the local Nazi Student Association (NS-Studentenbund, or NSDStB) were purged, and the branch of it at the University of Berlin was dissolved.[84]

The principal outcome of the insurrection was the victory that Hitler gained for his tactic of "legality." Under no circumstances did he desire another 9 November 1923. His success in suppressing the threat came in part from his centralized and highly loyal party organization—from local and district functionaries upward to Göring and the Reichs-Uschla. Stennes's failure, therefore, was not so much the result of a lack of support as of a lack of organization and nerve. Instead of standing his ground and unleashing the SA's alleged "revolutionary momentum" (as he termed it), he chose to play Hitler's game of pseudolegality and nonviolence. The consequence of his decision was the SA's first significant defeat at the hands of the NSDAP's political organization.

Another consequence of the revolt was the clear and unmistakable triumph that Hitler gained personally for himself and for his mythical image as the party's omnipotent Führer. Except for the Strasser affairs earlier, the Stennes action marked the only period in the NSDAP's early history when Hitler openly disengaged himself from the party's protective bureaucratic institutions (that is, the Uschla system) to put himself squarely at the center of an intraparty conflict. Revealing the degree to which he felt both himself and the movement to be threatened, he relied heavily in the initial stages of the crisis on his own Führer-image by demanding that all SA men give unconditional declarations of loyalty to him personally. If one was to believe the *Völkischer Beobachter*, such oaths of fealty were flooding Munich within hours after he made his demand.[85]

Especially crucial for the Uschlas and party justice, the uprising helped to produce a new Uschla directive, decreed by the Reichsleitung in mid April 1931, which officially outlined the jurisdiction (for the first time) of the Uschlas in cases involving SA and SS members. It will be recalled that meetings to draft the directive had begun much earlier, but disagreements between Buch and Röhm had slowed their progress considerably. In some respects, the lack of such an order during the Stennes rebellion worked to the Reichsleitung's advantage. It allowed Hitler a free hand to exercise his statutory right as party dictator to expel Stennes and his top aides immediately, without a formal hearing before the Uschla. Nevertheless, the Reichs-Uschla did command its Gau-Uschla in Berlin to "obtain as much incriminating material as possible" against Stennes "to prove his illegal views."[86] The absence of rigid guidelines also permitted Munich to bestow important emergency powers on its Gauleiters, which was aimed at purging disloyal members with the utmost speed.[87] But at the same time, the late appearance of the directive caused a good deal of pandemonium among Orts- and Gau-Uschlas that were forced to investigate many borderline cases. Such confusion was most prevalent in Potsdam, where it contributed to a lengthy delay in restoring working relations between the political leadership and the embittered SA.

Similar to GRUSA VIII (issued by the OSAF a year earlier), the new directive provided SA men with considerable protection before the Uschlas. Disputes concerning purely "SA and SS affairs" remained the preserve of each paramilitary group, and only high-ranking SA and SS officers were permitted to order the opening of Uschla proceedings against men under their command. In addition, at least one member of each Uschla had to be an SA or SS man. Orts-

Uschlas were competent to handle cases involving the rank of private only, and Gau-Uschlas handled cases of ranks through company and battalion commander. The jurisdiction of the Reichs-Uschla, according to the order, extended to cases involving colonels, senior colonels, lieutenant generals, and adjutants in the OSAF.[88]

In helping to compromise the disagreements between Uschla judges and SA leaders, the directive offered nothing new or significant. Above all, it tended to confirm the growing independence of the SA and to mirror the presence and influence of Röhm as its commander in chief. Whether or not the Reichsleitung recognized the directive's weaknesses is uncertain. The order apparently ended its search for a solution to SA-Uschla problems, however. With the exception of transferring cases involving the rank of colonel (despite the vigorous protest of Röhm) to the Gau-Uschlas two years later,[89] all guidelines regulating SA, SS, and Uschla relations remained unchanged until after the Nazi seizure of power.

The continued protection accorded SA men who were involved in Uschla proceedings was in part the result of Hitler's ambiguity in dealing with the broader problem of SA-party relations. Interested party leaders could not help recognizing the safeguards in the directive of 1931 that were designed to defend the SA man against an absolute accountability before the Uschlas. Yet, it appeared to the restless and hungry SA man on the street that the order was merely another blow aimed at curtailing his autonomy in the party. He noted, above all, that it was issued by the Reichs-Uschla (a party organization) and not by the OSAF, as was the case with GRUSA VIII and all earlier directives. Consequently, the order heightened the suspicion and resentment among many in the SA that Hitler was sharpening his policy of strict subordination of the SA to the political leadership of the party.

Except for the attempt to deal with the SA, the directive of 1931 was almost a carbon copy of the one issued in August 1929. The objectives, organization, and investigation and trial procedures of the Uschlas remained the same as before. Nevertheless, the order did define in more detail the jurisdiction of each Uschla, and it added several new punishments that the tribunals could inflict on disobedient party members. The Orts-Uschlas were competent to hear cases involving local members, and the Gau-Uschlas those concerning Ortsgruppenleiters, co-workers of the Gauleiter, Gau speakers, Nazi Landtag deputies, and members of the Gau Studentenbund. The Reichs-Uschla was empowered to judge Gauleiters, Reichstag and Landtag deputies, Reich speakers, members of the Reichsleitung, and entire Ortsgruppen whose expulsion from the party might be ordered.

In addition, the directive authorized the Uschlas to punish a member by ordering an "oral reprimand" *(mündlichen Verweis)* from his political leader, by preventing him from holding a party office, or by forbidding him to appear as a speaker for the movement. But while the order increased the Uschlas' theoretical powers in this respect, it deprived them of their right to remove quickly any party leader who "stands before the public," by requiring them to secure the "agreement" of their "superior Uschla."[90] The last was obviously a move to insure that those leaders who were popular among the people would not be expelled or would not receive bad publicity (which could jeopardize the NSDAP's campaign efforts in elections).

With the Stennes affair a thing of the past and with a set of new guidelines to govern the actions of the Uschlas, the work of the Reichs-Uschla settled back to normal toward the end of 1931. While the NSDAP had been busy restoring order in its own house, it had continued during the year to increase its total membership (estimated at seven hundred thousand in November), to expand its administrative organizations (for example, the full-time staff of most Gaus now exceeded one thousand), and to win election victories. In Landtag elections in Schaumburg-Lippe, Oldenburg, Hamburg, and Hessen the party captured an average 31.8 percent of the votes cast and 93 seats out of a total of 293.[91] The secrets to the movement's success remained the

97

tragic Depression, which had left over six million Germans unemployed by the end of the year, and the party's ability to blanket the nation with its hate-propaganda, which demanded the overthrow of the Republic. In early October, Hitler met Hindenburg for the first time and then made a feeble attempt at Harzburg to join forces with the other far-right parties and organizations (such as the DNVP and its paramilitary wing, the *Stahlhelm*, or "Steel Helmet"), which was aimed at demonstrating their collective unity and their opposition to the government of Chancellor Brüning.[92]

With the party rapidly increasing in numbers, the functions of the Uschla system in controlling membership applications and purging unwanted members became more apparent than ever. A concerted effort was begun by the Reichs-Uschla in October to tighten its own organizations and to police as carefully as possible the entire party membership. The Reichs-Uschla ordered its subordinate tribunals to examine closely all members suspected of belonging to Freemason lodges or any other "national or humanitarian" groups and to demand that such persons dissolve all past or present relations with their lodges.[93] The Court demanded the same treatment for members belonging to political organizations or paramilitary leagues outside the NSDAP, such as the Stahlhelm. Informing its lower Uschlas that "it is not possible for one man to serve two masters," the Reichs-Uschla directed that any Nazi who remained in another political group "simultaneously excluded" himself from Hitler's movement.[94] Along this same line, Hitler gave Gauleiters and Ortsgruppenleiters greater authority in removing rebellious or "unworthy" members, thus increasing their power over Orts- and Gau-Uschlas. As before, the Uschlas remained bureaucratic "tools" in the hands of their political superiors, who could use the Uschlas to purge anyone obstructing their orders.[95]

The NSDAP's rapid growth also necessitated another expansion and reform of the Uschla system. In January 1932 the Reichs-Uschla added a third assistant judge (besides

Frank and Graf) to Buch and Holzschuher, Wilhelm Grimm. Grimm was a long-time party member from Ansbach and a deputy in the Bavarian Landtag who had served since 1929 as Streicher's deputy Gauleiter of the Middle Franconia Gau.[96] Several months later the Reichs-Uschla was totally reorganized and expanded further as a part of Gregor Strasser's massive administrative reforms in the movement.[97] It was divided into three chambers, each having its own defined geographic jurisdiction over the party: Buch remained the chief justice and head of the first chamber, Holzschuher became chairman of the second, and Grimm of the third. The aims of the reorganization were to strengthen the centralization and cohesion of the Uschla system and to increase the Reichs-Uschla's efficiency in handling its growing workload.[98]

Although the NSDAP seemed no closer to winning political power at the beginning of 1932 than it had been a year earlier, many party leaders (including Buch) greeted the new year with confident optimism.[99] Few of them could foresee the frustrations that lay ahead of their expected victory. In January, Hitler was invited to address the powerful Industrie-Klub in Düsseldorf, where he appealed for the support of German big business by telling the industrialists present that they had no need to fear socialism from his party. While the address was a nominal success, the Nazi chief failed to win their massive financial backing, and this was to hurt the party in its future campaign efforts.[100] It was also to place additional strains on the NSDAP that would force some swift thinking by the party leadership and the Uschla to cement together the differing wings of the movement.

In the Reich presidential elections in the spring, Hitler captured a respectable 37 percent of the popular vote, but in a losing cause to the aging incumbent, Hindenburg. Within the party the campaign was significant, because it brought to the surface the tensions and personal animosities that were brewing in the Reichsleitung. A serious attack from within the party was made on the Osaf—Röhm—and several of his close aides. Not unlike his predecessor Pfeffer,

99

Röhm's personality, especially his distasteful moral reputation, brought him the sharp disapproval of several party politicos. Criticism of Röhm crystallized around Buch, Bormann (Buch's son-in-law and head of the Nazi Aid Fund), party treasurer Schwarz, and Paul Schulz (a close friend of Buch's and Gregor Strasser's and a member of the Reich Organization Department). The group was concerned above all with Röhm's homosexuality, which was well known in party circles. Most disconcerting to Buch and the others was the threatening possibility that Röhm's deviate behavior might become public knowledge and thus seriously jeopardize the growing prestige and respectability of the NSDAP.

Considering the danger that they believed Röhm's reputation posed, Buch, Schulz, and Bormann in particular attempted to convince Hitler that the SA chief should be removed.[101] But Hitler, who sorely needed his old friend and comrade to head the SA, flatly refused.[102] During the first presidential campaign in March, the type of open publicity concerning Röhm that his enemies feared most began to unfold. The SA leader's unsavory past became sensational headline material in several Socialist and liberal newspapers, and there appeared in Berlin a short, scandalous pamphlet accusing him of having "discovered" his homosexuality "as early as the year 1924."[103]

Although there was no conclusive proof, evidence was uncovered later that implicated Buch, Schwarz, and Schulz in a secret conspiracy that developed at the end of March—planned by two of Buch's old friends from Karlsruhe, Emil Danzeisen and Karl Horn—to murder Röhm and several of his staff in the OSAF (namely, Count Spreti, Count du Moulin-Eckart, and Röhm's foreign-policy adviser, Georg Bell). Such a resort to violence by enemies inside the party was indeed exceptional, yet what was certain was that the conspiracy did exist and that its central plan was to remove Röhm's aides and, if the opportunity presented itself, Röhm also.[104] But the plot misfired, and by early April it had become known to both the Munich police and the city's Socialist paper, the *Münchener Post*.[105]

At the beginning of July, Danzeisen was convicted in a civil court on charges of "conspiring to murder," and he was sentenced to six months' imprisonment. What remained unclear from the court's evidence was the role of Buch, Schulz, and Schwarz in the plot. Both Buch and Schwarz were called to testify at Danzeisen's trial, yet there was no airtight proof produced by the prosecuting attorney to link them or any other leading member of the Reichsleitung to the conspiracy.[106] For his part, Röhm was obviously shaken. Soon after the trial he surrounded himself with a personal bodyguard and countered his enemies by planting numerous articles against Schulz in the Socialist press in Berlin and Munich.[107]

These murky and obscure events—which reminded one more of an underworld organization than of a political party—were noteworthy for what they revealed about the NSDAP only months before it was to seize power. Not only did they suggest the growing animosity between Buch and Röhm and the broader antagonism between the SA and the political corps, but they reflected the frustrations building in the leadership over the party's failure to put Hitler into power. In view of such dissension and intrigue, the fact that Hitler was to be named Chancellor only months later probably seemed impossible. Yet both institutional and personal conflict was an integral part of behavior in the NSDAP, and this situation was to change little after the dawn of the Third Reich. The gangsterlike struggle for power between various individuals and cliques continued; feuds, quarrels, and competition for Hitler's cherished favor were often settled by intrigue, even by violence and murder. In this respect, one has only to recall the fate of Röhm in the bloody purge of 30 June 1934. His murder during that tragic night represented the culmination of a long and bitter vendetta waged by his enemies inside the party to see him removed.

Amidst the turmoil within the party leadership and because of Hitler's disappointing loss to Hindenburg, the NSDAP was able to keep its image as a winner by capturing victories in the Prussian and Bavarian Landtag elections at the close of April. But barely had the votes been counted, when the party found itself faced with another grueling test at the polls—the Reichstag was dissolved in May, when the Brüning government fell, and the new Chancellor, Franz von Papen, called for an election on July 31. To some in the party, such as Goebbels, fear and disillusionment surfaced at the thought that the movement was "winning itself to death in the elections" and playing itself out without having succeeded in its goal of gaining complete control of the German government.[108] To suppress such fears and any open display of dissension in the movement during the ensuing campaign, the Reichsleitung ordered all Gau organizations to forbid their members to disagree or quarrel in public and to demand that such differences be taken before the Uschlas.[109]

In the July election the party more than doubled both its supporters and its Reichstag seats. Almost fourteen million Germans voted National Socialist, sending 230 Nazis into the Reichstag and making them the largest delegation. But the extent to which the rapid succession of elections took their toll on party morale became particularly evident within the Uschla system during the second Reichstag election campaign in the autumn and during the first weeks of January 1933. Throughout the campaign for the election of 6 November (in which the NSDAP suffered a significant setback), the party's courts ceased to function almost completely, in the hope that this would lessen the mounting tension in the movement. All party members were commanded by their Gau organizations to familiarize themselves "in broad outline" *(in groben Umrissen)* with the Uschla directives and thus to avoid being dragged before the courts; and local Uschlas were instructed that all proceedings "not according to regulations" would be rejected by their Gau superiors.[110]

In addition, the Reichs-Uschla tightened its hold over the Gau-Uschlas and Gauleiters by warning them that "an expulsion can only be commanded on order of the Uschla." To insure that its orders were followed, the Reichs-Uschla notified the party's new national and state inspectors (*Reichsinspektoren, Landesinspektoren,* created by Strasser's reforms in the summer to control more effectively the Orts and Gau organizations) that they should review closely the operation of the Uschlas in their region.[111] The same relaxation in Uschla activities came at the highest party levels. On Hitler's orders, Buch flatly refused all requests for Reichs-Uschla investigations of Gau and Reich leaders, because "any dissension must be buried until the new election."[112] As with all party administrative organizations, the Uschlas (including the Reichs-Uschla) operated purely as a "means to an end"—that end being the NSDAP's total seizure of political power in Germany. Consequently, the Uschlas were forced at any time (when so ordered) to subordinate their decisions to those of Hitler and the entire movement.

In moves that revealed a further centralization and clampdown on the party's courts and the leadership corps, the Reichs-Uschla demanded that all Orts-Uschlas send the names, professions, and addresses of their members to the Gau-Uschlas for transferring to the Reichs-Uschla.[113] Moreover, to insure that the party was still being led (amid its massive growth) by the "Aryan" elite of German society, the Reichs-Uschla commanded the Gau-Uschlas to report the family genealogy of every political leader in their Gaus. Such work was busily undertaken by the Uschlas in cooperation with the party's Information Department (Nationalsozialistische Auskunft), and close records were kept on all party leaders. The NS-Auskunft, headed by Dr. Achim Gerke, was a department in the Reichsleitung that was concerned primarily with racial questions and research on family ancestry.[114] Along this same line, the job of the Uschlas to supervise membership applications was extended by a new Reichs-Uschla directive of 1 January 1933 (which replaced that of April 1931) to protect the "honor" of any party member, if he so requested, by engaging in research on his racial background.[115]

The January directive was definitely designed to enhance the prestige of the Uschlas and to free them from the iron rule of their political leaders. Beyond this, it differed little from the order of April 1931. The new guidelines officially designated the Uschlas as "courts of honor," and to emphasize this view of them, a "special court of honor" *(besonderer Ehrenhof)* for the Reichsleitung was created under Buch's chairmanship. The hearings of the "special court" were "strictly confidential," and its rulings were binding for the entire NSDAP; theoretically (that is, disregarding Hitler's power), there existed no possibility for an appeal against it. To increase the prestige of the Uschlas further, the directive noted that the chairman of a Gau-Uschla possessed the proud rank and service dress of a deputy Gauleiter, and the chairman of the Reichs-Uschla that of a department chief in the Reichsleitung.[116]

Moreover, the order explained that the members of each Uschla were now considered autonomous party officials and were no longer subject to being removed "against their own will" by their political leader. The chairman of an Orts- or Gau-Uschla was even given the right to request proceedings (by appealing to a higher court) against his political superior for any suspected "misuse of office" *(Amtsmissbrauch)*.[117] Thus, by the time of the Nazi seizure of power, the authority of the Uschla system had become theoretically and potentially as significant as that of any administrative organization in the party. The Uschlas could investigate all members of the party's political structure and the SA, and they were constitutionally independent bodies whose rulings were to protect and guide the entire movement.

Theory, however, rarely corresponded to reality. Despite their growing powers on paper, the Uschlas remained strictly subordinate to the orders of Hitler and the party leadership. As the secret political negotiations developed through mid January between von Papen and Hitler to unseat Papen's successor as Chancellor, General Schleicher, many in the NSDAP attempted one last time to suppress their utter despair at failing as yet to win control of the German government. The Reichsleitung suddenly moved to lessen the potentially explosive situation as much as possible and thereby to undermine again the authority of the Uschlas.

Whereas in the previous months the Uschla organization had been progressively tightened to stifle the party's frustrations and to keep the movement from flying apart, the leadership now executed some quick footwork to meet the needs of the moment. A confidential circular to the Gauleiters instructed that the Uschlas be called into session "only in the most extreme cases of necessity."[118] Few could have guessed, however, that within a matter of days the chains would be withdrawn, and the party's sense of frustration would turn into the ecstasy of triumph.

5

The Courts and the Nazi Revolution, 1933-1934

AT NOON on 30 January 1933 Hitler was named Chancellor of the government he had attempted to overthrow by violence a decade earlier; the "Third Reich" had begun. At last he had achieved the decisive chance to realize his wildest dream—to destroy the Weimar democracy and make himself the lord and master of Germany. Throughout the evening, thousands of Berlin SA and SS men, Hitler Youth, and other Nazi supporters marched amid a sea of torch lights and swastika flags past the Reich Chancellery as Hitler and the aging president of the Republic, Hindenburg, watched from the windows above. To Hitler, the party leadership, and the masses in the streets, the day was "like a dream," and it signaled the beginning of a "German revolution" and a "new Reich."[1]

The Nazi seizure of power began immediately, and it was fully consolidated by the end of 1934. While the remainder of the NSDAP conducted its brutal revolution from "above" and "below" on the outside, the Reichs-Uschla and its lower courts worked relentlessly within the movement to protect Nazi racial and political "unity" and to insure the party's total loyalty to Hitler and the Reichsleitung. In this respect the Uschlas became indispensable cogs in the party machine that ruthlessly overran Germany and transformed the nation into a one-party totalitarian state.

In the spring of 1933 Buch was reconfirmed as chief justice and disciplinarian of the Uschla system, and both he and Wilhelm Grimm (who replaced Holzschuher as chairman of the Reichs-Uschla's second chamber) were given the elite status of *Reichsleiter* ("national leader") in the party. On March 18 Hitler reaffirmed his command of April 1928 (extending the powers of the Uschlas) by ordering that Buch act in his "representation" for "ordering respectively the confirmation of expulsions."[2]

At the beginning of February the Reichstag was dissolved and new elections were set for March 5. In the days that followed, Hindenburg decreed a series of emergency laws (among them the law giving Göring practically full authority in Prussia, and the Reichstag Fire Decree of February 28) that laid the foundations for the power through which the National Socialists were able at will to control the nation, destroy their opponents, and win the March election. Göring, acting as a special Reich Commissioner *(Reichskommissar)* for the Prussian Interior Ministry, issued a series of commands that insured the Nazi takeover of the huge state. Ranking Prussian officials from the SPD and the Center Party were removed from their posts and were replaced by Hitler men or sympathizers from the DNVP.

Similarly, control of the police in most of the major Prussian cities went to leading SA or SS officers; in Berlin, the Police Presidium's Department IA (that is, the political police) was "cleansed" of republican elements, and the Gestapo first began to take form. Göring's orders also struck at the KPD and the SPD, with the aim of paralyzing and eventually destroying the leftist parties. These measures were complemented by orders to SA and SS terrorists to disrupt Communist and Socialist meetings and to join the police as *Hilfspolizei* ("auxiliary police") in combating "leftist radicals, particularly on the Communist side."[3] The same policy was applied with equal brutality in the smaller Nazi-controlled states of Thuringia, Braunschweig, and Oldenburg.

The Reichstag fire and the resulting presidential decree, giving Hitler the emergency powers that launched his dictatorship, had the effect of escalating the reign of terror and intimidation that had already begun. All basic civil rights of Germans were immediately withdrawn, and hundreds of Communists, Jews, and republicans were arrested and interned in the first "official" concentration camp being built at Dachau, and in the so-called wild camps at Sachsenhausen-Oranienburg, at Vulkanwerft in Pomerania, and near Berlin.

Despite the terrorism and coercion, the Nazis failed to receive a majority vote in the Reichstag election in early March. With their greatest successes coming in the rural areas of the north and east, they captured over seventeen million votes (43.9 percent of the total) and 288 seats of 647 in the legislature. The DNVP, blindly aiding the revolution, added its 52 seats to the NSDAP's fraction, giving the party the majority it desired. Hitler, seeking to minimize his party's disappointing showing, quickly labeled the election a further "revolution."[4]

The chief consequence of the election was that it formed the curtain raiser for the Reich government's *Gleichschaltung* ("coordination") policy, which was designed to destroy the political and economic freedom of those states still not under Nazi leadership. While SA and SS Kommandos (acting as Hilfspolizei) continued their terrorism, all state and local governments, beginning in mid March, were dissolved and reconstituted according to the Reichstag elections. In several major northern cities (Hamburg, Bremen, and Lübeck) and in some southern and central states (Hessen, Baden, Württemberg, and Saxony), the NSDAP captured the vital positions in government through the appointment of Reich Commissioners by Wilhelm Frick, the Nazi minister of the interior for the Reich. Bavaria was a major focal point in the "coordination" process. Franz Ritter von Epp (a retired general, former "free corps" leader, and long-time Nazi) was installed as a Reich commissioner, and he ruthlessly destroyed the state's republican government by naming

Dr. Frank as minister of justice, Gauleiter Adolf Wagner as head of the Ministry of the Interior, and Himmler as chief of police in Munich. Himmler thus began his successful attempt (which was culminated in April 1936) to bring the entire German political police under the control of the SS and himself.[5]

Hitler's dictatorship was further solidified and given the mask of legitimacy with the passage of the Enabling Law through the Reichstag on March 23. The assembly that gave Hitler dictatorial power for four years was hardly a legally constituted body. It had been elected in the face of extreme terrorism and coercion, its deputies were herded and harrassed into the Kroll Opera House by the SA and SS, and it was missing the entire KPD fraction and several SPD members who had been arrested and imprisoned.

Even with this, Hitler lacked the two-thirds majority for his proposed Enabling Law by almost forty votes. The decisive vote lay with the Catholic Center Party and its political adjunct, the Bavarian Peoples' Party (Bayerische Volkspartei), which together controlled ninety-two seats. With feverish last-minute negotiations and promises (which he scarcely intended to keep) to leaders of the Catholic Center Party, Hitler received the Catholic vote, and the Enabling Law was his. Only the SPD, represented at the podium by its veteran chairman, Otto Wels, who denounced the law, voted against it. But Wels was a "Jeremiah come too late."[6] Hitler, in his address answering the SPD and threatening the non-Nazi deputies, furiously declared: "I will also certainly not vote for you! Germany will be free, but not through you!"[7]

The most immediate problem produced for the Uschlas by the seizure of power was the tedious job of examining the sudden mass of applications for membership in the NSDAP. Not since the end of 1930 had the party experienced such an expansion in its membership. The terrorism of the SA and SS, the Reichstag election in March, and the granting of the Enabling Law had the effect of convincing thousands of Germans that they had better join the Nazi bandwagon as quickly as possible. Between January 30 and May 1 no less than one and a half million new members were admitted into the NSDAP.[8] To handle the flood of *Märzgefallene* ("March casualties," as the old fighters in the party cynically termed the new recruits), the Uschlas worked closely with the office of the National Treasurer of the party, Schwarz. Referring to the influx of new members as "colossal," Schwarz finally ordered a temporary restriction on membership *(Aufnahmesperre)* to begin on May 1.[9]

The task of the Uschlas was to supervise the membership freeze and make certain that Schwarz's guidelines were followed by all party organizations. With some exceptions, ceilings on membership were fixed for each Gau, *Kreis* ("county"), and Ortsgruppe. The only persons exempt from the restrictions were those in the Hitler Youth, those in the National Socialist Factory Cells Organization (NS-Betriebszellenorganisation, or NSBO), and those "expectant" of membership in the SA or SS (namely, members of the nationalist Stahlhelm, which was dissolved and incorporated into the SA in June). The party, revealing its suspicion of new members, ordered that membership cards be issued to them first, but only after a two-year "waiting period" were they given the right to have the cherished party membership book (possessed by the "old fighters" who had entered before January 30).[10] Despite the efforts to discourage the zealous from joining the party, the applications continued to mount on the desks of the Reichs-Uschla and the Treasurer's Office, and in the autumn Schwarz announced publicly that two million were still to be processed. Buch complained a few months later that his office and the party were still "deluged" with paper work.[11]

In examining membership applications, it was the duty of the Uschlas above all to ferret out and exclude Jews, Freemasons, Communist and Socialist saboteurs, and others whose "personal relations" prevented them from unconditionally subordinating themselves to the NSDAP. With Hitler now in power, the crucial function of Uschla justice became that of keeping the Jewish "poison" from penetrat-

111

ing the party's ranks and thus racially (or otherwise) contaminating the movement. In the minds of Hitler, Buch, and other party leaders, a racially "pure" party was an absolute necessity if the National Socialists were to lead the national rebirth of Germany and succeed in the "preservation of the German species."

Thus, the Reichs-Uschla ordered its lower benches in January 1934 to ban from entering (or remaining in) the party those persons with any trace of "colored or Jewish blood" in their family dating back to January 1800, those with marriage ties to anyone having "elements of colored or Jewish blood," and those with ties to such organizations as Freemason lodges and their "successor groups." In the Reichs-Uschla's view, the party's goal was not the "greatest possible mass of party members," but the "internal solidification" of a "fixed and united fighting community."[12]

Anyone entering the movement was forced to sign a sworn affidavit certifying that he was "of German descent and free of Jewish or colored racial mixture" and that he belonged to "no secret group, nor any other prohibited community or association" outside the NSDAP. To guarantee the validity of the statements, the Reichs-Uschla cooperated closely with the lower courts, other party organizations, and Nazi police authorities to gather extensive files on persons suspected of attempting to enter the party for subversive purposes. Such procedures were hardly foolproof, however, and *provocateurs* did manage to infiltrate the party to cause headaches for some organizations.[13]

Since the party equated Freemasonry with the "world Jewish conspiracy," a vigorous effort was begun by the Uschlas in the spring of 1933 to remove former Freemasons from party offices and to shut the door tight on those who now wished to enter the movement. In May the Reichs-Uschla warned all party organizations that "no Freemasons need enter the party." It also alerted the movement to guard against "new attempts of Freemasons seeking a way to influence the NSDAP by transforming their lodges into so-called orders, etc., and by abandoning their ritual."[14]

Party members who held government posts and had once belonged to lodges faced immediate harrassment from the Uschlas and even faced release from their jobs. In June, Bruno Schüler, a state commissioner in Dortmund and a former Freemason, was investigated by his Uschla and threatened with expulsion from the party and dismissal from his office. Schüler was saved, however, when the Uschla discovered that he had entered a local lodge at the order of his Gauleiter, Josef Wagner, to gather secret information on the lodge's activities.[15] The Reichs-Uschla's policy on Freemasons caused considerable pandemonium and excitement, particularly since it was discovered that many "pure Aryans" in party organizations had once been affiliated with lodges.[16]

The Uschlas also followed a rigid policy with regard to readmitting former party members who had left the NSDAP prior to 1933. Eugen Munder, the Gauleiter of the Württemberg Gau who had been forced to resign his post in 1928,[17] begged Hitler in April 1933 to permit him to rejoin the NSDAP. Munder's request was given to the Reichs-Uschla, which abruptly rejected it on the basis that Munder had shown a continued "disinterest" in the party since his resignation. Protesting to Hitler's deputy Führer, Hess, that the Reichs-Uschla's decision was "very harsh" and failed to take into account his "personal reasons" for leaving the party, Munder was ultimately to plead with the Reichsleitung for two years before finally being allowed to recover his membership in August 1935.[18]

A group of former members in Insterburg (East Prussia Gau) was not so fortunate. They had committed the sin of rejecting the NSDAP in July 1932 by continually refusing to follow the orders of their Gauleiter, Erich Koch. Koch and his Gau-Uschla had dissolved the entire Insterburg Ortsgruppe and had removed the rebels from the party. During the autumn of 1934, the latter began an attempt to gain readmittance through the Gau-Uschla. Upon a careful examination of the applications, however, the Gauleitung and the Reichs-Uschla ruled in March 1936 to deny membership to most of them, and they were thus never permitted to rejoin the party.[19] Without exception, the Nazi leadership never forgot a grudge.

In this respect, the significance of the work of the party's courts for the average German was that, unless he belonged to the NSDAP, he could probably expect to live under the shadow of suspicion and could scarcely anticipate a bright future in his job or community. This was especially true of those in the professions—teachers, lawyers, doctors, and civil-service employees *(Beamten)* in the government. With Hitler's appointment as Chancellor, members of such groups apparently began to recognize the dismal facts of life immediately, inasmuch as thousands from each rushed to join the party in 1933 and 1934. By January 1935, for example, some 307,205 civil servants in Germany were members of the NSDAP, and approximately 250,000 entered the party between 30 January and 30 April 1933. The same mass influx was true of teachers and lawyers.[20] The minimal fate that a lawyer or judge who failed to join the party could expect was complete exclusion from privileged promotions and repeated denial of even normal professional advancements.[21]

On the other hand, if a member of the NSDAP was expelled from the party by his Uschla (and the action was upheld by the Reichs-Uschla), he most assuredly faced a greater catastrophe. According to Buch, "no one wants to associate with him."[22] Once expelled, an individual and his family became "outcasts," losing everything, including their jobs, social respectability, and the privilege of associating with their friends who remained party members. In some instances, those who were banished even found themselves arrested by the Nazi-controlled police and whisked off to prison or concentration camp. In September 1933 a great many SA and SS men from Munich were put under "protective custody" by the Bavarian political police and were interned in Dachau. Their alleged offenses against the NSDAP ranged from stealing party money to engaging in "Communist intrigues" and wrongfully wearing party insignia.[23] Because of the serious nature of expulsion from the party and because of the close cooperation of the Uschlas with the police authorities, the Uschlas formed another instrument in Nazi Germany to coerce and intimidate the individual. Hess explained most clearly the plight of those purged when he warned the party in April 1934: "Exclusion from the Party is the severest punishment known to it."[24]

The policing and supervising of the NSDAP's bulging membership lists was not the only problem that faced the Uschlas during the early months of the party's seizure of power; another difficult problem was that of the party's relationship to the state. In the early summer of 1933 the NSDAP was declared the only legal party, and the remaining parties simply dissolved their organizations or went underground. To give the semblance of "legality" to his coup and to ensure the process of coordination of the state and provincial governments, Hitler appointed a large number of leading party officials (primarily Gauleiters and SA officers) to powerful government positions. Special Reich commissioners (such as Göring and Epp) and provincial presidents *(Oberpräsidenten)* were appointed in Prussia, and Reich governors *(Reichsstatthaltern)* in the smaller states. Such duplication of high party and state offices, especially the uniting of the post of Gauleiter with the office of Reich governor or provincial president, led to endless conflicts over authority and jurisdiction in government matters. In some disagreements, the Reichs-Uschla was commanded by Hitler to investigate and settle the quarrels as quietly as possible.

An example was a case that the Reichs-Uschla handled during the summer and autumn. In July the Gauleiter and newly appointed provincial president of East Prussia, Koch, expelled (in agreement with his Gau-Uschla) three party members who had been sent to Königsberg as peasant leaders by the Reich government and by the Nazi minister of food and agriculture, Walter Darre. Darre, who was well known for his squabbles with other party leaders, maintained that the three were sent as advisers to help Koch implement in the east the federal government's new agrarian policy, which was designed to curtail mass unemployment and win the

115

peasantry to the NSDAP. But Koch, loathing Darre's interference into "his district" and referring to each of the advisers as a "saboteur and troublemaker" *(Saboteur und Miesmacher)*, accused them of slanderous remarks against him and immediately ordered their expulsion from the party. Moreover, to show Darre his political muscle, the irate Koch imprisoned one of the advisers and threatened to send him to a concentration camp.[25]

Outwardly, at least, it appeared that the issue at stake was the implementation of the federal government's new agricultural policy for East Prussia. Considerable confusion existed among the peasant leaders over whether they should receive their orders from Koch (as Gauleiter and provincial president) or directly from Darre's office in Berlin. Yet the real problem, according to the Prussian Ministry of Agriculture, was not so much agrarian policy as personal "differences of opinion" between Koch and Darre. Consequently, the ministry requested the Reichs-Uschla to intervene and settle the conflict.[26] As usual, the Reichs-Uschla was bombarded with letters from numerous party members and organizations—Koch, Darre, the OSAF, and the Gau-Uschla of East Prussia. To complicate matters, both Koch and Darre claimed to have acted on orders issued directly by Hitler.[27] In the final analysis, therefore, the quarrel centered around who possessed the power of command in the province.

A final decision by the Reichs-Uschla came at the close of 1933. Expressing its concern for the "confidence of the rural population of East Prussia in the authority of the National Leadership of the NSDAP" and the "agrarian policy advocated by the Führer," the Reichs-Uschla refused to confirm Koch's expulsion of the peasant leaders and ordered him to release the one that he had imprisoned. The decision acknowledged that the advisers had apparently been the "victims" of a personal disagreement between "old Party Comrades whose service and leadership . . . should not remain unnoticed" in the last judgment.

But the Reichs-Uschla, attempting to satisfy Koch (who was a favorite of Hitler's among the Gauleiter corps)[28] as well as Darre, also issued a warning to the advisers and condemned them for speaking out against the district leader.[29] In addition to the official ruling, Buch also sought to persuade Koch and Darre to meet personally in order to iron out their differences. His efforts were apparently unsuccessful. Koch informed him a year later that "a discussion between Party Comrade Darre and myself has still not occurred."[30]

The conflict illustrated the most confusing problem that confronted the Reichs-Uschla (and its lower courts) once Hitler and the NSDAP had captured control of the German government. Hitler's duplication of party and state offices and his continuing practice of "divide and rule" within the party made it extremely difficult in many instances to decide exactly where the jurisdiction of the Uschlas ended and the competence of another authority began. But as the quarrel also revealed, the Reichs-Uschla's methods of handling personal strife had changed little since its creation seven years earlier. Its strong concern that the confidence in the authority of the Reichsleitung be protected and that the prestige of the NSDAP not be injured by disagreements in public among its leading functionaries was another reflection of the highest principle of Nazi legal philosophy in practice—the movement means more than the individual member. Finally, the Reichs-Uschla's attempt to restrict Koch's power as Gauleiter and to enhance the Reichsleitung's authority were policies that it had pursued since 1926.

Until late in 1933 the Reichs-Uschla and its lower courts experienced few major organizational changes. Beginning in December, a series of state and party laws was enacted that increased significantly the penal and disciplinary powers of the Uschlas. On December 9 an Uschla circular officially renamed the committees, calling them simply Parteigerichte ("party courts"). The Reichs-Uschla became the *Oberstes Parteigericht* ("Supreme party court," or OPG), each Gau-Uschla a *Gaugericht* ("district court"), and each Orts-Uschla an *Ortsgericht* ("local court"). Inasmuch as party organizations had also been formed at the Kreis ("county") level, the order provided for the renaming of the Kreis-Uschlas; they became *Kreisgerichte* ("county courts") and were to function administratively between the Gaugerichte and the Ortsgerichte.[31] A month later the Oberstes Parteigericht was formally redivided into two chambers, with Buch remaining as chairman of the first chamber (assisted by Dr. Frank and Ludwig Schneider) and Grimm becoming head of the second (assisted by Graf and Konrad Hofer). The first chamber was mainly responsible for supervising the southern and western Gaus, and the second chamber the northern and eastern districts. In addition, a large Zentralamt functioned as the OPG's business office, employing a mass of secretaries and bureaucrats.[32]

Within the constitutional framework of the Third Reich, the Parteigerichte were established as official legal institutions in the German state by the Act for the Securing of the Unity of Party and State, which was decreed by the Reich government on 1 December 1933. According to that Act, all Nazi members had "increased obligations to the Führer, the People, and the State," and if such duties were not performed to the satisfaction of the movement (that is, Hitler and the Reichsleitung), those members who were disobedient were "subject to a special jurisdiction of the Party."[33] That "special jurisdiction" was the party judiciary, and particularly the powerful OPG. Beyond legalizing the Hitler regime as a totalitarian "one-party state," the Act increased tremendously the powers of the Parteigerichte and authorized them to punish government officials who were party members. Moreover, with the total identification of the NSDAP with the state, any crime now committed against the party was considered a crime (in the strict sense of the Act) against "the Führer, the People, and the State."

Consequently, expulsion from the movement or other punishment by the Parteigerichte (for example, issuing a warning to a member or barring him from holding a party office) was serious business and the worst fate that could befall a member. According to the Act, the Parteigerichte could even resort to "detention or imprisonment" beyond the "usual disciplinary measures" used as punishment. Buch, in something of an understatement, argued that the Act "significantly increased the responsibility of the Parteigerichte." In his judgment, it was now their foremost task to "watch over" the party and to ensure that its "entire political apparatus becomes saturated with the spirit of National Socialism."[34]

THE PARTEIGERICHTE, 1933–1945

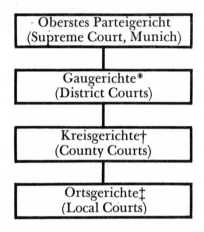

* In 1938 there were forty Gaugerichte, or district courts.

† The number of Kreisgerichte within a party district varied. In January 1936, for example, there were thirty Kreisgerichte under the jurisdiction of the Pomerania Gaugericht.

‡ The number of Ortsgerichte in a party district or county also varied. Some districts had several hundred Ortsgerichte within their jurisdiction.

Until 1942 and the last years of World War II, the basic law governing the Parteigerichte was a directive issued by the Reichsleitung on 17 February 1934. The order was the result of a great deal of planning, which began with a

119

memorandum on party justice drafted by Hitler the previous September. According to the memo, Hitler believed that it was necessary to ensure the NSDAP's existence "as a state within [the] state" *(als Staat im Staate)* by establishing "special laws" *(besondere Gesetze)*. The jurisdiction of the Parteigerichte, as he envisioned it, should extend only to the "crimes" that threatened "the existence" of the party's "political leadership":

> *That means, therefore, that it is the task of party justice to establish and to punish those crimes that have stood—because they have not endangered the existence of the state—hitherto outside prosecution in the general penal code, but that are crucial for the survival of the party and its internal organic life!*[35]

It is interesting (but not surprising) that Hitler considered himself (and not Buch or the OPG) to be the Supreme Judge of the party and its courts. He ended the memo by noting that the Supreme Justice *(Oberster Gerichtsherr)* was the "Leader of the Party" and that party law would be "pronounced in the name of the people."[36]

Hitler's draft was dispatched from his Chancellery at the end of September to the Reich minister of the interior, Frick. Frick interpreted Hitler's statement about crimes that threatened the party's "political leadership" as meaning: "Violations against discipline and order in the party, rebellion against legal commands of the Führer, undermining the prestige of the party and its Führer, and similar behavior, for example, slipping into the party under false pretenses."[37] In a lengthy note to Hess, Frick stated that the critical issues raised by the memorandum centered around the place of the NSDAP in the German constitution and, more specifically, "whether it [the party] should be made a corporate body of public justice for holders of legal political obligations and rights." Frick's chief concern was not to formulate guidelines to govern the objectives or formal procedures of the Parteigerichte. The most vexing problem, as he explained to Hess, was answering a question that concerned the dual relationship between party and state: should the Parteigerichte be allowed to prosecute public officials in the government?[38] Ultimately, the answer was affirmative. The Act for the Securing of the Unity of Party and State legally established that any state official who was a member of the NSDAP was subject (in addition to being accountable to the public courts) to the "special jurisdiction" of the Parteigerichte.[39]

The result of Hitler's memo and further exchanges between Frick, Hess, and Buch was the directive for the Parteigerichte issued by the Reichsleitung in February 1934. In the new guidelines the value of the Uschla system was particularly evident. There was very little in the directive, in fact, that distinguished the Parteigerichte of the Third Reich from their predecessors. Theoretically, at least, the Parteigerichte's primary goals, their competence as judicial bodies, their technical procedures for investigations, and their organizational structure remained basically the same. The overriding purpose of the Parteigerichte was to "protect the common honor of the party and [its] individual members as well as to arbitrate, if necessary, differences of opinion in the best possible manner." The chief functions of the Parteigerichte were constitutional and judicial: to discipline unruly party members, expel unwanted elements, settle strife in the movement, and examine closely party membership applications. Each tribunal was to be controlled by its competent political leader (that is, its Ortsgruppenleiter, Kreisleiter ["county leader"], Gauleiter, or Hitler), who possessed the powers of appointing and removing his court chairman, ordering his court into session, and executing its decisions. The Gau and Kreis benches were directed to divide themselves into two chambers (on the model of the OPG), and each chamber was to include three judges (a chairman and two assistants) and two alternate members who could be called on to serve in the absence of the regular members.[40]

The competence or jurisdiction of the Parteigerichte was also defined. Ortsgerichte and Kreisgerichte could investigate and bring to trial one or more members in an Ortsgruppe, while the Gaugerichte could hear cases against Ortsgruppen-leiters, Kreisleiters, co-workers of Gauleiters, Reich and Gau speakers, and officers in the SA and its subordinate organizations (namely, the SS and the Nazi Motorized Corps [Nationalsozialistische Kraftfahrer-Korps, or NSKK]). In addition, the Gaugerichte served as appeal instances for decisions of the lower courts. The OPG was competent to handle cases involving Gauleiters, Reichsleiters, ranking officers in the SA, and those party members who were ministers of state, secretaries of state, and Reich ministers in Hitler's cabinet. Except for Hitler, the OPG was the party's court of last resort for appeals.[41]

The directive of 1934 apparently solved the nagging problem of the party courts' relationship to the SA and its subgroups (SS, NSKK). The Parteigerichte could not judge "SA affairs" involving "violations of discipline and appeals" by SA men or "differences of opinion and strife" among SA members. For these, the SA and SS had their own courts and disciplinary institutions. However, in instances where an SA man (who was not a member of the party) accused a party member, the Parteigerichte were competent. The party benches could also bring to trial SA members who were expelled from their organization (or from the SS or NSKK), but who still belonged to the party; in fact, the removal of an individual from the SA usually meant an automatic inquiry by his Parteigericht to ascertain whether or not the man deserved to remain in the NSDAP. Nevertheless, SA men were given considerable protection before the Parteigerichte. At least one member on each bench had to be a ranking SA officer, and before an investigation could be opened against an SA man, his "competent leader" (that is, his commanding officer) had to be notified and given an opportunity to defend his subordinate during the trial proceedings. With the demise of the SA and the rapid rise of Himmler and the SS following the Röhm Purge in June, more extensive orders were issued by the OPG, specifically outlining which SS offices were permitted to advise the Parteigerichte and defend their men.[42]

The proceedings of the Parteigerichte during the Third Reich were complicated affairs. As was the case with the Uschlas, they involved a preliminary investigation *(Voruntersuchung)* and a closed trial *(Hauptverhandlung)*. During the preliminary inquiry, written affidavits and oral testimony from the witnesses and contending parties were gathered, examined by the judges, and made ready for trial. If the Parteigericht ruled that a trial was necessary, the accused, or defendant, was made aware immediately that the proceedings had become serious business: he was removed from all party offices and his membership book (or card) was confiscated for the duration of the trial. Once in the courtroom, all participants (namely, witnesses, defendant, and plaintiff) were warned not to perjure themselves or give false testimony (which carried the penalty of expulsion from the party). The trial thus began, and the contending parties (who were denied legal counsel) were interrogated by the judges, and opinions from "expert witnesses" (for example, SA officers or political leaders) were heard. The accused was then given an opportunity to present a concluding statement before the judges rendered their verdict. In the event that the party itself was the plaintiff accusing a member, the accused still retained the right to have the final word.[43]

Yet, when the moment of reckoning arrived, the party and its judges obviously held the trump card. Following a private deliberation, the Parteigericht pronounced one of several decisions that it could render: incompetence to decide the case, acquittal of the accused, expulsion of the accused from the party, warning to the accused, and reprimand to the accused. Moreover, the Parteigericht could decree what amounted to an excommunication *(Ausstossung)* of the accused from the party "if the accused has violated in a particularly severe manner the endeavors of the NSDAP and his actions definitely suggest a vile way of thinking and unprincipled behavior." In most instances the sentence meant immediate arrest by the police, a long imprisonment, and perhaps even execution. At the same time, however, the comparatively milder punishments of a warning or a reprimand most assuredly damaged a member's party status and left an endless cloud of suspicion hanging above him. He was denied the right to hold a party office for three years or to appear as a party speaker, and the record of his punishment was entered in his membership book, to remain for five years.[44]

Beyond possessing these vast powers, the Parteigerichte had the arbitrary authority to expel members without a regular hearing and to usurp the right of the public or state courts and police to retain privileged information. The directive of 1934 provided for what were termed summary proceedings *(Schnellverfahren)* before the Parteigerichte. Through such proceedings, political leaders could order their Parteigericht chairman to expel a member if the latter suddenly posed a "danger" to the NSDAP or embarrassed it in public. The political leader simply issued a temporary order *(einstweilige Verfügung)* for expulsion, and the banished member had eight days in which to appeal the decision. Undoubtedly, the objectives were to speed up justice and to deprive the accused of a thorough examination of the charges against him. Moreover, appeals in such instances had little chance of being acknowledged; nowhere in the party's laws was it stated that a member was entitled to or guaranteed a regular court hearing.

The Parteigerichte were also granted the authority to infringe (grossly, if necessary) on the constitutional rights of the state courts and police. When disagreements between party members brought them before a public court in a civil action or complaint, a trial could not begin without the official approval of the members' competent Parteigericht. In addition, for their proceedings the Parteigerichte were empowered to obtain any type of information or legal aid *(Rechtshilfe)* from the state judiciary and police authorities. Although trials of the Parteigerichte were closed to the public and their judges were sworn to unconditional silence *(unbedingtem Schweigen)*, they were obligated to return the favor.[45] Thus, the party and state courts cooperated closely, and disobedient party members found that there were few loopholes through which one could beat the Nazi penal system.

A further question raised by the directive was that of the competing jurisdictions of the party and state judiciaries in cases involving government officials or civil servants who were members of the NSDAP. Through a series of Civil Servant Laws enacted by the Reich government in the spring of 1933, a systematic purge was begun to remove Jewish, Socialist, Communist, and "liberal" civil-service employees at all levels of government. Although the attempt to "nazify" the bureaucracy was limited, hundreds of National Socialists became government officials, and the civil-service employees who remained outside the NSDAP were rigorously indoctrinated in the party's ideology.[46]

Revealing the broader problem of party-state dualism, Nazi civil-service employees throughout the Third Reich faced possible "double jeopardy" if found guilty of an offense against the government or the party. If, on the one hand, they were convicted by a state court, they could be hauled before their party tribunal, tried again for bringing "injury to the party," and removed from the NSDAP.[47] On the other hand, once a civil servant was banished from the party, he was quickly categorized as "politically unreliable" (which placed him only a notch above Jewish or "half-Jewish" officials and equal with those formerly belonging to the KPD, the SPD, the Catholic Center party, and other parties), and the loss of his job was well-nigh automatic. The long arm of the party judiciary reached into the halls of every government ministry to punish and remove officials who were Nazi members,[48] and the party eventually devised a system for retaining a close record of those expelled.[49]

During the summer of 1933 the National Socialist district president of Magdeburg, Dr. Helmut Nicolai, incurred the wrath of the Magdeburg-Anhalt Gauleiter, Wilhelm Loeper. Nicolai refused to overlook criminal excesses by several party members, and he even had the courage to order them punished. Loeper disagreed and attempted to have Nicolai taken before the Magdeburg Gaugericht; but the president also held a minor office in the Reichsleitung, and he was therefore punishable only by the OPG. In November, Nicolai was called by Frick into the Reich Ministry of the Interior. Loeper finally convinced the OPG to introduce proceedings against Nicolai, and after a lengthy investigation, the latter was expelled (despite Frick's protests) from the NSDAP and removed from the government.[50]

The interference by the party judiciary into the affairs of the government and the state courts represented an example of the naked "perversion of justice" in the Third Reich.[51] To justify the practice, the National Socialists combined their innate disrespect for law of any kind (except their own) with the philosophy that had always dominated the actions of the Parteigerichte: the community (or nation) is everything, and the individual (or citizen) nothing. Dr. Frank expressed this cruel maxim most clearly when he boasted to the diplomatic corps and foreign press in January 1934 that "the internal essence of Parteigericht justice" was that "the National Socialist has no special rights; he has only duties to the Führer and the people."[52] Thus, the Parteigerichte—added to the Gestapo, the SS, the Special Courts (Sondergerichte) and the People's Courts, and the orders for death sentences issued by Hitler to set aside milder punishments by the regular courts—became an integral part in the Nazi arsenal of intimidation that was aimed at forcing "reluctant" Germans to support the NSDAP and the government.

Indirectly, the verdicts of the Parteigerichte sent countless numbers of expelled or disobedient NSDAP members to prisons and concentration camps in 1933 and 1934. To avoid trials of party members before state courts and thereby to avoid risking adverse publicity for the NSDAP or one of its organizations, the Parteigerichte were used to "convict" a member for an alleged offense, and he was then arrested by the police and imprisoned. Although the Parteigerichte rarely issued formal decisions ordering arrests and imprisonment, they did work closely with state and local authorities to keep the latter informed of court actions against individual members.

In fact, once a member was expelled or punished severely by his Parteigericht, his arrest by the local police, Gestapo office, or county executive *(Landrat)* was nearly automatic.[53] In addition, rebellious members were frequently incarcerated before a party proceeding was opened that could legally remove them from the NSDAP. In March 1934, for example, an SA man and party member from Zwickau, Alfred Seifert, was interned at the protective-custody camp in Hohnstein (Saxony). Following a quarrel with his Ortsgruppenleiter, Seifert had been expelled without a party hearing, and he was arrested soon thereafter.[54] Such procedures were hardly surprising; party justice often meant depriving the individual of his rights instead of protecting them!

An example illustrating the power of the Parteigerichte to condemn a party member to prison was a case handled by the Franconia Gaugericht in the spring of 1934. The Gaugericht opened a formal proceeding in April against a long-time Nuremberg member and SS leader, Ludwig Böck. Böck was proven guilty of swindling his employer out of a substantial sum of money, but during his trial he denied having committed the fraud. In fact, he threatened the Gaugericht by alleging at the trial that he was in possession of incriminating material against the chairman of the court and one of the assistant judges. Obviously angered at Böck's threat, the judges closed the proceedings by ordering that he be expelled from the party. Condemning Böck's allegations and behavior in the courtroom, the Gaugericht noted in its verdict that "whoever fights with such dishonorable methods is no National Socialist."[55]

Within days, Böck found himself under arrest and taken into "protective custody" by the Nazi-controlled Nuremberg-Fürth police. The chairman of the Gaugericht, Georg Gradl, had informed the police chief (who was the leader of the Gau SS) of Böck's removal from the NSDAP, and the police immediately accused him of endangering "public order" by making the "most unbelievable personal slander and insults" against the Franconian Gauleiter, Streicher.[56] Although the authorities produced several witnesses, the charges against Böck were clearly fabricated and designed to justify his imprisonment. It was only following a barrage of letters exchanged among local police, the Bavarian Political Police, and Reichsstatthalter Epp that he was finally released (albeit grudgingly) later in the summer.[57]

In June, Hitler moved suddenly and with little warning to crush the last organized element of opposition in the party: the SA and other radical advocates in the NSDAP who demanded the continuation of the Nazi "revolution from below." During the fateful "night of the long knives," 30 June–1 July, the SS brutally murdered Röhm and countless other SA leaders who were suspected of "treason" and of leading a "revolt" against Hitler, and Gregor Strasser and General Schleicher were "sacrificed" for their part in opposing Hitler's bid for power at the end of 1932.

Although Buch opposed the killing of his friend Strasser,[58] he took an active role in planning and organizing the SA purge. After his attempt to persuade Hitler to remove Röhm in 1932 because of the latter's homosexuality, Buch had worked secretly with Bormann and Hess to gather a mass of incriminating material from Gauleiters and other party officials against the SA chief and his most "intimate" friends. Buch had also collected several hundred complaints from SA men and parents of members of the Hitler Youth, and he had in his possession "love letters" that Röhm had sent to male friends of his in Bolivia (where Röhm had once trained officers).[59]

Several months before the purge, Buch took his impressive evidence to Hitler, but the latter still refused to release the SA leader. Beyond accusing Röhm, the chief justice worked to eliminate Röhm's close aides in the OSAF: Count Spreti, Count du Moulin-Eckart, and Georg Bell. In April 1933, Bell had already been stalked and shot to death at the Austrian border by the SS after the OPG had refused

128

to open an investigation into his homosexual relations and informer activities with the Socialist press.[60]

When Hess, Bormann, and Buch were joined in the spring of 1934 by the power-hungry trio of Göring, Himmler, and Heydrich, the fate of Röhm and the SA was sealed. For his part, Buch was a decisive figure in organizing the SS for the bloody murders of SA leaders in Bavaria. Röhm, Spreti, and many others were shot, and Eckart was sent to Dachau to reflect on his "continual treason to the *Münchener Post*" during the Kampfzeit.[61] Despite his villainous role in the purge, Buch was a hero to several people who might well have been victims of the Nazi "long knives." On June 27, for example, he secretly warned the former Catholic Center party leader and Chancellor, Brüning, of the pending massacre. Brüning had once been Buch's commander in the army, and the latter's warning (given to Brüning at his Berlin home by an anonymous SS man) enabled Brüning to flee the country.[62]

Immediately after the crushing of the SA, Hitler addressed the remaining brown-shirt leaders in the Senate Hall of the Brown House, the party's headquarters in Munich. He praised Buch for being the man who had called his attention to Röhm's perversion, and he noted that Buch had been the only party leader to oppose vigorously Röhm's appointment as Osaf in 1931. A bit later, Hitler wept and complained to Buch about his great disappointment in Röhm, and he queried Buch about who should become the new Osaf. Buch strongly recommended an old friend, Victor Lutze—a married man with children, who was modest and who would not try to become a public figure.[63]

In addition to ridding the party of Röhm, Buch was extremely pleased to have the old and nagging rivalry between the SA and the Parteigerichte finally settled. Röhm's successor, Lutze, never challenged Buch about the Parteigerichte's jurisdiction over the SA, and Buch's difficulties with the military groups now switched to the SS and its rapidly rising leader, Himmler. The SS, however, was to have its own disciplinary organizations and courts, and Buch was never to attack Himmler (whom the chief justice admired) as he had attacked Röhm.

After the Röhm affair, the nature of Buch's work and the business of the OPG became veiled in an ever-increasing secrecy. He was frequently asked to travel from Munich to Berlin to meet with Hitler on important Parteigerichte matters. Appearing only occasionally at party meetings, however, the OPG chairman began to avoid publicity, and his influence on general party policy began to dwindle. He now confined himself almost exclusively to his disciplinary functions, and he made certain that party orders were carried out fully and promptly. In September 1934 he was awarded the rank of honorary general in the SS (*Obergruppenführer*, which was commensurate with his party Reichsleiter status), and he was appointed to positions in the SS's Race and Settlement Main Office (Rasse- und Siedlungshauptamt) and the Council of Experts on Population and Race Policy (Sachverständigenbeirat für Bevolkerungs- und Rassepolitik) in the Reich Ministry of the Interior. He also became a ranking member of the German Academy of Law.[64]

Although the OPG and its chairman became less active publicly by the end of 1934, both continued to be involved "behind-the-scenes" in mediating dissension among the party's leaders at the Reich and Gau levels. In this respect, the Röhm revolt and the mass influx of new members into the NSDAP in 1933 and 1934 had the effect of reshaping the party leadership (especially at the lower echelons) and decreasing much of the strife and rebellion that had characterized the movement during the Kampfzeit. The party's old political conflicts were now safely suppressed; Strasserism and socialism were no longer a threat, and the political leadership had settled its score with Röhm and the "revolutionary" SA. This is not to say, however, that intraparty rivalries stopped. They continued until the end, but those that arose during the Third Reich were primarily organizational and personal in nature, and they involved party "bigwigs" who quibbled with one another over the authority and power delegated to them by Hitler.

Pursuing his practice of combining party and state offices, Hitler carefully erected a web of competing offices within the party organization itself. Aside from the familiar instance of competition between Gauleiter and Reichsleiter, the classic example of overlapping offices was Robert Ley and Hess (and later Bormann). Although their titles differed, their functions were much the same. In propaganda, Goebbels's office rivaled that of Otto Dietrich (Hitler's press chief) and that of the newspaper czar Amann. In culture and art, Alfred Rosenberg and Göring were given positions that competed with Goebbels's, and similar duplications were created in the Nazi labor movement (for example, Ley and Fritz Sauckel) and education (which was supposedly controlled by Bernhard Rust). There was little or no definition of authority in the party hierarchy, and the higher the office, the more confused and unclear were the definitions of its jurisdiction. The results were nothing new for the NSDAP: there was a steady flow of bickering and backbiting, and one could note the continued success of Hitler's old tactic of "divide and rule."

Hitler's use of the OPG to encourage a certain amount of conflict was evident in the autumn of 1934 when Hess attempted to have it open proceedings against Ley. The latter (who also had difficulties working with Himmler, Bormann, and Rosenberg) was the nominal head of the party organization, and he carried the official title of staff leader of the Supreme Leadership of the Political Organization *(Oberste Leitung der Politische Organisation)*. Moreover, Ley was leader of the rapidly growing (but poorly administered) German Labor Front (Deutsche Arbeitsfront, or DAF), which was designed to replace "Marxist" trade unions and to win the working-class masses to National Socialism.[65] A power struggle between Ley and Hess began as early as the spring of 1933 over the issue of who controlled what in the Reichsleitung. Hess's position was strengthened when Schwarz supported him and when Bormann was added to Hess's staff and named Reichsleiter.

By the beginning of 1934, relations between the rivals

131

had deteriorated to the point where Ley refused to follow orders issued by Hitler under Hess's signature. Hess (who was normally quiet and timid and who rarely was one to challenge the sacred work of the Führer) attacked Ley and attempted to subordinate the latter directly to his office. In October, Hess ordered the OPG to investigate the rebellious Ley, but Hitler, again revealing his old lack of respect for the party judiciary, intervened in Hess's favor before the conflict could reach the OPG and thus create a major embarrassment for the Führer.[66]

Hess, a few days after his command to the OPG, issued a firm statement to the party, which noted that Hitler had made him "responsible" for the "uniformity in the line of political leadership" and that such leadership lay "solely and alone" with the NSDAP's "leading functionaries, thus with me, the Gauleiters, Kreisleiters, and Ortsgruppenleiters." A month later, Ley's official party title was changed to Reich organization leader *(Reichsorganisationsleiter)*, thus eliminating the misleading conception that he was head of the Supreme Leadership of the Political Organization.[67] Without much success, Buch continued to harass Ley by pushing for an investigation of Ley's excessive drinking in public and its effect on the NSDAP's reputation. Ley appealed to Hitler, however, and the latter prohibited the inquiry.[68]

In settling the incessant quarrels among leaders and in exercising its disciplinary powers, the OPG was far more effective with the Gauleiter corps and other functionaries below the Reich level. When the Gauleiter of Schleswig-Holstein, Lohse, protested to Hess in November that the Reichsleitung's rigid policy against Freemasons was leading to "nothing but petty difficulties" in his Gau, Hess reprimanded the Gauleiter and ordered Buch to introduce proceedings against him. Lohse then attacked Buch, but when faced with the serious charge of "violating the endeavors" of the NSDAP, for which he could be expelled, he quickly made his peace with his superiors.[69]

The OPG also crushed party members in educational

132

and cultural circles who refused to follow orders from Rosenberg, Goebbels, or Rust in publishing literature on the NSDAP and its ideology. In October a Nazi author and propagandist from Berlin, Dr. Engelbert Huber, was expelled by the OPG for writing a short booklet that supposedly stood in the "strongest opposition to the clear and distinct will of the Führer and the view of the party leadership." Huber thus discovered too late that attempting to define or delimit Nazi philosophy was an unforgivable sin.[70]

By the end of the year, however, personal conflict was not the crucial problem facing the Parteigerichte. With Hitler declaring at the Nuremberg rally in September that the Nazi "revolution" was at an end and that the NSDAP would be "for all time the select political leadership of the German people," the chief concern of the Parteigerichte continued to be that of protecting the movement's racial and political "purity."[71] At the rally a special conference of Parteigerichte chairmen gathered to hear Buch, Grimm, and Ludwig Schneider discuss the urgency of the courts' task. Buch opened the meeting by warning that all party judges must be totally loyal to the NSDAP and its work. "Only with completely pure hands," he noted, "should justice be handled." Grimm and Schneider followed, and they emphasized that all applications for party membership should be examined rigorously by the Parteigerichte, which should never hesitate to punish party members who violated public law. In closing the assembly, Buch set the tone for the future work of the Parteigerichte when he commanded his subordinates that "above all in the race question and in the Freemason question," they rule without compassion and according to the "conscience of the German people." To this he added: "He [the party judge] has to fulfill his difficult office solely with loyalty to himself, loyalty to the Führer, and loyalty to the movement."[72]

6

Iron Clamps of the Movement, 1935-1939

THE ESSENCE of the Third Reich was the National Socialists' efforts to bring national unity and European hegemony back to Germany. To display the former, the NSDAP held its massive party rallies at Nuremberg and countless other propaganda functions to show the world that Nazism and Hitler represented "all" of Germany. Yet, in sharp contrast to what Nazi propaganda maintained, the secret proceedings of the Parteigerichte between 1935 and 1939 told a far different story. Not every German was a fanatical, heel-clicking, and hand-raising National Socialist, and numerous party members became disenchanted enough with Hitler to oppose the NSDAP and open themselves to a rigorous trial before the competent Parteigericht.

While Hitler and the party carefully attempted to rearm Germany, strengthen the nation's economy, and destroy external opposition to the government from the churches and the Wehrmacht, the Parteigerichte became what Chief Justice Buch often termed the "iron clamps" of the movement.[1] In Hitler's view the Parteigerichte should operate as "tribunals of war of the army," and their judges should be "former officers" or party members who possessed some experience in the "state judiciary." In other words, the Parteigerichte were "militarized" (as was every aspect of life in the Third Reich), and they functioned as though the

NSDAP were under a continuous state of emergency.[2] Their punishments were to be harsh and were to be decreed in Hitler's name, in the interest of the party, and in total disregard of personal circumstances or hardships.

Although the major functions of the Parteigerichte changed little, their powers over the party and over government employees who were NSDAP members were steadily expanded and consolidated. The position of the Parteigerichte as bodies of justice within the state was reconfirmed in March 1935 by the Reich government's Second Act for the Securing of the Unity of State and Party. According to this Act, the NSDAP was an entity of public law, and it was composed of its own organizations *(Gliederungen)* and so-called affiliated associations *(angeschlossene Verbände)*.

Most party groups possessed their own disciplinary department or court, but when the actions of one of their members seemed to harm or endanger the entire movement, he was quickly bound over to the authorized Parteigericht for trial. As party "organizations," the Act recognized the SA, the SS, the NSKK, the HJ, the NSDStB, and the Nazi Frauenschaft ("women's auxiliary"). It defined the affiliated associations (which were legal entities in themselves, yet subject to the financial control of Schwarz) as the party's DAF, League of German Lawyers, Teachers' League (NS-Lehrerbund), Doctor's League (NS-Arztebund), Welfare Association (NS-Volkswohlfahrt, or NSV), War Victims Society (NS-Kriegsopferversorgung, or NSKOV), Reich League of German Civil Servants (Reichsbund der Deutschen Beamten, or RDB), and League of German Technicians (NS-Bund deutscher Techniker).[3]

To extend its control over the mass of groups and the party members or provisional members *(Parteianwärter,* meaning those admitted provisionally to the movement for two years until they could "prove" themselves worthy of full membership) enrolled therein, the OPG issued in the autumn of 1935 a series of varied commands. For example, it threatened members of the Lawyers' League with expulsion from the NSDAP if they represented a Jew in a civil trial or in a state court. The OPG also began a campaign (which was to continue into 1937) attacking members in any organization who refused to pay their monthly dues. Those who were found guilty of having fallen more than three months behind in their payments and of "purposely refusing to pay" were ruthlessly purged.[4]

The OPG even collaborated with the Reich Treasury Office to warn groups and affiliates to exercise greater caution in their use of official party automobiles and trucks. In a circular to the Gauleiters, Schwarz complained bitterly about members driving both official and privately owned motor vehicles that were not insured by the NSDAP (which operated a massive insurance program). He also noted that party-insured autos were involved in an increasing number of accidents, which raised "intolerably" the "financial burden" of the party. He thus threatened all offenders with serious consequences: "In especially gross instances (drunkenness, excessive speeding, driving without a license or without an auto registration or before acquiring insurance) . . . I will order an investigation by the proper Parteigericht."[5]

The powers of the Parteigerichte in this regard were later extended by Hitler. Because of the alarming accident rate and because of injuries to leading party personalities (such as Ley and several Gauleiters), the Führer's attitude toward automobiles was becoming progressively more conservative. A "passionate automobilist," he loved his Mercedes and high speeds, and during the Kampfzeit he had always commanded his chauffeur to drive at great speeds to overtake any cars ahead. But in November 1935 he gave formal notice through Hess that "in the future, party members who deliberately violate traffic regulations will be removed from their offices, and where necessary, punished by the Parteigerichte."[6]

Acting as watchdogs over the party's numerous organizations was only one of many tasks facing the Parteigerichte. A concerted effort was made during the summer and autumn by the OPG and its forty Gaugerichte to tighten their control over the countless Kreisgerichte and Ortsgerichte and to en-

137

sure the smooth functioning of the entire court system. Aside from the OPG's annual meeting with Gaugerichte chairmen at the Nuremberg Reichsparteitag in September, the OPG coordinated its activities with the lower courts by publishing an official monthly journal (begun the previous year), *Der Parteirichter*, and by holding a special Gau Judges Conference in Munich in July.

As guests at the meeting were the special commissioners *(Beauftragten)* of the party leadership and representatives from the disciplinary courts of the SA, the SS, the NSKK, the HJ, and the Lawyers' League. Addressing the group, Chief Justice Buch stressed the same dull themes that the OPG had always emphasized to its judges (namely, the glorification of Hitler, the importance of the party judge to the NSDAP, and the concept that the "community is all and the individual nothing"). Obviously exaggerating the significance of court members, he noted that "whoever desires to become a party judge must think of himself as a priest of justice." Added to this, he demanded from his listeners that they conduct their lives and judge others according to the principle that had supposedly been the "secret" to Hitler's greatness: "He [Hitler] wants nothing for himself and everything for others. Anyone who associates closely with a person possessing such massive willpower will become even stronger."[7]

Especially at the Gau and Kreis levels, a serious attempt was made by the Parteigerichte and their political leaders to clamp down on "agitators and mischief-makers." Any party member caught uttering "untrue or grossly distorted statements" that threatened the "welfare of the nation or the reputation of the NSDAP" and its "leading personalities" was now subject to maximum punishment by the party (that is, expulsion and a sojourn in prison).[8] Furthermore, the Gaugerichte were ordered by the OPG to create a central penal file *(Strafkartei)* containing every decision of the Kreisgerichte and Ortsgerichte in their districts.[9] Thus, a closer record could be maintained on troublemakers who had appeared before the courts and who might endanger the lower organizations. As with the Gestapo and the SS, the Partei-gerichte and Nazi leaders were often more eager to "anticipate" opposition than they were to stop it once it arose.

Continuing its efforts (begun in 1928) to control carefully the subordinate tribunals and ensure that their judges were genuine "priests of justice," the OPG gathered extensive information on all assistant judges as well as court chairmen (Ortsgerichte included). Adding to the veil of secrecy surrounding the courts' activities, no judgment could be published in the press (such as, for example, in the *Völkischer Beobachter*) without the written consent of Buch or the OPG's Zentralamt. Only in "apparently urgent cases" could approval be obtained by telephone or teletype.[10]

Critical instances often arose, when the Parteigerichte found it necessary to expel a member who was a government employee or civil servant. Throughout the Third Reich the NSDAP vigorously attempted (with varying degrees of success) to "purify" the government bureaucracy by removing elements suspected of being republican or Jewish and rebellious party members from its ranks.[11] Expulsion of a civil servant from the party, of course, meant that the unlucky official was almost certain to lose his job and be prosecuted by the state. In January 1935 Alfred Meyer, the Gauleiter and Reich governor of Westphalia-North, discovered that his personal adjutant, Graf von Zech, had pilfered four thousand marks from the Gau treasury. Zech was immediately ejected from the movement, and notice was served in the party press (obviously to show what could happen to members caught stealing from the party) that he had been bound over to the district prosecutor.[12]

In the following year a major coup occurred for the OPG when it forced out of the party a prominent Berlin member and ranking secretary in the Prussian Ministry of the Interior, Dr. Ludwig Grauert. A Göring protégé, Grauert had been a continual critic of the NSDAP's attack on the civil service, and he had argued that the party should instead focus on building a political elite in the government. Opposition from party leaders quickly mounted against

Grauert, and he soon became another sacrifice to the OPG. As early as 1934 the OPG began to assemble incriminating material against him, and on 30 June 1936 he "voluntarily" resigned his post in the hope of avoiding a proceeding that could have sent him to prison.[13]

During 1935 and 1936 Hess's office and the OPG issued orders to Gau organizations, demanding quick notification to the Reichsleitung of civil servants who were expelled from the party by Gau (or lower) courts or who left the NSDAP of their own free will. Bormann informed the party in July 1935 that the Reich and Prussian ministers of the interior were "in agreement" with him that "civil servants who resign from the NSDAP should be excluded from favored promotions." He also ordered that any person leaving the party should be reported by the Gauleitung to the proper Reich ministry and the Deputy Führer's office.[14]

The witchhunt for disloyal civil servants intensified in 1936, particularly as the Hitler government became more aggressive in foreign policy. In the spring it was announced that civil servants being tried by the Parteigerichte were to be "put on leave" or "removed from their offices" for the duration of the proceedings. Furthermore, Hess ordered a "searching examination" of the "reason" that each civil servant gave for resigning from the party. If an investigation proved that an official had left "because he rejected the program or the political attitude of the party, then he will no longer be able to remain a civil servant."[15] Later, the OPG moved to ensure that no civil servant expelled from the party and released from his job could slip unnoticed past the party leadership or state authorities. The OPG ordered its lower courts to forward the names of such persons to both the Reich Ministry of Justice and the Deputy Führer's office.[16]

In ministries that were headed by fanatical National Socialists, the "purge" system worked effectively. An example was Goebbels's enormous Ministry for People's Enlightenment and Propaganda. Not only did the OPG reach into the halls of his Reich office,[17] but the lower courts proved themselves worthy bloodhounds in removing the ministry's officials at the Gau and Orts levels. The Partei-gerichte especially kept party-press reporters and news correspondents under close surveillance to ensure rigid loyalty in propaganda and party affairs.[18]

Even disloyal mechanics and garage attendants employed by the ministry were ferreted out and punished. In the spring of 1937 Hans Grabow, the chief attendant at the Reich broadcasting station in Cologne, was expelled from the SS for stealing money from that organization. Later, the Gestapo discovered that Grabow was courting the wife of a man suspected of being a Communist and a Jew, and Grabow was immediately taken before the Kreisgericht in Cologne. When the court issued him a "warning" and ordered him to break off his "relationship," Grabow lost his job and was transferred to "another Reich broadcasting station."[19]

Such cases involving moral offenses of ordinary party members rarely became significant for the functioning of the NSDAP or for preserving its reputation. But Buch, who suddenly rediscovered in early 1935 the importance of the family in National Socialism and in German culture, demanded in a series of articles in *Der Parteirichter* that the immorality of ranking party leaders be judged severely by the OPG. Buch's crusade, however, touched several sensitive nerves; a number of party notables were known to be unfaithful to their wives, including Goebbels, Streicher, and Wilhelm Kube (the Kurmark Gauleiter).

Consequently, Buch soon found himself up against a brick wall of opposition that counted among its adherents the bachelor and non-family man Hitler. The chief justice nevertheless continued to write articles in the OPG's journal, and it was only in November 1935 that he was forced to halt his crusade. Hitler, in a move that was to mark the beginning of the demise of Buch's authority (which was to culminate during the war), commanded him to resign as head of the OPG's first chamber (in favor of Buch's deputy, Schneider). In addition, the Führer called him to Berlin, whereupon Buch experienced what was surely a shattering blow to his blind confidence in his master—Hitler berated him verbally and ordered the humbled judge to stop playing the role in the party of the self-righteous country parson.[20]

With respect to the general question of civil-service employees and the power of the Parteigerichte to prosecute them, the diplomats in German embassies and consulates abroad were hardly safer than their bureaucratic brothers who served the Reich and the Führer at home. The Gaugericht that supervised the party's Foreign Countries Organization (Auslands-Organisation, or AO) kept close tabs on Nazi diplomats and officials around the world, and when one made himself suspect, the court arranged for his recall to Germany and a trial to decide his fate. In the spring of 1937 a ranking German official in Argentina, Arthur Koch, was spotted selling military secrets, and the Gaugericht AO cooperated with the state police in Hamburg in arresting Koch when he returned to the Reich in May. Moreover, Koch was attempting to reenter the NSDAP (which he had left several years earlier) prior to his arrival, but the Gaugericht dealt him a further reversal by refusing him readmittance. It was thus not surprising that a state court soon sentenced him to imprisonment and hard labor for life.[21]

Retaining accurate records on traitorous or suspect diplomats, officials, and NSDAP members abroad was no easy task for the Foreign Countries Organization. Correspondence with party locals around the globe (established by the AO) was only as fast as the mail could be transported, and members abroad were never as accessible to the NSDAP as were those at home. The result was often embarrassing confusion about who had been removed from the party and who was still a member.

A classic instance was the uproar in the Reichsleitung and AO when it was discovered in early 1938 that Kurt Lüdecke, a former Nazi official in Washington, D.C., who had left the NSDAP and Germany in 1934, was still listed as a party member. When, in 1937, Lüdecke published his memoir, *I Knew Hitler*, Schwarz began to check the master membership file and could find nothing on Lüdecke's status. He then queried the political leader of the AO, Gauleiter

Ernst Bohle, about Lüdecke's membership in his organization, but the result was another zero. Bohle maintained that his records showed that Lüdecke had never belonged to the AO.[22]

The Gauleiter finally contacted Hess to clarify the situation. According to the Deputy Führer, Lüdecke "had been in a concentration camp before his escape abroad, and at that time, he had already been excommunicated from the party." Hess further ordered Bohle and Schwarz to enter Lüdecke's expulsion in the membership file and to place his name on the party's famed "black list."[23] The "black list" was reserved for persons who had especially incurred the hostility of the party, and once on the list (which was sent regularly to all party organizations), one could never enter or reenter the NSDAP. It frequently contained, moreover, the names of Jews and Communists who were caught attempting to join the movement.

Although the Parteigerichte did their share of devastating numerous departments in the vast civil service, not every court trial ended in catastrophe for the defendant. A police captain and Nazi member in Ludwigshafen, Albert Buchmann, survived both Himmler's animosity toward him and a trial before the Saar-Pfalz Gaugericht in 1936 to become a ranking member of the Bavarian Political Police. Buchmann was fortunate enough to have friends who were willing to testify to his long-time sympathy for nazism.[24] Unquestionably, members who had entered the NSDAP before 30 January 1933 (that is, the "old fighters") or who could produce witnesses to testify to their service to the movement in the Kampfzeit fared much better before the Parteigerichte than did the newer members.[25]

Yet, at the same time, civil servants who were National Socialists faced the terrifying prospect of being ruined professionally, socially, and economically if they opposed the party and were convicted by both party courts and state courts. Considerable friction arose between Frick and Hess over this issue of "double jeopardy." Frick contended that according to the numerous civil-service laws, a civil servant could not legally be tried by two different judicial agencies. In every individual case of vital importance (for example, Grauert's), strife arose over whether and how far affairs of government officials should be subjected to the judgment and scrutiny of the party.[26] Naturally enough, it was the Deputy Führer who prevailed. In early 1938 Bormann announced that a government employee's resignation from the NSDAP was "alone" an "important basis" for his removal from office "without consideration for the alleged basis of the resignation."[27]

Hess did attempt, nevertheless, to make life somewhat easier for expelled civil servants and others. In his view it was the "task of Parteigericht justice to keep the ranks of the party pure and to remove harmful elements from the movement." Yet, he clearly recognized the drastic consequences of expulsion, and in January 1937 he ordered that, wherever possible, mercy be shown those rejected by the party:

> Removal from the party and its organizations is such a hard punishment for honor-loving citizens, that I can only believe it right that in especially grave instances, they should still be able to work and bring bread to their wives and children.
>
> That should especially be true for the old fighters from the period of struggle—which is the sad part—who must be removed from the ranks of the movement because of serious violations.[28]

One "old fighter" who hardly received much sympathy for his sins was the long-time Kurmark Gauleiter, Kube. In April 1936 Kube attempted to even the score with Buch (who disapproved of Kube's keeping a mistress) by writing an anonymous letter (signed "Some Berlin Jews") to Buch, accusing his wife of being half Jewish. The letter also noted that Buch's son-in-law, Bormann, was not married to a woman who was of "pure Aryan descent" (namely, Gerda Buch). Revealing an obvious disdain for Buch personally and for his job as OPG judge, Kube cynically wrote: "You

144

are mainly charged with having condemned hundreds of people for the same tragic fate that has befallen your wife. What conclusions do you draw, you wise and unbiased judge! We are happy that you may count yourself as one of us."[29]

The letter was quickly and quietly dispatched to the Gestapo, and within weeks it was discovered that Kube was the author of the note. When questioned by Hess, the Gauleiter admitted that he had written it. To absolve Buch and Bormann of any suspicion, however, the SS and the Office for Race Policy in the Reich Ministry of the Interior busily investigated Frau Buch's family background, and (not surprisingly) they found her to be of "pure Aryan" stock. Kube was stripped of his party office, taken into custody, and imprisoned for several years in a concentration camp. Only Himmler's intervention in 1940 resurrected him and saved him from dying there.[30]

Ironically, by 1936 Buch was also beginning to encounter difficulties with Bormann. One of the "Feme murderers" of 1924, the ambitious Bormann had joined the NSDAP three years later and was eventually "adopted" by Buch and taken into the latter's home in Solln, near Munich. Buch viewed the far-right assassins as national heros, and in 1929 he was instrumental in securing the release from prison of one of the killers, Paul Schulz.[31] In September 1928 Bormann married Buch's eldest daughter, Gerda, and Hitler was present at the ceremony. From that moment, Bormann counted himself a member of a prominent circle in the Reichsleitung that included Buch and Schwarz. Through his work as head of the party's insurance program (supervised by Schwarz), he was promoted to staff leader under Hess and to the post of Reichsleiter in 1933.[32]

Although Buch and Bormann collaborated in the Röhm revolt, the latter's rapid rise in the party hierarchy and his increasingly close relationship with Hess and Hitler apparently made Buch envious and jealous. Moreover, the two came from entirely different cultural backgrounds. Buch was a former officer and was not the type of individual that fit comfortably (as did Bormann) into the inner circles of the barracks-oriented, lower-middle-class NSDAP leadership. As early as October 1933, Bormann issued orders in Hess's name, torpedoing Buch's pet idea for the creation of a Supreme Senate in the NSDAP (on the model of Mussolini's Fascist Grand Council in Italy).[33]

Evidently, Buch disliked having to receive commands from his son-in-law, and consequently, their relationship declined progressively into a purely business affair. They rarely saw one another except at functions of the party, and their correspondence was cold, abrupt, and totally lacking in affection.[34] As Buch continued to withdraw from party policy-making to concentrate on his work in the OPG and as Bormann moved nearer to Hitler, the resentment on both sides grew more intense. During the war, Buch was to pay dearly for his attitude as Bormann ruthlessly and systematically reduced Buch's role as chief justice to almost nothing.[35]

The greatest bone of contention between the two was over authority and power of command. Inasmuch as the Deputy Führer's office was the only party office that could give orders to the OPG (and even overrule the OPG), Buch often received commands related to the OPG that were issued by Bormann. At the beginning of 1938, for example, the OPG was informed by Bormann that Hitler had decreed a special "amnesty" for party members involved in court proceedings. Moreover, Bormann ordered in July that the Nazi leadership and Parteigerichte were to remove preachers from positions of leadership in the NSDAP and that they were to replace them with "suitable substitutes." Bormann, who was notorious for his dislike of religion and for his persecution of the churches throughout the Third Reich, noted that preachers were unable to help lead the Nazi party, because, being men of the cloth in a nation ruled by those determined to destroy religion, they lacked the "presumed freedom of decision" in the "church strife."[36]

Another point of contention was that the Deputy Führer's office seemed (at times) to encroach on the OPG's power of serving as the party's "court of last resort." Not only did Hess's office possess a department for appeal cases of members who felt themselves cheated by the Partei-gerichte, but it handled its share of personal conflicts involving questions of authority among Reichsleiters and other party leaders. For instance, when Ley criticized Schwarz's continued supervision of the DAF's finances, he complained to Hess, not to Buch or the OPG.[37] The tactic of approaching Hess (and later Bormann) instead of the OPG to curry Hitler's favor on such issues remained popular among the party elite until the end of the Third Reich. The task of settling disputes over authority at the highest levels was one that Hitler always preferred to retain for himself and his deputies, and the OPG rarely intervened.

If personal conflict was not a concern, supervising the party's membership was a problem for the OPG. The problem had two sides to it: controlling the types of persons who entered the NSDAP and disciplining those who were already within the fold. At the Reichsparteitag meeting of court chairmen in Nuremberg in September 1935, Buch stressed to his subordinate judges the necessity of building an elite and devoted membership, and he quoted Hitler by remarking that "all Germans should be National Socialists, the best of them being party Comrades."[38]

With Schwarz's membership ceiling of 1933 still intact, the OPG continued to screen applications for admission to the party. Only "provisional members" who had served their two-year waiting period in a party organization or affiliate, members of the Hitler-Jugend who were eighteen years of age, and members of the League of German Girls (Bund Deutscher Mädel) who were twenty-one years old were given the coveted red membership book. Above all, the OPG was to keep out Jews and subversives, and it ruled that no former Freemason could hold a party office even in a local group in a foreign land.[39]

Since the NSDAP represented the only legally constituted organization in Germany, it strictly forbade its members to belong to other groups (political or otherwise) without the consent of the Reichsleitung. It was the OPG that decided which organizations outside the movement a member could enter. The OPG's regulations were rigid, and, in effect, members were only permitted to join groups whose leadership was heavily National Socialist.

As an example, the OPG ruled that party members could join the Guttemplerorden ("Independent Order of Good Templars"), because the group's executive committee consisted of seven Nazis and because the institution had "nothing to do with Freemasonry." Furthermore, the OPG advertised that the Good Templars dedicated themselves "solely and alone to the combatting of drunkenness and the enlightenment of the young about the dangers of alcohol."[40] At the same time, organizations like the Rotary Club were off-limits for members. Beyond labeling the Club "American in origin," Buch described it as being one that "believes personal association with Jews is possible. National Socialism does not."[41]

At the beginning of 1937 Hess issued a major command dealing with the recruitment and acceptance of new members. He decreed that "under no circumstances" was "force or pressure to enter the party to be exercised." Instead, the "basis of spontaneity as one of the most valuable and important symbols of the movement" was to "be preserved completely." Only persons (irrespective of professional or economic status) who had "fulfilled the general conditions for acceptance and who leave hope by their relations in the past years that they promise to be Party Comrades ready for valuable work" were to be considered for entrance into the hallowed halls of nazism.

In Hess's view the party members and institutions that were crucial to the selection process were the Parteigerichte, "for the moral judgment"; the personnel offices, "for the political judgment"; the local leaders; and the party treasurers, who were to make certain that a prospective member was in a position to pay monthly dues. Finally, the Deputy Führer reminded the Parteigerichte and the other concerned offices that their supreme duty was to keep the NSDAP absolutely free from its archenemy, Judaism. As before, applications were to be refused categorically if the spouse of the applicant "was not free of Jewish or colored racial mixture," if the prospect possessed "half-breed" children, if the applicant belonged to a Freemason lodge or "secret organization," or if the applicant had been punished for "shameful conduct."[42]

Apart from guarding the membership rolls, the OPG continuously revised the procedures for the system of Parteigerichte and issued new regulations to the lower courts. The OPG was most concerned with trials against Nazi Reichstag deputies, SS officers, and members in the various party organizations and affiliates. To protect Reichstag members before the Parteigerichte (Hitler, of course, had to have his "rubber stamp" parliament), the OPG was required to inform the fraction leader, Hans Fabricius, that proceedings were about to begin against a deputy. Fabricius was then to aid the accused by offering him counsel and by advising the OPG concerning his "character" and value to the NSDAP.[43]

Similarly, if the accused in the proceedings was a ranking SS officer, the OPG was obligated to contact the man's superior and seek his opinion of the defendant before the trial opened. In trials involving SS leaders from the rank of brigadier general *(Oberführer)* upward, Himmler's office was immediately contacted, and the Reich Leader of the SS advised the OPG on the officer's character and his service to the SS and the NSDAP.

When Karl Wolff, Himmler's adjutant and liaison man with Hitler until 1943, became the victim in 1936 of a real estate swindle that involved a construction company connected to the DAF, the OPG and Schwarz's office were called on to investigate. Himmler, in a note to Schwarz (which was forwarded to Buch), sought to secure his adjutant's full exoneration by explaining that Wolff possessed a "pure and unimpeachable character" and one that he (Himmler) had "learned to know daily and hourly in the past eight years." In fact, at the powerful SS leader's request,

149

Schwarz helped to "fix" the matter for Wolff, and Buch gladly permitted it to drop without further investigation.[44]

While the SS was clearly the most important organization with which the Parteigerichte had to deal, the other party organizations and affiliates were supposed to receive the same treatment. Once a member of the DAF or the NSV, for example, was suspected of committing an offense against not only his institution but the entire Nazi movement, he was tried by his organization's disciplinary court and handed over to the Parteigerichte. Some groups tried to punish their members by assessing them money fines, but in August 1937 Bormann strictly prohibited that practice.[45]

At least one judge on the Parteigericht was to be a ranking member of the defendant's organization, and the man's boss was contacted by the court for an "opinion" of the accused before proceedings could begin. Each organization and affiliate coveted such rights and the chance to protect its own people. This was especially true of the SA. When the Parteigerichte began investigations of SA men for their brutality in the anti-Jewish riots in November 1938, the chief of the OSAF's Judicial and Legal Office urged SA commanders to sit as assistant judges on the courts.[46]

If the OPG served as the heart and the nerve center of the party judiciary, the subordinate courts at the Gau, Kreis, and Orts levels were the system's arms and legs. By 1936 and 1937 the lower tribunals (especially the Gaugerichte and Kreisgerichte) were functioning smoothly under the rigid control of the OPG. The average Gaugericht was divided into two chambers that employed from seven to nine judges (that is, a chairman, two assistants, and four to six alternates) who had jurisdiction over approximately thirty offices in the Gau organization, forty Kreisgerichte, and several hundred Ortsgerichte. (See tables 2 and 3.)

As a rule, only OPG judges and Gaugerichte chairmen were full-time, salaried party officials. Chairmen of Kreisgerichte and Ortsgerichte worked part-time, and their labor was "honorary" (that is, unpaid). The highest paid judge, of course, was Buch—the chief justice earned twelve hundred

TABLE 2. POMERANIA GAUGERICHT, 1936

Name	Position	Profession
Chamber 1:		
Dr. Ernst Volkmann	Court Chairman	Lawyer
Rudolf Gladrow	Assistant Judge	—
Gunter Eyrich	Assistant Judge	—
	Four Alternate Judges (Including an SA and an SS commander)	
Chamber 2:		
Ludwig Förster	Deputy Court Chairman	County Executive, Greifenhagen
Hermann Hofrichter	Assistant Judge	Assessor
Dr. Rasch	Assistant Judge	Government Counselor (District)
	Six Alternate Judges (Including five SA or SS commanders)	

SOURCE: Pomerania Gaugericht, "Geschäftsordnung," 2 January 1936, BA, NS 26/Folder 152.

TABLE 3. GAUGERICHTE CHAIRMEN, 1936

Name	Gau
Otto Hüssn	Baden
Karl Götz	Bayerische Ostmark
Kurt Kapeller	Danzig
Karl Engel	Düsseldorf
Wilhelm Kattwinkel	Essen
Schulz	Franken
Paul Franke	Gross-Berlin
Kurt Otto	Halle-Merseburg
Hans J. Sievers	Hamburg
Freiherr von Lynder	Hessen-Nassau
Paul Brauer	Koblenz-Trier
Wolfgang Utendorfer	Köln-Aachen
Karl Bolte	Kurhessen
Paul Martin	Kurmark
Hartmann	Magdeburg-Anhalt
Alfons Ilg	Mainfranken
Paul Röper	Mecklenburg-Lübeck
Joachim von Moltke	München-Oberbayern
Grauenhorst	Ost-Hannover
Ewald Oppermann	Ostpreussen
Emil Gauer	Saarpfalz
Wilhelm Jördens	Pommern
Otto Eckart	Sachsen
Günther Ungermann	Schlesiens
Hans Wilhelm Lütt	Schleswig-Holstein
Anton Wolf	Schwaben
Gentzen	Süd-Hannover-Braunschweig
Constantin Rembe	Thüringen
Gustav Bertram	Weser-Ems
Hans Erich Ummen	Westfalen-Nord
Robert Keimer	Westfalen-Süd
Otto Hill	Württemberg-Hohenzollern

SOURCE: "Gauleitung . . . der NSDAP," undated (probably 1936, however), BA, NS 26/Folder 240.

marks per month (roughly three hundred dollars).[47] While most of the Parteigerichte's main offices were in the party's Gau and Kreis headquarters, the trials of Gaugerichte and Kreisgerichte were held in the rooms of the state courts. When a party proceeding was pending, the Parteigericht chairman simply contacted the local public court and reserved its rooms for the trial.[48] The NSDAP believed that nothing was sacred with the state judiciary—neither its privileged testimony nor its physical facilities!

It will be recalled that "legal aid" for the Parteigerichte was required of the state courts (and police) for trials and for condemning party members. Similar aid was required for party promotions. For significant promotions in Gau and Kreis organizations, the Parteigerichte examined thoroughly (for the Kreisleiter or Gauleiter) the personal background of those being considered for new jobs. One aspect of the Parteigerichte's scrutiny was delving into the prospects' court and prison records, and this information was acquired from the public judiciary.[49]

At the same time, the Parteigerichte themselves traded trial records and personnel files freely, and if a court needed the testimony of a party member who did not live nearby, it could request another court to get it. In January 1938 the Kreisgericht in Bingen sent affidavits to the Gaugericht of Munich–Upper Bavaria to help the Gaugericht prosecute Bernd Lembeck, a member in Deisenhofen (near Munich) who was accused of swindling several thousand marks from his fellow members.[50] Thus, thieves or "confidence men" (like Lembeck) who were party members and made their living moving from one Gau or Kreis to another, bilking innocent members, usually discovered that the cards were stacked against them. If they did not fall prey to the Gestapo and the countless public courts, they became victims of the Parteigerichte.

Creating a cohesive and smoothly functioning operation among the lower courts was not achieved without headaches. In this regard, the key to the system was the Gaugerichte. Just as the OPG carefully controlled the Gaugerichte, so the latter (following the Führerprinzip) rode herd over the Kreisgerichte and Ortsgerichte. Until 1936 and 1937, when the lower courts became solidly established and when they included experienced, full-time chairmen, the Gaugerichte were forced to discipline and scold them regularly. Many Ortsgerichte failed to follow the directive of 1934 for the Parteigerichte in interrogating witnesses, handling documents and evidence, writing minutes of court proceedings, and preparing a chronological index for all documents used in trials and investigations.

Moreover, there were some courts in small locals that forgot (or refused) to report their expulsions at the first of every month to the Gaugericht (for transferral to Munich). The Gaugerichte were especially interested in acquiring records on government officials who had been expelled and who had once belonged to Freemason lodges.[51] In performing their daily administrative duties, the Gaugerichte that impressed the OPG the most were those of Pomerania (whose chairman, Dr. Ernst Volkmann, was promoted to the OPG late in 1936), East Prussia, and Württemberg-Hohenzollern. Consequently, they sometimes received the proud honor of being named the "ideal" courts at the annual Gau Judges Conference.[52]

The lower courts, although they were cussed, discussed, and viewed as "necessary evils" by most NSDAP members, served the party well in providing members with a reasonable (and private) forum through which to voice their complaints against one another. Every party comrade was led to believe that the Parteigerichte represented the party's "official" means of settling personal conflict, and those persons who tried to solve their differences outside the movement (for example, in a public court) faced the prospect of punishment by the Parteigerichte.[53] As during the Kampfzeit, the image of a united and monolithic party had to be maintained at all costs.

Also as during the Kampfzeit, a predominant number of quarrels among NSDAP members in the Third Reich focused on the embezzlement of party funds and the slandering of one comrade by another. In countless instances the conflict was petty and inconsequential in nature; it was motivated more by jealousy and envy than by serious accusations. In Bingen in 1938 the directors of two party music groups (one for the SA and one for the DAF) haggled over who was the best choral and orchestra leader, and the Kreisgericht was called on to bring them back together. Although the court made no effort to judge who was the "blue ribbon" winner at directing, it did arbitrate the differences between the antagonists, and they apologized and shook hands.[54]

Some party members, seeking to retain their sacred "honor" as National Socialists, requested the Parteigerichte to protect that nebulous entity against remarks made by non-Nazis. For several years, Josef Schilgen, a leading jute-manufacturer and party member in Munster, fought with Paul Bahr, Schilgen's competitor, who remained outside the NSDAP. The squabble, which centered around Schilgen's assertion that Bahr was homosexually inclined, was heard by a state court in Hamburg and by two disciplinary or honor courts in the Reich Ministry of Economics.

The result was that each court exonerated Bahr and condemned Schilgen for his accusations. The latter finally turned for help in March 1941 to the Westphalia-North Gaugericht, and for the "protection of his honor," he asked the court to open proceedings against Bahr. Working mainly through the OPG and Hess's office, the Gaugericht was able to apply pressure on the Ministry of Economics and was able to overturn the anti-Schilgen rulings of the honor courts. Furthermore, the Deputy Gauleiter of Westphalia-North, Peter Stangier, urged the Gaugericht to acquit Schilgen.[55] Thus, while Bahr stood by helplessly, the Parteigerichte robbed him of legal judgments in his favor and simultaneously reassured the wealthy Schilgen (in his mind, at least) that he was still a respected National Socialist and that his accusations against Bahr were not unfounded.

While the lower courts settled personal conflicts, they also punished rebellious members and stifled intraparty dissent. Despite numerous past efforts to the contrary, the

155

Parteigerichte remained effective weapons in the hands of tyrannical political leaders who wanted to destroy opposition to their personal rule. As was the case with Ley, Streicher, Kaufmann, and others in the Kampfzeit, most Gauleiters ruled their Gaus with an iron hand; they could appoint and remove their court chairman, and they used their power mercilessly to force the Parteigerichte to decide cases as they wanted them decided.

Karl Florian, the Gauleiter of Düsseldorf, ordered his Parteigericht in July 1937 to investigate the Gau's long-time leader of the RDB, Paul Maass. Maass was accused of bringing "harm to the authority and reputation of the Gauleiter" by his "slanderous utterances," and he was immediately "put on leave" from his office and forced to surrender his membership book to the court. It was only after Maass had apologized and reached a reconciliation with Florian that the Gauleiter "retracted" his command to prosecute Maass and then restored him to his old position.[56]

Along with serving as an instrument of repression for political leaders, the Parteigerichte viciously punished Nazis who associated with Jews and thus threatened to "contaminate" the party racially. Although Hess ordered a stop to the practice in 1935,[57] the Parteigerichte were still regularly trying such cases three years later. In some instances, the investigations drove "provisional members" away from the NSDAP,[58] and in others, the Parteigerichte showed little sympathy with National Socialists who shopped in Jewish businesses or mixed socially with Jewish friends.

By the beginning of 1938, being accused of mingling with Jews was the "kiss of death" for party members. Most who did so were ruthlessly expelled for violating the party's sacred racial philosophy, and only a few "old fighters" survived a court proceeding with the milder punishment of a "warning." Not only did the Parteigerichte believe themselves to be the party's protector of political unity, but they viewed their duty as being the iron guardians against the race "pollution" of the movement. In condemning a comrade for inviting a Jew to his home and drinking a glass of wine with the guest, a Kreisgericht noted that the

> Party Comrade embodies the movement; he is its propagandist and its defender in all that he does. He should be the model for all fellow citizens. It will not do, therefore, for a National Socialist to indulge in comfort in order that he not miss a few [business] dealings. He is instead obligated to support the party at every opportunity in the fight against Judaism.[59]

More often than not, the subordinate tribunals showed greater mercy and compassion in their judgments than did the OPG. In their verdicts the Parteigerichte followed the example of the state courts in Nazi Germany in failing to achieve a solid uniformity and consistency.[60] One problem lay in the composition of the Parteigerichte; to become a court chairman, one did not have to be a practicing lawyer or judge. Another difficulty was that the office of chairman of an Ortsgericht or Kreisgericht was hardly the most envious job in the Nazi party. The Parteigerichte were extremely unpopular and feared by the average party member, and often a chairman found himself presiding over a trial involving a close friend. An objective and rational judgment in such instances was well-nigh impossible. Moreover, Kreisgerichte and Ortsgerichte chairmen were under considerable pressure from their political leaders, who controlled the courts' activities in much the same manner that Hitler dominated the OPG.

Thus, without trained and free lawyers guiding the system, the actions and decisions of the Parteigerichte varied from one level to another. Ortsgerichte and Kreisgerichte, for example, tended to issue milder punishments than did Gaugerichte and the OPG. Yet, at the same time, the OPG frequently rejected the rulings of the Gaugerichte as being too lenient, and where expulsions or admittance of new members to the party (for example, former Freemasons) were involved, the OPG proved far more ruthless and arbitrary.[61]

This was particularly true of the OPG's relationship

to the Gaugericht of the Auslands-Organisation. The Gaugericht AO, the most unique of all the Parteigerichte, was overruled repeatedly by the OPG.[62] Inasmuch as the persons that the Gaugericht AO dealt with lived many thousands of miles away in foreign lands and overseas, it was difficult for that court to secure evidence and hold regular trials. Most investigations, therefore, were undertaken without personal testimony of defendants and witnesses, and the testimony that could be obtained on paper proved far less valuable than the testimony that could be acquired through live interrogations.

The Foreign Countries Organization, formed in 1931 and headed by Gauleiter Bohle, was a party rival to the German diplomatic corps and Foreign Office. The AO was mainly concerned with the manipulation and coordination of ethnic German groups abroad and with instilling in such groups a consciousness of the German "race" and a feeling of allegiance toward the German Reich. In addition, the AO used stalwart German Nazis to spy on Germany's diplomatic missions, and the organization acted as a sort of fifth column whose duty was to gain the support of foreign missions for Hitler.[63]

To accomplish its goals, the AO established party groups of ethnic Germans all over the globe: London, Cairo (where the party local was headed by Hess's brother, Alfred), Rio de Janeiro, New York, San Francisco, and Shanghai. Ortsgruppen were even created among work crews and officers aboard German passenger ships sailing the high seas. Since each Ortsgruppe possessed its own disciplinary court, the Gaugericht AO (whose office was in Berlin) was responsible for supervising the lower courts, helping them to settle personal strife in their groups, and excluding from the NSDAP foreign Germans who (in Bohle's words) were not "worthy representatives of the new Germany." In the latter task, the court was rigid in its policy to let only "morally pure" ethnic Germans into the NSDAP. It refused party membership to former Freemasons and persons from other "Jewish-dominated" organizations, and if a foreign German had been convicted for a crime by the country in which he lived, he was denied membership.[64]

The Gaugericht AO also exercised a strong influence in the hiring, releasing, and promoting of German diplomats abroad and of members of the Foreign Office. In the first years of the Nazi regime, appointments and promotions in the Foreign Service began slowly to depend on party membership, and in 1937 membership became a condition *sine qua non*. This was especially true following Bohle's appointment in January as Chief of the Foreign Countries Organization in the Foreign Office and the founding of an Ortsgruppe Foreign Office in the AO. The trend of the party's influencing the personal affairs of the Foreign Office continued, and during the war, diplomats were dismissed for not being NSDAP members.[65]

While the Gaugericht AO was unique in the Parteigerichte system, that tribunal was similar to its sister courts in its close cooperation with police authorities and with its Gauleiter, Bohle. As with the other Gauleiters, Bohle used his court to suppress opposition within the AO and to expel critics of his policies. In January 1934 he replaced Georg Wagner as head of the AO's Ortsgruppe in Budapest. Wagner, who had organized the Ortsgruppe two years earlier, protested his removal and complained to Bohle and Franz Hasenörhl, the leader of the AO's department in the Reich Propaganda Ministry. A year later, Wagner was expelled from the NSDAP by the Gaugericht AO, and when he returned to Berlin, he was harassed by the Gestapo, which accused him of espionage against the Reich. Wagner was readmitted to the party in 1939, but his attempts during the war to get the OPG to prosecute Bohle and a member of the Gaugericht were fruitless.[66]

The AO's Gaugericht was one of the few subordinate Parteigerichte that had the opportunity to deal directly with the highest SS and police officials. In early 1938 Reinhard Heydrich, Himmler's trusted chief of the Security Police (Sicherheitspolizei, or Sipo) and of the Security Service (Sicherheitsdienst, or SD), commanded the AO court to

159

prosecute the captain and first officer (who were Nazi members) of the German passenger ship *Milwaukee*. The officers, Arthur Jost and Karl Dancker, were accused by Heydrich of tolerating disrespect toward Hitler and other Nazi leaders on board the ship and of being involved in a homosexual clique.

Apparently, Heydrich had sailed on the *Milwaukee* on a pleasure cruise (presented as a gift to him by Himmler) to Greece in the spring of 1937, and he had been a first-hand witness to the officers' behavior. In addition to emphasizing their homosexual inclinations, Heydrich testified to the Gaugericht that Jost and Dancker had refused to celebrate properly Hitler's birthday and that they had tolerated jokes in "extraordinarily tactless ways" about Göring, Ley, and the DAF. Many aboard were German workers who had "won" a vacation from the DAF's much ballyhooed organization Strength through Joy (Kraft durch Freude).

When the liner returned home to Hamburg, the Gestapo made "a number of arrests and convictions," and Jost and Dancker were taken into protective custody.[67] Furthermore, Heydrich proposed to the Gaugericht AO that Dancker be expelled from the NSDAP and removed from his job and that Jost be given a warning and a new post on the ship where he would not come into "contact with any passengers." Hardly surprisingly, the court followed his advice, and the following year, Dancker committed suicide.[68]

The Gaugericht AO and Heydrich were mainly concerned with forcing Germans on passenger liners (such as the *Milwaukee*) to be enthusiastic about the Hitler regime and to put forth a favorable image for the foreigners on board. The principle behind such reasoning was the same maxim that had guided the actions of the Parteigerichte since 1926: that which serves the NSDAP is justice. Yet, in the name of Hitler and "justice," the Parteigerichte succeeded in decreeing some of the modern world's most criminal injustices. Probably the most extreme example was the OPG's response to the famed *Kristallnacht* ("night of broken glass") against the Jews on 9–10 November 1938.

During that fateful night, members of the party, the SA, and the SS (most of them camouflaged in civilian clothes) rioted against the Jews, and the savage acts of criminality and destruction that occurred brought such an outcry of protest from several Gauleiters and numerous other party officials that the OPG was ordered to investigate the worst offenses.

Violent attacks by barbaric SA men on Jews were nothing new to Nazi Germany. Sporadic outbursts and the destruction of Jewish property in Baden and other districts in the summer of 1935 had prompted Hitler to order a stop to "single actions against Jews by party members."[69] With his regime barely two years old and the world wondering about his motives and policies, Hitler was still concerned enough about foreign reaction and public opinion to attempt to discourage such "actions." But the massive pogrom in 1938 was ordered by Hitler himself and Goebbels, apparently in retaliation for the shooting on the morning of 7 November of Ernst vom Rath, a third-rate German diplomat in Paris. Rath's assassin was a young Polish-German Jew, Herschel Grünspan, who was quickly labeled by the *Völkischer Beobachter* as the "criminal tool of international Jewish murderers."[70]

When vom Rath died from his wounds on the afternoon of the ninth, Hitler decided to use the murder as a pretext to move against the Jews and thereby to put pressure on English politicians such as Winston Churchill to halt their public attacks on his expansion in Czechoslovakia and eastern Europe. Late that evening, while he was in Munich to celebrate the fifteenth anniversary of the Putsch, Hitler gave Goebbels an oral command to order a spontaneous anti-Jewish riot by the SA and sympathetic party officials.[71] The propaganda minister, whose relationship to his boss had slowly declined since 1934, was anxious to win back the Führer's favor, and he gladly consented. Moreover, he and other vigorously anti-Semitic party men had wanted for some time to play a greater role in the Jewish destruction

161

process that was being carried out steadily by the SS and the government.[72]

Minutes before midnight, Goebbels informed a group of party leaders assembled at a "Comrade's Evening" in the Alten Rathaus that anti-Jewish demonstrations had begun in the districts of Kurhessen and Magdeburg-Anhalt. Jewish businesses were being destroyed, he said, and synagogues were in flames. He further noted that Hitler and he had decided not to discourage the demonstrations in the event they might spread "spontaneously" throughout the Reich. The attentive listeners understood Goebbels's words to mean that the party should not outwardly appear to be the instigator of the riots (for example, SA and SS men should wear civilian clothes), but that it was in fact to organize and carry them out.[73]

With this in mind the leaders immediately telephoned and teletyped the order to their Gau headquarters. While Heydrich ordered the Sipo and the SD to stand by as "supervisors" and to guard against destructive "plundering" of Jewish property (which was insured by Aryan insurance companies),[74] the riots spread with lightning quickness. In Berlin, windows in Jewish businesses were smashed and 3 synagogues were destroyed (except for their outer walls) by fire.[75] In Nuremberg, 70 Jewish businesses and 236 houses were badly damaged, and the city's Fire Department helped the plain-clothes SA burn down the synagogues. (Despite the criminality, Streicher told a mass party meeting the following evening that the "demonstrations in Franconia" were "generally disciplined, clear and far-sighted.")[76] Even in the smaller towns and villages such as Xanten and Geldern (Westphalia-South Gau) and "Thalburg" (Hanover Gau), the burning and ransacking proceeded through the night.[77]

Added to the physical destruction of property, individual SA men and groups of SA "vigilantes" molested Jewish women and cold-bloodedly murdered Jews in a number of cities. Jews were slain in Chemnitz, Munich, Innsbruck, Küstrin, Lünen, and Linz (Hitler's boyhood home), among

162

other places. As morning dawned on the tenth, 177 synagogues in the Reich lay demolished or in burned rubble, streets were full of shattered glass from 7,500 damaged Jewish stores, and over 20,000 Jews were being rounded up like cattle by the police for transfer to concentration camps.[78]

When news of the Kristallnacht reached the rest of the world, the reaction was extremely negative. Foreigners were horrified at the display of barbarism and destruction. English officials and other Western politicians did not cease their criticism of Hitler's aggression in Czechoslovakia. The NSDAP, however, acted totally surprised; the *Völkischer Beobachter* noted that the "demonstrations" were a "spontaneous" answer to the "provocation in Paris" and to the "cowardly Jewish murder."[79] Furthermore, in the midst of the pogrom, Goebbels dispatched a circular to the party, ordering the action to stop "immediately." A bit later, a command from Hess's office forbade the burning of Jewish businesses, and the order disclaimed any responsibility by the party for the riots.[80]

The response of a number of ranking party leaders to the night of unrestrained violence was one of shock and opposition. As soon as they learned what was happening, several Gauleiters and Deputy Gauleiters—among them Kaufmann (Hamburg), Joachim Eggeling (Magdeburg-Anhalt), Albert Forster (Danzig), Adolf Wagner (Munich–Upper Bavaria), and Paul Wegener (Kurmark)—either refused to obey or issued counterorders. Göring, who disliked the destruction of property because it hurt his efforts (as head of the Reich's Four Year Plan) to rebuild the economy, was likewise angry. Even Heydrich promised a group of Gauleiters and Gaugericht judges on November 20 that severe measures would be taken against all participants.[81]

During the last week of November the OPG received steady reports from the Gaugerichte, indicating that numerous cases of rape, plunder, and murder by Nazi members were under investigation by the police and the state courts. Fearing a public inquiry that might uncover the real culprits in the riots, thus seriously embarrassing the NSDAP, Hess suddenly ordered Buch and the OPG to intervene and bring the party members to trial secretly. Simultaneously, Göring was appointed as Hitler's "special commissioner" to cooperate with the OPG and the Gestapo in getting the state investigations stopped. Through such moves it was also hoped that the party leaders who had opposed the pogram would be convinced that the movement was genuinely interested in punishing the guilty.[82]

The Gestapo, the state police, and the OPG began their joint investigations immediately, and in mid December the OSAF was informed by the OPG that proceedings were pending against a number of SA men. Lutze and his staff were instructed that the OPG intended "to establish which instances from the [anti-Jewish] actions could and must be justified and which cases sprang from personal and beastly motives."[83] Within a few days, thirty SA, SS, and party officials had been seized and moved to Munich for trial; their offenses ranged from murdering and raping Jews to plundering Jewish property.

Basing their cases on evidence produced by the Gestapo, the OPG began the trials on December 20. Because of the unique and unusual circumstances of the cases, each of the OPG's two chambers was transformed into a special senate *(Sondersenat)*, and included in each senate (in addition to the regular OPG judges) were "jurors," who cooperated in the proceedings and the decisions. The jurors were selected carefully; they included ranking officers from the OSAF and the SS and several Gauleiters who had opposed the riots (namely Kaufmann, Eggeling, Forster, and Wagner).[84] Obviously, it was the Reichsleitung's plan to involve the disgruntled Gauleiters so as to soothe their feelings and halt criticism of the party by giving them a part in the trials. However, since only one Gauleiter was permitted to participate in each proceeding, the group found itself badly outnumbered when decisions on punishments were made.

During the remainder of December and into January and February 1939, the senates went through the motions of trying the guilty. Their judgments made a shambles of the concept of justice. The OPG, being far less concerned with the murder of Jews than with uncovering sexual offenses and guarding the party's racial "purity," dispensed National Socialist justice, which was entirely different from Western liberal-democratic justice. The acquittals flowed fast and heavy, and except for three instances involving the rape of Jews, the punishments were next to nothing. Revealing a hint of the perverted mentality that later produced the Jewish extermination plan, the "final solution," the OPG coldly excused the murder of twenty-one Jews as being the result of "unclear or unavoidable commands" or hatred of the Jews and as revenge for the death of vom Rath.[85]

The OPG issued three basic verdicts: expulsion from the NSDAP, warning from the movement, and no punishment. Expulsion, the severest punishment, was ordered for four SA men who either raped or molested Jewish girls in Niederwerrn, Linz, and Duisburg. In each instance, the convicted was vigorously condemned for violating the NSDAP's hallowed racial laws and sent to prison.[86] In Linz a group of drunken SA men had searched Jewish homes, and two had captured a young girl, commanded her to disrobe, and molested her shamefully. Although the men were "old fighters" who begged the OPG to give them mild punishments, the OPG expelled them, because they had done "things" that were "not in common with the fight of the party against the foreign-blooded Jewry."[87]

The OPG also expelled an unskilled factory worker who was an SA man from Rheinhausen, Heinrich Frey, for having raped a thirteen-year-old schoolgirl. While visiting nearby Duisburg, Frey posed as a police official, abducted the unsuspecting child, and forced her to accompany him to his home, where the crime was committed. When questioned by the OPG, Frey denied the accusations; but the OPG called on a police officer and a physician (who had examined the girl) to testify against him.[88] The last rapist expelled and imprisoned was Gustav Gerstner, an SA leader from Niederwerrn who had also been charged with plundering and stealing Jewish property.[89]

For the criminals who had cold-bloodedly murdered Jews, the OPG decreed either pardons or warnings. Franz Norgall, an "old fighter" and rowdy SA leader (who had also served five prison terms) from Heilsburg (East Prussia Gau), had used the pogrom to go on a personal murder spree. Upon hearing that the town's synagogue was about to be burned, Norgall raced to it to capture a Jew, Seelig, who was suspected of being a Communist. Norgall forced his way into the darkened synagogue, where he heard Seelig and his wife attempting to flee. Without a word of warning, Norgall emptied several shots into the darkness, killing the pair.

As its chief witnesses the OPG called on two of Norgall's political leaders, who testified that the defendant was unaware that people were in the synagogue and that the shootings were clearly justified. Accordingly, the Court ruled that the "motive" for the murders could

> only be Jewish hate and particularly the common dislike in the ranks of the Heilsburg party members and SA men for Seelig, who was a known Communist in the period of struggle, was active in confrontations with National Socialists, and displayed provocative relations from the time of the seizure of power down to the present.[90]

Thus, the OPG accepted the biased testimony of Norgall's friends, and it did not occur to the judges that it was anything but a "coincidence" that the persons killed were active opponents of the Nazis. While Norgall was given a warning and was banned from holding a party office for three years, the OPG praised him as an "old fighter in the period of struggle" who "has inserted himself solely for the movement without regard to his person."[91]

Another warning was given to four Chemnitz SA and SS leaders who went during the Kristallnacht to the villa of a Jewish family named Fürstenheim. They rapped on the door, and then forced their way inside to drag the terrified mother and father out of bed. The father was beaten, thrown down the cellar steps, and then shot to death. Defending themselves later before the OPG, the accused contended that Fürstenheim was shot when he tried to attack them. The OPG found it hard to believe, however, that "even a Jew" would challenge "four armed men," and it refused to accept the story. Nevertheless, except for giving them a warning and forbidding them to carry weapons for a year, the OPG did nothing to the thugs.[92]

The OPG tried several other groups of drunken SA and SS vigilantes. However, the more vicious and extensive the crime, the lesser was the punishment decreed by the Court. In a wild and totally undisciplined night in Neidenburg (East Prussia Gau), six SA men stabbed and killed two Jews in their beds, and an Aryan was likewise injured. Saying that the murderers had "acted in good conscience" and had followed the orders of their Gauleiter and Kreisleiter, the OPG dismissed the charges and gave the accused no punishment.[93]

Similarly, the OPG refused to punish two Innsbruck SS men for stabbing and beating three Jews until they died. It was revealed at the trial that the murders were partly the result of a vendetta by the SS men, who had longstanding "personal differences" with their victims. It was also discovered that the Innsbruck SS headquarters had been ordered by its Gauleiter, Franz Hofer (Tirol Gau), to conduct a sort of "night of the long knives" against the Jews. According to an SS brigadier general named Feil, Hofer had in turn received his orders in a discussion late on the night of 9 November with Goebbels. In completely acquitting the killers, the OPG noted: "Both of the accused are irreproachable men who have not been punished before. Both have done considerable service for the National Socialist movement. . . . Their competent SS leader said of them that they were ready at any time to make any sacrifice of property and life for the movement."[94]

Finally, one of the bloodiest uprisings during the night of 9–10 November occurred in Lünen (north of Dortmund). Two persons were killed by SA and party leaders, and the

167

Ortsgruppenleiter, Fritz Österreich, used the riots as an opportunity to shoot a Jewish shopkeeper named Kniebel, who "had been a known Marxist" and was "generally hated by the Lünen party comrades." Yet, despite the coincidence that an active opponent of the Nazis had been eliminated conveniently in the riots, the OPG noted in pardoning Österreich: "The Court is convinced that Österreich, who also does not give the impression of being a particularly impulsive or violent person, did not intend to kill the Jew before entering Kniebel's home."[95]

The mass of trials finally ended on 9 February 1939, and the OPG immediately informed the Reich Ministry of Justice that the OPG was requesting Göring and Hitler to halt all state investigations or court proceedings against Nazi members who had just been acquitted by the party. Several days later, Buch and Ludwig Schneider (who had presided as chairman at most of the trials) sent Göring a ten-page report on the OPG's proceedings, and the request to Hitler was contained in it. Twenty-six of the thirty men tried by the OPG were released with warnings or with no punishment, and the report justified the sentences by saying in effect that one could not prosecute the "little man" while Goebbels, the instigator, went unpunished. In addition, the report concluded with a surprising bit of logic and realism: "Also the public knows down to the last man that political actions such as those of 9 November are organized and executed by the party, whether this is admitted or not. When, in just one night, all synagogues burn down, that must have been organized somehow, and it could only have been organized by the party."[96]

As was the case with the trials, the OPG's report remained secret, and its contents only became public at Nuremberg. The OPG was ordered into the whole affair for three reasons: to purge party members who had raped Jews or mingled sexually with them, to keep the party murderers away from the state courts (and, therefore, the public), and to satisfy the political leaders in the NSDAP who disapproved of the excessive violence. Although the trials and their results remained basically secret, rumors circulated throughout the party, and the proceedings were able to create the impression (amongst the ranking party and government leaders who knew of them) that the movement was making a serious effort to prosecute the worst of the criminals. Thus, while the party in fact punished very few of its members, it was able to save its face somewhat by at least holding the trials.

Through its judgments the OPG seemed to operate on the principle that the worse the crime, the less the punishment. Many SA men—predominantly "old fighters" and drunken thugs that had spent terms in prison—used the Kristallnacht as a pretext or "license" to kill their Jewish enemies. Realizing that they would probably not be held accountable for their actions by the party, they set out to settle old scores. Some who went too far and committed sexual crimes were made to pay by the party, however; the reason for the punishment being that such activity was the worst sin a member could commit against the NSDAP (and thereby the Führer). Moreover, the OPG's attitude toward the deeds of nihilistic barbarism foreshadowed the type of mentality that was to justify the "final solution" during the war. Chief Justice Buch himself exemplified this mentality when he wrote in 1938 in the journal *Deutsche Justiz*: "The Jew is not a human being. He is a symbol of decay."[97]

Having settled the urgent business surrounding the "night of broken glass," life for the Parteigerichte returned to normal by the spring of 1939. In May they were presented with a wave of new membership applications to examine after Schwarz lifted the "membership ceiling" of 1933. Two months later, he and Buch cooperated in issuing a new set of directives for accepting members. The order reminded the tribunals and their political leaders that they must admit into the hallowed halls of National Socialism only the "best" Germans, those who "are ready and willing to fight and to work for the Führer and his movement." Above all, no one was to be forced or persuaded into the NSDAP; in the future the party would welcome into its ranks former soldiers (who were healthy), and it would outlaw all preachers, priests, and "other fellow citizens who are strongly bound confessionally."[98]

Revealing a further stiffening of opposition by the party toward the churches, Bormann extended the ban against clergymen entering the movement to include theology students. The Parteigerichte were commanded to shut the doors permanently on churchmen and not to admit them even for "special circumstances."[99] Despite such restrictions, the NSDAP and its entire attitude toward party membership was beginning to undergo a fundamental change. No longer was the party to form an elite cadre to lead the nation; instead, it was to transform itself into a mass organization (which, in Hitler's view, should include about one-tenth of the population) that could control and discipline the people more effectively. An active campaign was to begin immediately to enroll in the party most of the "leading men of the state and the economy" as well as "the manual laborer, the peasant, and the German wife."[100] Thus, as the threatening winds of war were beginning to blow with a greater intensity over the issue of Poland's freedom, Hitler was preparing his party and the Reich for the storm that lay ahead.

7

Epilogue:
The War Years

THE EARLY MONTHS of World War II brought few
changes in the nature of work done by the Parteigerichte.
As the Wehrmacht and Göring's *Luftwaffe* ("air force")
smashed Poland, Scandinavia, the Low Countries, and
France by June 1940, it was almost "business as usual" for
the Parteigerichte and their judges. As the war progressed,
however, this comfortable situation changed. Not since the
Kampfzeit had the NSDAP been confronted with such internal strains and pressures as those presented by the war.
Similarly to the Uschlas in the tense days of 1931 and 1932,
the Parteigerichte became intent on brutally ensuring that
no National Socialist forgot the needs of the party and that
all members gave their bodies and souls to the war effort.
Where the Parteigerichte were concerned, the war brought
to the surface the ugly corruption of ranking Nazi leaders,
and it unmasked the hideous perversion of party justice.

To increase the cooperation between the NSDAP and
the Wehrmacht, an agreement of honor *(Ehrenabkommen)*
was signed at the beginning of September 1939 by the army
and the Parteigerichte. With numerous members of the SA,
the SS, and the NSKK being thrown together suddenly in
wartime conditions with Wehrmacht soldiers, conflicts frequently arose. Aside from the covert social and professional
enmity that had always existed between the army and the
party groups, public arguments and brawls broke out in

171

bars, barracks rooms, and officers' quarters. In order to define the position of party members in such altercations and to protect the members from being subject to punishment according to the army's rigid code of justice, Buch and the OPG were ordered by Hitler to come to an agreement with the Wehrmacht.

The formal understanding that was completed by Buch and General Wilhelm Keitel provided for the establishment of special courts to hear only arguments among Nazi members and Wehrmacht soldiers. Each court was to consist of five judges: a president (who could be either a party member or army officer), two party members, and two army men. Thus, the purpose of the courts was to bring a reconciliation among the party men and the professional soldiers, and any disciplinary action was left to the respective organizations (that is, the Parteigerichte or the Wehrmacht).[1]

Also revealing that Germany was at war, the Parteigerichte focused much of their attention on ensuring the loyalty of German citizens and diplomats in foreign countries who were either members of the NSDAP or who aspired to join Hitler's party. For officials abroad who wanted to become party members, the OPG and the Gaugericht AO made greater use of Gestapo secrets to weed out former Freemasons and political "subversives." A number of ranking diplomats in German consulates were threatened if they did not join the party, and others were refused entry into the movement if it was discovered that they had belonged to Freemason lodges.[2] Furthermore, when a Nazi diplomat defected, he was promptly removed from the Foreign Service roster and ejected from the party.[3]

In the spring of 1940 the Parteigerichte were made responsible for prosecuting party members who refused to cooperate actively in the war and in service to the NSDAP. Bormann, noting that increasing numbers of party leaders were being called to the battlefront and that the "tasks of the party in wartime" were "greater and more numerous," ordered that any member could be drafted for a full-time party office. Those who refused, he stressed, violated the

172

"interests of the party," and they were "to be punished by the Parteigerichte."[4]

Consequently, if a member ran afoul of the party or the state, he found himself in endless difficulties. The NSDAP now possessed another means of punishment: sending its rebels to the front. In October 1941 Eugen Wolbert, the Ortsgruppenleiter of Neudenau (Baden Gau), was fined and sentenced to prison by a state court for plotting to falsify information to the police. Wolbert was quickly "put on leave" from his office and ordered into the Wehrmacht. When he returned from military duty, he faced both the term in prison and a trial before the Baden Gaugericht.[5]

Several ranking party officials became victims of the pressures and troubles caused by the war, and in some instances the OPG was directly responsible for their demise. In 1940 Streicher was removed by Hitler as Gauleiter of Franconia at the urging of Göring and the OPG. Streicher and the man who was still second in command to Hitler had been personal antagonists since Streicher had claimed that Göring's daughter was fathered by artificial insemination. In 1939 it was Göring who created a special party commission to scrutinize Streicher's private life and particularly his business transactions.[6]

Since the early years of the Kampfzeit, Streicher had been renowned for his elaborate financial dealings and personal vices, and Hitler's toleration of him had angered several politicos in the Reichsleitung, including Göring and Buch. Although Streicher had been a loyal Hitler disciple since 1922, he had become a major source of embarrassment to the NSDAP after the seizure of power. Now, at a time when Germans were asked to deny themselves the barest material necessities, the party could hardly afford to support a rogue who publicly flaunted his wealth and his shady business dealings.

Streicher's last fraudulent transaction (as a party official) was concerned with the Aryanization of Jewish property in Nuremberg and Fürth following the Kristallnacht in 1938. Along with his deputy, Holz, and the district DAF, he used extortion and physical force to make Jews sign over to the Gau (and, therefore, to local party leaders) their property at less than 10 percent of its real value. One Jew after another was called in to sign legal papers transferring his property to the Gau, the city of Nuremberg, or some other purchaser.[7]

By early December 1938 Göring, who was charged with supervising the Aryanization process, was receiving complaints from Nuremberg court officers and policemen. He quickly decreed that all irregular Aryanizations were invalid, and on December 9 he met in Berlin with police officials and members of the OPG to discuss the affair. In addition to appointing a commission to investigate Streicher, Göring ordered the OPG to inquire into the Aryanization abuses.[8] From the Nuremberg police and Gestapo files, the OPG discovered that the local population was aware of Streicher's swindle and that the people viewed it as "the worst kind of corruption."[9]

The confiscating of Jewish real estate to enrich himself and his cronies and the slandering of Göring were only two of the charges leveled at Streicher. In addition, he was accused of having an illicit sexual relationship with a teen-age Nuremberg actress, which had become the subject of gossip in beer halls and coffee houses throughout the city. Hitler, realizing that something had to be done to blunt the growing unrest over his loyal Gauleiter, finally commissioned Buch to open a proceeding before the OPG against the Franconian boss. The Führer, however, reserved the final judgment on Streicher for himself.

Streicher's trial lasted for a week during February 1940, and several days were devoted to lengthy interrogations of the defendant. The hearing was conducted by the chairman of the OPG's first chamber, Schneider. Buch and Hess attended as observers, and six of Streicher's peers from the Gauleiter corps were invited to the proceeding. The OPG found Streicher guilty on all counts, and Buch reported the decision to Hitler. The Führer immediately suspended Streicher from his party office and forbade him to make any public speeches. The demoted leader, however, was allowed to continue operating his vulgar propaganda organ, *Der Stürmer*.[10]

Given the serious nature of his crimes, Streicher could have been punished far more severely than he was. The fact that he was not expelled from the NSDAP and arrested revealed once again how Hitler honored and protected men who were the worst types of criminals. Moreover, the affair illustrated how the Parteigerichte were utilized by the Führer to legitimize his perverted decisions. Streicher, revealing his pathological personality, later explained his suspension: "In February 1940 I requested to be suspended as Gauleiter. All those years I had had no rest. I wanted to write my life story."[11]

If Streicher's removal revealed both the gross inequities in party justice and the control that Hitler had over the Parteigerichte, the ensuing months were to witness an intensifying of such trends. When Hess suddenly flew to England in May 1941, thereby shocking Hitler, the party, and the world, a decisive blow was struck at the internal functioning of the NSDAP, and especially at the independence of the Parteigerichte. Hess's successor as head of the party Chancellery was Bormann, the man who was to become Hitler's shadow and the "grey eminence" of the Third Reich in its last years. When the news of Hess's flight reached Bormann's archenemy, Buch, the latter must surely have winced and trembled at the thought of what obviously lay ahead for himself and his courts.

Buch's suspicions quickly became a sober reality. Bormann's encroachment on the OPG's authority became evident at the end of 1941. In a wave of cases brought before the OPG that stretched into the following year, Bormann systematically "helped" the OPG form its decisions. In other instances, the new "Leader of the Party Chancellery" thwarted and sabotaged Buch's efforts to punish ranking party leaders caught taking advantage of the wartime situation and indulging themselves in scandalous activity and corruption. In this respect, Buch emerged as the party's "good guy," seeking to clean up the leadership and salvage a degree of respectability within it. In doing so, however, he was to frustrate himself immensely and destroy completely his position in the party.

Bormann's obstruction of justice began when he ordered Buch not to prosecute the Nazi newspaper czar and Reichsleiter Amann, who had shamefully beaten another old party member and then boasted openly of the deed. Although Amann's brutality was the talk of Munich's streets, Buch became aware of the incident through the Danzig Gauleiter, Albert Forster, whose parents lived in the Bavarian capital. Buch discussed the affair with Schneider, and the two judges concluded that something had to be done to punish Amann. Buch interrogated Amann's victim (who was so ill that he could hardly answer the questions) and presented the evidence to the party Chancellery.

Bormann responded to Buch's report by suggesting that the matter be settled through a "personal discussion" between Amann and the OPG chairman, not through a trial before the OPG. Revealing the extent to which Bormann's power already functioned as a protective umbrella for delinquent leaders is the fact that Amann never appeared at the OPG's headquarters to discuss the matter, despite several written requests from Buch that he do so. The hands of the chief justice were tied, and Amann emerged untouched.[12]

In December 1941 Bormann interfered in a similar manner to protect Otto Telschow, the Gauleiter of East Hanover. According to a mass of complaints from Telschow's Gau functionaries, the Gauleiter was scurrilously chasing everyone's skirts except those of his wife. The protests were examined closely by the OPG, which requested that Bormann (acting on Hitler's behalf) give permission for the opening of a proceeding against Telschow. Again, Bormann frustrated the OPG and Buch by answering that the problem could be satisfactorily handled through a "personal discussion" with the playboy-Gauleiter.[13]

Several examples of corruption that was condoned by

176

the party Chancellery developed as a direct result of the war. As the Germans reached the peak of their military expansion in France, eastern Europe, and Russia in mid 1942, the party's ruthless commissioners and governors general who were sent to the occupied areas attempted to feather their pocketbooks through numerous shady means. Exploiting the people and the countries that they governed, they embezzled money, involved themselves liberally in "black market" transactions, and stole whatever luxury goods could be found.

An example was Dr. Frank, the governor general of Poland. Through the chairman of the Ortsgericht in Cracow, which was prosecuting one of Frank's subordinates, the OPG learned of several gross improprieties of the governor general and his wife. Apparently, Frau Frank had acquired many fur coats and a considerable amount of jewelry on "shopping sprees" in Jewish ghettos, and her husband had sent a very expensive painting (which was state property) to his estate in Bavaria. Buch dispatched a critical letter to Frank and reported the matter to Bormann, but the latter informed his father-in-law that the OPG was to do nothing and that Hitler himself would contact Frank.[14] Although the Führer eventually removed Frank from his post in Poland (mainly because of Frank's disagreements with the SS over the treatment of the Jews) and threatened him with a Parteigericht proceeding, nothing was done to punish the governor.[15]

Frank's case was hardly unique. During 1942 so many cases of corruption in the occupied regions were reported to the OPG that Buch had Schneider draft a lengthy memorandum to Hitler, recommending that the Parteigerichte be allowed to use stronger forms of punishment—such as depriving disobedient party members of their life or liberty.[16] On several occasions, when the party refused to discipline its political elite, other authorities with penal powers boldly stepped forward to render the service. When the OPG ignored an officer in the SA's Motorized Corps who was smuggling large amounts of wine and schnaps from France for sale to the luxurious Regina Palast Hotel in Munich, the

Wehrmacht eventually punished the culprit.[17] As Rosenberg, Hitler's quarrelsome head of the occupied eastern territories, noted later, most Nazi leaders came to believe that the Parteigerichte could not touch them and that Hitler would intervene in their favor.[18]

The last shred of the OPG's independent authority was destroyed in the autumn of 1942 when the OPG and Buch decided a case against Hitler's wishes and flatly disobeyed the Führer. The affair centered around Josef Wagner, the Gauleiter of Westphalia-South and a commissioner in the Reich government. At the close of 1941, Wagner was stripped of his offices and ordered out of the NSDAP by Hitler because of his reputed ties to the resistance group "Catholic Action." Relations with any Catholic or religious group were totally forbidden for ranking party functionaries. At Bormann's prodding, Hitler attacked Wagner at a conference of Gauleiters in Munich, and the Führer ordered a full investigation of Wagner by Buch and the OPG. Hitler believed that the OPG, as always, would be a rubber stamp that would automatically approve his action. Moreover, he felt that calling in the OPG would at least give the appearance to the other party leaders that Wagner had been given an equitable chance to defend himself.

Wagner's trial, conducted by Schneider and held before Buch and several other Gauleiters (who were added to the OPG to form another "special senate" as in 1938), lasted through January 1942. Wagner was charged with a variety of party crimes: giving classified party information to Franz von Pfeffer (the former Osaf who had been out of favor with Hitler since 1930), sending his children to a Catholic school in Breslau, and allowing Frau Wagner to oppose vigorously the marriage of their pregnant daughter to an SS man. A devout Catholic, the mother had written a particularly provocative letter against the marriage, and the note found its way into Himmler's hands.[19]

In a long and eloquent oration during the trial, Wagner denied having established close ties to Catholicism. Buch, Schneider, and the Gauleiters that were sitting in judgment were sufficiently impressed with the defense; and to everyone's surprise (and amazement), the OPG voted to overrule Hitler's expulsion and to acquit Wagner. At the beginning of February, Buch forwarded a report of the proceeding to Bormann and Himmler, and they completely disagreed with the verdict. In fact, Bormann was furious, and Himmler sent Buch a highly critical letter, arguing that the OPG should have examined more closely "what influence Frau Wagner had on her husband" (which, Himmler believed, was "very great") and that the OPG had decided the case solely on "a few actions and facts."[20]

Hitler was also enraged with the decision, and he expressed his desire to other party leaders "not to take it into account in any way!"[21] Thoroughly embarrassed, he recognized that calling in the OPG had been a drastic mistake, since it had clearly decided against his wishes. Buch's motives for acquitting Wagner and disobeying Hitler were varied. He was sympathetic to the demoted leader, because Wagner was an "old fighter" who had done more than any other party leader to develop the NSDAP in Westphalia and parts of the Ruhr. Furthermore, Buch's ruling was designed to counter the opinion of his bitterest rival, Bormann. While the latter demanded Wagner's crucifixion, Buch fought his powerful "son" by issuing an acquittal. Finally, there were some in the Reichsleitung, such as Goebbels, Amann, and Ley, who believed that Buch had become mentally deranged and that he saw himself as "a judge even of the Führer."[22]

Buch's final test of power with Bormann was obviously a losing cause. Hitler's first move was to call Buch to his headquarters in the east; then, in a raging fury, he shouted obscenities at the embattled judge for almost an hour. In addition, Buch was commanded by Bormann to remove his chief assistant, Schneider, and to replace him with a loyal Bormann favorite, the Deputy Gauleiter of the Moselland, Reckmann. Although Schneider begged to be sent to the front to atone for his sins, he was demoted and given the lowly position of Kreisleiter in Silesia. Nor was this all. Bormann soon informed Buch that he should relieve all of the OPG judges that had formal judicial experience and appoint in their places old party comrades who would form the "correct" decisions.[23]

The Wagner affair was allowed to smolder through the spring and summer as Hitler hesitated to take final steps to settle it. While he procrastinated, however, he picked up considerable support in the Reichsleitung against Wagner and especially Buch. At the end of May the gossipy Goebbels noted: "Buch is nothing but a laughing stock among the circles of old party members; he is a male governess."[24] In October, Hitler revealed his contempt for his own party law by ordering Buch to expel Wagner. Buch swiftly signed the decree, and within days, Wagner was doing hard labor in a concentration camp.[25]

Unquestionably, Buch's behavior represented a serious breach of party discipline. For the first time in his long career as the party's loyal "judge of honor," he had committed the cardinal sin, for which he had condemned so many of his comrades: he had openly placed his own wishes above those of his Führer. Hitler allowed him to remain in his post, because Buch had been sufficiently humiliated in the party and because Bormann was readily available to control and counter him.

Yet, although he remained in his office, Buch's power was officially reduced to zero. Having suffered the disgrace of losing Hitler's favor and being the outcast of the Reichsleiter corps, he became completely a figurehead and, thus, another victim of the war. In a new set of directives for the Parteigerichte, decreed by Hitler in November 1942, Hitler's orders of 1928 and 1933 (which had granted Buch considerable power) were formally thrust aside, and Bormann was given the authority to confirm (in the Führer's name) all decisions of the OPG. Without the signature of the leader of the party Chancellery, the OPG's judgments were invalid and illegal.[26] After the publication of the new order, Buch finally admitted to himself that he had failed in his mission to persuade Hitler that he should remove the evil satans around him. Bormann, he knew, had now become (by Hitler's delegation) the NSDAP's supreme justice (*Oberster Gerichtsherr*).[27]

By the early months of 1943 the war was grinding down heavily on Germany, and the initiative in the conflict was beginning to shift to the side of the Western democracies. In January, German troops surrendered at Stalingrad, thereby sealing Germany's fate in the Soviet Union. Increasingly, waves of Allied bombers hit German cities and towns, and the Reich "situation reports" of the SD began to note the "deepest excitement" among the people concerning the course of the war. In August the same reports emphasized a growing sense of defeatism and a belief among the masses that with a change of government, "something could still be rescued."[28]

Expressing words of defeatism and shirking one's duty to the NSDAP could never be justified, even on grounds of ill health or a heavy work load. Throughout 1943 and much of 1944 the Parteigerichte spent many hours exchanging information on AWOL Nazis with the military tribunals of the Wehrmacht.[29] In addition, the Parteigerichte became utterly ruthless in condemning party members who revealed the least bit of opposition to the government or the war effort. When the plot to assassinate Hitler on 20 July 1944 failed, the Parteigerichte worked closely with the party Chancellery to expel the National Socialists who had taken part in the abortive revolt. Although several elaborate proceedings were held, most of the accused were not removed from the party in the official manner. Their expulsions were made known to Buch by letters from the party Chancellery, which noted that Hitler had already done the OPG's work for it. There were roughly two dozen party members involved in the conspiracy, and among them was Count Wolf von Helldorf, president of the Berlin police.[30]

At all levels of the party and the government, the Parteigerichte granted little mercy to those persons who had served the party and the Reich with distinction and who suddenly began to rebel. In January 1944 the Kreisgericht in Waldshut (Baden Gau) expelled from the party and sent to prison a "record perfect" young member named Herbert Zehnle. Zehnle had joined the Hitler Youth in 1931 (at the age of ten), his mother and father had been active National Socialists since the Kampfzeit, and his younger brother was enrolled in an Adolf Hitler School.[31] Furthermore, Zehnle had served in the Wehrmacht, and before being discharged, he had been wounded severely on the eastern front and had been decorated for his heroism.

When he returned from the war, Zehnle was an embittered and crippled veteran who found it difficult to readjust to civilian life. The Waldshut NSDAP, lacking able-bodied men to fill its offices, made him a political leader and involved him busily in the Kreis's work. However, Zehnle slowly proceeded to destroy himself by acquiring the wrath of his Kreisleiter. Among other charges, he was accused of using the Kreisleiter's party auto and gasoline without authorization, giving "immoral commands" to the secretaries in the party office, misusing the office for "wine and schnaps," and uttering "untrue statements" about the Kreisleiter. In a meeting with the Kreisleiter, the chairman of the Kreisgericht, and the leader of the Kreis organization, Zehnle admitted to the accusations, and he was promptly expelled and imprisoned.[32]

Members who were proven guilty of spreading a "defeatist" attitude about the war and of disobeying party commands suffered the same fate. Karl Behr, a *Blockleiter* (party leader of a block in an urban area) in Gladbeck (Hessen-Nassau Gau), was a long-time National Socialist who had lost his enthusiasm for the NSDAP during the war. In fact, he sometimes behaved as though he was ashamed of being a party leader. His superiors viewed him suspiciously because he entertained more non-Nazis than party comrades in his home and because he failed to affix his Blockleiter sign to the front door.

When questioned by another leader about the sign, Behr replied that since the Italians had "laid down their arms" (in the spring of 1944), there "was no further reason" for him to retain either the sign or his office. The implication of Behr's remark, of course, was that the war would soon be over and that Germany would be defeated. His words were reported to the Kreisleitung; and in a lengthy trial before his Kreisgericht in June, Behr was condemned for preaching defeatism, refusing to follow party regulations, and associating with "persons of very doubtful character" (that is, non-Nazis). Not surprisingly, he was ejected from the party.[33]

Thus, throughout the final stages of the war, it was the job of the Parteigerichte to "educate" members continuously about what was expected of them and what they could anticipate if they acted contrary to the party leadership. In March 1945 the Gaugericht in Bayreuth (acting as an appeal court) expelled a state judge from Regensburg, issuing the following explanation:

> According to directive 15/44 of the head of the Party Chancery, every party comrade is subject to serve the country in time of war. The pitiless harshness of this struggle demands, especially from the party members, the unconditional pledge of their person. The person incapable of doing this and not being able to fulfill the special and greater obligations incumbent upon him by reason of being a member of the NSDAP, is only a burden upon the party. The accused, apart from the fact that he is only a recent member of the movement [he entered in May 1935] and can show no merits for the party, must therefore be removed from the NSDAP.[34]

The ideology behind such rulings was nothing new to the Nazi movement. It had always been the philosophy that had guided decision-making in the party: what served the party was just; what did not was unjust and had to be destroyed. Apparently, however, neither the party nor its judicial system enjoyed much success, toward the end, in hammering home this lesson to members. As the war situation deteriorated, increasing numbers of members were hauled before the Parteigerichte. In August 1944 Bormann issued a command ordering that all Parteigerichte proceedings be halted and that members be left free to cooperate totally in the war effort. Consequently, future disciplinary actions were to be executed quickly and without prohibitive red tape by the competent political leaders.[35] The courts, therefore, were again sacrificed to the needs of the party and the state, and (except for hearing appeal cases) they ceased to function in the final days of the war.

Had the war ended with Germany the victor, the Parteigerichte would probably have been resurrected and utilized extensively to prosecute ranking party leaders who used the grave situation in the last moments to disobey orders. One functionary scheduled for scrutinization by the OPG, for example, was Alfred Frauenfeld, a former Gauleiter and the general commissioner for the occupied Crimea-Tauria region. Frauenfeld was accused by the SS of demoralizing the local population and other party officials in his Gau by living "excessively" and associating with persons who were known criminals and who exploited the "black market."[36]

Moreover, Buch himself would probably have faced impeachment and removal as chairman of the OPG. Despite sporadic praise for him in the *Völkischer Beobachter* and despite his appearance next to Bormann, Himmler, Goebbels, and other Reichsleiters at important party conferences,[37] Buch's relationship with Bormann worsened during 1943 and 1944. The latter, increasing his power daily, controlled Hitler's schedule and handled all of the major intraparty quarrels over authority. Even before the Wagner case had been settled, Bormann suggested to Hitler that Buch should be dismissed, and he began to collect material that could be used against his "father" in the future. He started by quietly asking Himmler's "view" of the OPG chief.[38] Gerda Bormann, in a note to her husband that revealed her own antagonism toward her father, remarked: "The fact that my Father, of all people, is causing you your greatest official difficulties . . . and that you have constant trouble through him makes me deeply sorry. . . . The situation between you and him is one of the reasons why my own relationship with my Father has been highly artificial and nothing more."[39]

The hostility between the two Reichsleiters was common knowledge in high party circles, and the head of the Reich Chancellery in the government, Heinrich Lammers, testified after the war that Bormann had finally succeeded in convincing Hitler to remove Buch.[40] Whether or not the contention was true will probably never be known. When the war ended, Buch was captured by the Americans as he fled to the west (the OPG headquarters in Munich lay in rubble from Allied bombing), was interrogated at Nuremberg, and was interned in a prison camp, where he followed the example of other ranking Nazis by committing suicide in 1949.[41]

His death marked the end of a career that had become both pitiful and tragic. As his beloved Germany crumbled around him and the news reached him that Hitler had apparently committed suicide, Buch found himself totally alone, detested by his former party comrades and condemned by the Allied enemy. Not only had he been deserted by his political master, Hitler, and his party cronies, but he had turned to alcohol during the war and had lost what he always claimed was uppermost in his life—his family. Ironically, the one-time Nazi preacher of the concept of the virile German family had been divorced by his wife (of some thirty years) and rejected by his children.[42]

Equally important, when Buch died, he was fully aware that National Socialism had failed to reestablish Germany's greatness and that he personally had failed to divert Hitler from the latter's disastrous course. Dejectedly, he once noted, "The Fuehrer had stopped listening to me many years ago."[43] Indeed, there is little else more tragic than one who feels that his entire life has been wasted while he has labored at a task that has produced no visible, worthwhile value. At Nuremberg, Buch told his interrogators:

> I would like to ask you to consider the position of a man who for seventeen years was forced to do

against his will, a job which he didn't like. I kept asking that I be relieved of my functions, and be permitted to return to my original profession as a regular army officer. This was particularly true during the war when my boys were out in the field, and my mind was not on my job as much as it was on the military situation.[44]

The structure of the Parteigerichte, which Buch so carefully helped to create, was dismantled immediately after Germany's surrender in May 1945. The Parteigerichte were officially abolished when the Allies suspended the German state courts.[45] Yet, through their brief history of two decades, the Parteigerichte had destroyed countless lives with their judgments, and they had contributed significantly to Hitler's transformation of Germany from a liberal *Rechtsstaat* (a state based on the rule of law) into a *Polizeistaat* dominated by fear and terror. Such considerations, of course, were hardly contemplated by Buch and his comrades at Nuremberg. For his part, Buch was more concerned with justifying what he had done and in explaining to the world that Hitler had been misled by the satanic forces in the NSDAP (such as Bormann) that he, Buch, had fought unsuccessfully to purge from the movement.

As the story of the Uschlas and the Parteigerichte revealed, the party's naked perversion of justice was no accident. In part, it was the logical conclusion of a morally bankrupt system of jurisprudence carried to its cruelest extreme. The system, in retrospect, was a vital part of what has often been termed the "German catastrophe"[46]—the total rejection of such concepts as the sanctity of the individual and the need for certain checks in the exercise of state power.

As had been the case with respect to the Uschlas before 1933, Hitler never considered himself bound during the Third Reich by either the Parteigerichte or the state courts.[47] "Justice" in his Reich was nothing more than that which served him. As bodies of law that developed a consistent philosophy and a firm set of precedents, the Parteigerichte were a failure. But as instruments of dictatorship and mechanisms for managing conflict (whether by encouraging or by stopping conflict), they were highly effective. Dissension in the Nazi movement was always a product whose supply far exceeded the demand for it. Hitler never desired the total suppression of conflictive behavior, because he recognized that it was far more trivial in nature than it was substantial enough to challenge his person and authority. At the same time, however, he had the wise foresight to note that if such frivolous conflict were allowed to exist unchecked or unguided, it could paralyze the organization of the NSDAP and even destroy it. With this in mind, he created the party's judiciary.

Despite the attempt by the Parteigerichte to establish such a monster, Hitler's dictatorship over his party was not the result of a highly structured, monolithic political organization that obediently executed his every command. Instead, his control rested fundamentally on his magnetic appeal and mythical image in the movement, and on his ability to exploit successfully dissension among party members and to manipulate his highest lieutenants. The Parteigerichte, inasmuch as they provided him with convenient tools that controlled yet permitted discord in the NSDAP, aided him considerably in each respect. They were, in a sense, the mechanisms that institutionalized his Führer-figure image.

Hitler also cleverly utilized the Parteigerichte to give his party dictatorship a semblance of legality and democracy. All of their faults notwithstanding, the Parteigerichte gave National Socialists an official appeal instrument through which members could be heard and could seek a redress of their grievances. For the average "little man" in the German middle classes who followed Hitler most fanatically, this was in part the early promise of nazism. He joined the NSDAP with the hope of making himself heard and respected by the rest of the world; in the end, however, he achieved the former and destroyed the latter.

Like the other suppressive elements of Hitler's regime, the Parteigerichte embodied the brutal nature of National

Socialism and European fascism. As Hitler and his movement developed out of the Weimar chaos to become eventually the masters of Germany, the Parteigerichte increased their powers correspondingly. During the "revolution" of 1933 and 1934 the NSDAP erected for itself (using the solid foundation provided by the Uschlas) a judicial system whose authority was at times greater than that of the German state judiciary. Not only did the Parteigerichte have full access to the criminal records of the police and the state courts, but they were empowered to condemn rebel Nazi members to prison. In this regard, one could have believed Hitler's repeated contention that the "party controlled the state."

One of the worst marks against the Parteigerichte was their significant contribution to the vulgar racism of the Nazis. Their rigorous guarding of the racial "purity" of the NSDAP against Jews and other "non-Aryans" revealed the totally fanatical commitment that the party had to anti-Semitism, and it revealed the deep penetration of the movement's racism into its general legal philosophy. On the one hand, the Parteigerichte ruthlessly condemned party members who mixed either socially or sexually with Jews, while, on the other hand, the OPG blithely acquitted members who cold-bloodedly murdered Jews during the pogrom in 1938. Thus, the Jew—who was the sworn archenemy of nazism—joined the National Socialist who failed to cooperate fully in Hitler's madness. In an ironic twist of fate, both became acquainted with the Parteigerichte and with their power not only to coerce but to sanction race discrimination and nihilism. Yet, when one ponders this situation seriously, it could hardly have been otherwise; such ugly elements, in short, mirrored the essence of nazism.

Finally, the Parteigerichte represented another method through which Hitler was able to deceive both his party followers and his fellow Germans. By attempting to paper over and suppress the irrationalities of the NSDAP and its leaders, the Parteigerichte helped to distort the true nature of nazism. When the OPG began refusing to perform this function during the war, it was stripped of its authority, and it practically ceased to operate altogether (except to stamp a "yes" to decisions already made for it in the party Chancellery). Thanks to the Parteigerichte and their secret trials, Germans before 1933 were never permitted anything close to an objective examination of the fanatics, adventurers, and criminals that Hitler was employing. After his seizure of power, it was too late to examine his movement.

Notes

The following acronyms and abbreviations are used in the notes:

AO	Auslands-Organisation
BA	Bundesarchiv, Koblenz
BDC	Berlin Document Center
DVO	Deutscher Vaterländischer Orden
FT	*Fränkische Tageszeitung*
GL	Gauleiter, Gauleitung
GRUSA	Grundsätzliche Anordnungen der SA
IfZ	Institut für Zeitgeschichte
IMT	International Military Tribunal
MP	*Münchener Post*
NA	National Archives, Washington, D.C.
NS	Nationalsozialistische
NSDAP	Nationalsozialistische Deutsche Arbeiterpartei
O.Gr.	Ortsgruppe, Ortsgruppenleitung
Ogrl.	Ortsgruppenleiter
OPG	Oberstes Parteigericht
Osaf	Oberster SA-Führer
OSAF	Oberste SA-Führung
PK	Parteikorrespondenz
RFSS	Reichsführer SS
RG	Record Group
RGBl	*Reichsgesetzblatt*
RL	Reichsleitung
SA	Sturmabteilung
SABE	"SA-Befehl"
SD	Sicherheitsdienst
Slg. Schu.	*Sammlung Schumacher*
SS	Schutzstaffeln

191

1. INTRODUCTION: HITLER AND THE SETTLEMENT OF CONFLICT IN HIS PARTY

1. As prescribed in "The Statutes of the Communist Party of the Soviet Union," quoted in *Man, State, and Society in the Soviet Union*, ed. Joseph L. Nogee (New York, 1972), p. 101. See also William G. Scott, *The Management of Conflict: Appeal Systems in Organizations* (Homewood, Ill., 1965), pp. 17–90; Attila Chanady, "The Disintegration of the German National Peoples' Party, 1924–1930," *Journal of Modern History*, 39:65–91 (1967); and Ossip K. Flechtheim, *Die KPD in der Weimarer Republik* (Frankfurt/Main, 1969).

2. To my knowledge, the only scholarly study focusing on the Parteigerichte is John Brown Mason's "The Judicial System of the Nazi Party," *American Political Science Review*, 38:96–103 (1944).

3. This image of Hitler held by party members is discussed in considerable detail by Dietrich Orlow, *The History of the Nazi Party: 1919–1933* (Pittsburgh, Pa., 1969), especially pp. 4–5, 300–308. For his assessment of the importance of the Parteigerichte to the "Hitler myth," see p. 80.

4. Joseph Nyomarkay, *Charisma and Factionalism in the Nazi Party* (Minneapolis, Minn., 1967), pp. 3–5.

5. Hermann Rauschning, *The Voice of Destruction* (New York, 1940), pp. 216–217.

6. Philip Bouhler, *Kampf um Deutschland* (Berlin, 1939), pp. 33, 97.

7. Otto Dietrich, *Mit Hitler in die Macht* (26th ed.; Munich, 1938), p. 20. Having survived the holocaust of World War II and the judgment of the Nuremberg Trials, Dietrich apparently changed his attitude. See his *Zwölf Jahre mit Hitler* (Cologne, n.d.), pp. 125–132.

8. Note Joseph Goebbels, *Vom Kaiserhof zur Reichskanzlei* (35th ed.; Munich, 1942), especially p. 285, the entry for 20 Mar. 1933; Hermann Göring, *Aufbau einer Nation* (Berlin, 1934), p.

42; and Walter Buch, "Niedergang und Aufstieg der deutschen Familie," *Der Schlesische Erzieher*, 3:294 (1935).

9. Buch to Wilhelm Holzwarth (NSDAP member of the Bavarian Landtag, or state legislature), 29 Mar. 1928, BDC, OPG, Folder *Wilhelm Holzwarth*.

10. Konrad Heiden, *Adolf Hitler: Das Zeitalter der Verantwortungslosigkeit* (Zurich, 1936), pp. 121–125; and Wolfgang Horn, *Führerideologie und Parteiorganisation in der NSDAP (1919–1933)* (Düsseldorf, 1972), pp. 308–310.

11. See, for example, Heiden, *Hitler*, pp. 124, 408–409; Alan Bullock, *Hitler: A Study in Tyranny* (New York, 1961), p. 97; and Otto Strasser, *Mein Kampf: Eine politische Autobiografie* (Frankfurt/Main, 1969), p. 44.

12. Useful socioeconomic studies of the NSDAP and its appeals to various groups are Orlow, *The Nazi Party, 1919–1933*, pp. 118–119, 131, 171–174; Max H. Kele, *Nazis and Workers: National Socialist Appeals to German Labor, 1919–1933* (Chapel Hill, N.C., 1972); and David Schoenbaum, *Hitler's Social Revolution: Class and Status in Nazi Germany, 1933–1939* (New York, 1967).

13. As an example, see Karl Kaufmann (Ruhr GL) to *Reichs-Uschla* (Supreme Court of the NSDAP before 1933), 18 May 1927, BDC, OPG, Folder *Karl Kaufmann*. Also note Hitler to Ernst Schlange (Berlin GL) and Wilhelm Klaunig (Brandenburg GL), 23 Apr. 1926, BA, NS 36 *(Untersuchungs- u. Schlichtungsausschuss, Reichsleitung)*/Folder 10.

14. Erhard Klöss, ed., *Reden des Führers: Politik und Propaganda Adolf Hitlers, 1922–1945* (Munich, 1967), p. 18.

15. Buch to Dr. Rudolf Butmann (NSDAP member of the Bavarian Landtag), 31 Dec. 1928, BDC, OPG, Folder *Robert Ley*.

16. Dietrich, for example, tells of Hitler's commanding Goebbels and Joachim von Ribbentrop (the chief's most trusted diplomat and Germany's foreign minister after 1938) to lock themselves in a room and not to leave until their differences over propaganda releases were resolved (*Zwölf Jahre*, pp. 129–130).

17. See above, particularly chapters 4 and 6.

18. Adolf Hitler, *Mein Kampf* (16th ed., 2 vols.; Munich, 1933), 1:243.

19. See "Satzungen des Nationalsozialistischen Deutschen Arbeitervereins, e.V. Sitz München," copy dated 9 Mar. 1922, BA, NS 26 *(NSDAP Hauptarchiv)*/Folder 79; and Dietrich Orlow,

"The Organizational History and Structure of the NSDAP, 1919–1923," *Journal of Modern History*, 27:219–220 (1965).

20. "Satzungen," 9 Mar. 1922, BA, NS 26/Folder 79; and Georg Franz-Willing, *Die Hitlerbewegung: Der Ursprung, 1919–1922* (Hamburg, 1962), pp. 121–122.

21. See the Munich police report, "Bericht über eine persönliche Unterhaltung mit Hitler und persönliche Warnehmungen im Parteibüro," 14–16 Nov. 1922, BA, NS 26/Folder 1480.

22. NSDAP, "Rundschreiben Nr. 4," 10 Sept. 1921, BA, NS 26/Folder 97.

23. Ibid. See also, NSDAP, "Rundschreiben Nr. 10," 22 Oct. 1921, and "Rundschreiben Nr. 15," 10 Dec. 1921.

24. The German word *völkisch* is an exceptionally difficult term to translate precisely. Basically, it refers to extreme rightwing groups in German politics that rejected Western democracy and liberalism and sought to construct a new political system for Germany based on racial, rather than legal, similarities among the German people.

25. Heinrich Bennecke, *Hitler und die SA* (Munich, 1962), pp. 27–32.

26. In 1920 there existed (among numerous others) nineteen major far-right and "free corps" organizations (including the Nazis) in Bavaria. In Munich alone no less than forty-nine political parties and organizations were registered. See Werner Maser, *Die Frühgeschichte der NSDAP: Hitlers Weg bis 1924* (Frankfurt/Main, 1965), p. 168.

27. Much of this took place despite the ban against the Nazis and other radical rightist groups in all the German states except Bavaria. The ban resulted from the assassination in June 1922 of Walter Rathenau, the Reich foreign minister. See R. G. L. Waite, *Vanguard of Nazism: The Free Corps Movement in Postwar Germany, 1918–1923* (New York, 1969), pp. 255–258.

28. Orlow, *The Nazi Party, 1919–1933*, pp. 42–43.

29. Maser, *Die Frühgeschichte*, p. 463.

30. The best accounts of the Putsch are Harold J. Gordon, Jr., *Hitler and the Beer Hall Putsch* (Princeton, N.J., 1972); and Hans Hofmann, *Der Hitler Putsch: Krisenjahre deutscher Geschichte, 1920–1924* (Munich, 1961).

31. Also, Hitler's prestige in the völkisch movement rose as a result of his conduct at his Munich trial in February and

March of 1924. His proud assumption of the responsibility for the Putsch contrasted sharply (and favorably, for völkisch leaders) with the attempts by the army and by conservative leaders to disclaim responsibility for the uprising. See Jeremy Noakes, *The Nazi Party in Lower Saxony, 1921–1933* (London, 1971), pp. 46–47.

2. RECONSTRUCTING THE PARTY: 1925–1927

1. Maser, *Die Frühgeschichte*, pp. 355–356.

2. The divisions are best discussed in Joseph Nyomarkay, "Factionalism in the National Socialist German Workers' Party, 1925–1926: The Myth and Reality of the Northern Faction," *Political Science Quarterly*, 80:29–31 (1965); Dietrich Orlow, "Conversion of Myths into Political Power: The NSDAP, 1925–1926," *American Historical Review*, 72:909–910 (1967); and Jeremy Noakes, "Conflict and Development in the NSDAP, 1924–1927," *Journal of Contemporary History*, 1:5–10 (1966).

3. Albrecht Tyrell, ed., *Führer befiehl: Selbstzeugnisse aus der 'Kampfzeit' der NSDAP* (Düsseldorf, 1969), pp. 107–108. In November 1923 the NSDAP claimed 55,787 members, Maser, *Die Frühgeschichte*, p. 463. At the end of 1925, the party could claim only 27,117 members. See Hans Volz, *Daten der Geschichte der NSDAP* (9th ed.; Berlin, 1939), p. 21.

4. Ernst Röhm, *Die Geschichte eines Hochverräters* (5th ed.; Munich, 1934), p. 335.

5. Karl Bracher, *Die deutsche Diktatur: Entstehung, Struktur, Folgen des Nationalsozialismus* (Cologne, 1969), p. 135.

6. *VB*, 26 Feb. 1925.

7. Ernst Deuerlein, ed., *Der Aufstieg der NSDAP in Augenzeugenberichten, 1919–1933* (Düsseldorf, 1968), p. 246.

8. Because of different administrative reorganizations, the number of Gaus increased steadily after 1925 from 25 to approximately 40 by 1933. See Tyrell, *Führer befiehl*, pp. 216–220. Concerning Hitler's appointment of the Gauleiters mentioned, note BA, NS 26/Folder 91.

9. Article 7, "Satzung des Nationalsozialistischen Arbeiter-Vereins e.V. Sitz München," 21 Aug. 1925, BA, NS 26/Folder 91.

10. "Richtlinien für Gaue und Ortsgruppen der Nationalsozialistischen Deutschen Arbeiter-Partei," 1 July 1926, Tyrell,

Führer befiehl, pp. 230–232; and "Verzeichnis der Gau-Uschla-Vorsitzenden," Oct. 1930, IfZ, F 28 *(Dr. Korn, Private Dokumente, 1927–1938)*, pp. 40–41 (photocopy).

11. Articles 4 and 7, "Satzung des Nationalsozialistischen Deutschen Arbeiter-Vereins e.V. Sitz München," 22 May 1926, BA, NS 26/Folder 91.

12. "Richtlinien für die Untersuchungs- und Schlichtungs-ausschuss der Nationalsozialistischen Deutschen Arbeiterpartei (Uschla)," Aug. 1929, NA, Microcopy T-81 (Records of the National Socialist German Labor Party), Roll 164/Frame 303395.

13. Graf von der Goltz, *Ehre und Gemeinschaft: Grundsätzliches zum nationalsozialistischen Ehrenschutzgedanken* (undated), p. 7, BA, NS 22 *(Reichsorganisationsleitung der NSDAP)* /Ordner 387.

14. Note, for example, Reichs-Uschla, "Beschluss," 9 Oct. 1931, BDC, OPG, Folder *Walter Stennes.*

15. Article 3, "Satzung," 22 May 1926, BA, NS 26/Folder 91.

16. Ibid., Article 7, "Satzung," 21 Aug. 1925. For Heinemann's appointment, see *VB*, 10 July 1926.

17. Heinemann to the Reichsschatzmeister ("national party treasurer"), 23 Jan. 1935, BDC, PK, Folder *Bruno Heinemann.* For further biographical information on him, see *VB* (Munich ed.), 25 Jan. 1938, and *Münchner Neueste Nachrichten*, 25 Jan. 1938.

18. Goebbels's appraisal is in Joseph Goebbels, "Das Tagebuch von Joseph Goebbels, 1925/26" (ed. Helmut Heiber), *Vierteljahrshefte für Zeitgeschichte*, 9:71 (1961), Goebbels's entry for 13 Apr. 1926.

19. "Fragebogen für die ersten Mitglieder der N.S.D.A.P. (D.A.P.)," 2 Oct. 1933, signed by Ostberg, BDC, PK, Folder *Karl Ostberg.*

20. Walter Görlitz and Herbert Quint, *Adolf Hitler: Eine Biografie* (Stuttgart, 1952), p. 146. From 1919 to 1923 Graf was Hitler's continuous escort *(ständige Begleiter)*, according to *VB* (Munich ed.), 6 July 1938.

21. "Die Ereignisse im Münchener Bürgerbräukeller am 8. November 1923, abends," in *Die Weimarer Republik: Das kritische Jahr 1923*, Vol. V of *Ursachen und Folgen: Vom deutschen Zusammenbruch 1918 und 1945 bis zur staatlichen Neuordnung Deutschlands in der Gegenwart*, ed. H. Michaelis, E. Schraepler, and G. Scheel (Berlin, 1958), p. 435. His role in

196

protecting Hitler during the Putsch is best described by Röhm, *Geschichte eines Hochverräters*, p. 248.

22. Reinhard Kühnl, "Zur Programmatik der National-sozialistischen Linken: Das Strasser-Programm von 1925–1926," *Vierteljahrshefte für Zeitgeschichte*, 14:319 (1966).

23. Orlow, *The Nazi Party, 1919–1933*, p. 66; and Kele, *Nazis and Workers*, pp. 97–98.

24. Orlow, *The Nazi Party, 1919–1933*, p. 70; and Noakes, "Conflict and Development," p. 32.

25. "Bericht über die Entwicklung der Stellung der Landes-leitung, der Gauleitung Ostsachsen zum Tannenberg-Bund und Frontbann," 27/28 Jan. 1926, BA, NS 36/Folder 6.

26. Ibid., telegram, Goss to Hitler, 31 Jan. 1926; and Mutschmann to Hitler, 2 Feb. 1926.

27. Ibid., Reichs-Uschla, "Beschluss," 15 Mar. 1926; and Reichs-Uschla to Goss, 8 Apr. 1926.

28. "Rundschreiben an die Gauleitungen und selbständigen Ortsgruppen der N.S.D.A.P.," 5 Feb. 1927, in Tyrell, *Führer befiehl*, pp. 165–166. Hitler's attitude toward his fellow travelers on the Right is summarized in *Mein Kampf*, 1:395–400.

29. Hitler to Schlange and Klaunig, 23 Apr. 1926, BA, NS 36/Folder 10. The sociological composition of the early Berlin NSDAP is discussed by Martin Broszat, "Die Anfänge der Berliner NSDAP, 1926/1927," *Vierteljahrshefte für Zeitgeschichte*, 8:85–88 (1960).

30. *VB*, 1/2 Aug. 1926; and "Vollmacht," 22 July 1926 (for Heinemann and signed by Hitler), BA, NS 26/Folder 1290. Such dispatching by Munich of national leaders like Heinemann was hardly uncommon. At the end of 1926 Gregor Strasser was sent to the Hamburg Gau to settle a feud between the Gau member-ship and the Gauleiter, Klant. See Werner Jochmann, ed., *Nationalsozialismus und Revolution: Ursprung und Geschichte der NSDAP in Hamburg, 1922–33 (Dokumente)* (Frankfurt/Main, 1963), pp. 264–265, 293; and Albert Krebs, *Tendenzen und Gestalten der NSDAP: Erinnerungen an die Frühzeit der Partei* (Stuttgart, 1959), pp. 42–44.

31. For example, "Otto Telschow [Lüneberg-Stade GL] v. O.Gr. Wilhelmsburg," BA, NS 36/Folder 1; and "Robert Wagner [Baden GL] v. O.Gr. Constance," BA, NS 36/Folder 2.

32. Hitler to Gunzenhausen and Rothenberg/Tauber O.Gr., 11 June 1926, BA, NS 36/Folder 1.

33. Together with the Munich members, the Ortsgruppen that were expelled included Bergen, Blankenburg, Heimberg, Gunzenhausen, Bad Kissingen, Rothenberg/Tauber, Weissenstadt, Mainz, Udenheim, Framersheim, Cadolzburg, Burgerbernheim, Colmberg, Ergersheim, Hofheim, Ipsheim, Konigshofen, Oberwohlsbach, Murnau, Neunkirchen (Saar), Neuses bei Coburg, Obermenzing, Wilhelmsburg, Walderbach, Schwarzenbach, Stadtsteinach, Laufamholz, and Constance. All Uschla files are in ibid.

34. Bracher, *Die deutsche Diktatur*, p. 134.

35. Reichs-Uschla to Dinter, 16 Sept. 1927; and Dinter to Heinemann, 13 Nov. 1927, BDC, OPG, Folder *Arthur Dinter*.

36. "Verlag 'Der Nationalsozialist:' Revision der Geschäftsbücher für die Zeit von 1 Juni 1925 bis 31 Januar 1927," by Dinter, BA, NS 36/Folder 7.

37. Ibid., "Anmerkungen zu dem 'Revisionsbericht' des Herrn Dr. Dinter und der Anklage gegen Dr. Ziegler," 25 June 1927, by Ziegler; Sauckel to Hitler, 17 June 1927; and Sauckel to the Reich organization committee (Heinemann), 24 June 1927.

38. Ibid., Sauckel to Hitler, 17 June 1927.

39. Ibid., Heinemann's memo to himself dated 23.6.27 at the end of the letter.

40. Ibid., organization department to Sauckel, 12 July 1927.

41. Ibid., Eher Verlag (Amann) to Reichs-Uschla, 2 July 1927.

42. *VB*, 2/3 Oct. 1927.

43. Fritz Ertl (chairman of the Nazi delegation in the city council and head of the Orts-Uschla) to Heinemann, 10 Sept. 1927, BDC, OPG, Folder *Karl Holz*.

44. Ibid., Nuremberg Orts-Uschla, "Beschluss," 5 Sept. 1927; and Ertl to Heinemann, 9 Sept. 1927.

45. Ibid., Klegraefe to Frank, 20 Sept. 1927. Such a considerable sum for SA music was rather questionable inasmuch as the Nuremberg SA's music groups had been in existence for some time and appeared to have no serious financial problems. See "Niederschrift über die Bezirksführersitzung v. 30 August 1927."

46. Ibid., Reichs-Uschla, "Beschluss," 6 Oct. 1927; and Reichs-Uschla to the Nuremberg O.Gr., 15 Mar. 1928, BA, NS 36/Folder 4.

47. *Landgericht* Nuremberg to Frank, 14 May 1930, BDC, OPG, Folder *Karl Holz.*

48. Heiden, *Hitler,* pp. 230–232, 276–277; Karl Bracher, Wolfgang Sauer, and Gerhard Schulz, *Die nationalsozialistische Machtergreifung: Studien zur Errichtung des totalitären Herrschaftssystems in Deutschland, 1933/1934* (2d ed.; Cologne, 1962), pp. 844–848; and Bennecke, *Hitler,* passim.

49. Pfeffer to Paul Schmitz (treasurer of the Ruhr Gau), 30 Mar. 1927; and Kaufmann to Reichs-Uschla, 2 Apr. 1927, BDC, OPG, Folder *Karl Kaufmann.*

50. Ibid., Kaufmann to Reichs-Uschla, 18 May 1927.

51. Ibid., "Akten-Notiz über Aussage des Dr. Goebbels," 27 May 1927.

52. Ibid., Reichs-Uschla (signed by Bouhler) to Kaufmann, 1 June 1927; and Kaufmann to Heinemann, 24 June 1927.

53. Reichs-Uschla (signed by Bouhler) to Pfeffer, 1 June 1927, BA, NS 36/Folder 8.

54. The letter that Bouhler opened without Pfeffer's authorization was from Hans Wystrack (Nazi member in Breslau) to the national SA leadership in Munich (*Oberste SA-Führung,* OSAF), 3 May 1927, ibid. Pfeffer's comment in the margin of Wystrack's letter was: "Ist mir unterschlagen!" ("It was intercepted from me!").

55. Pfeffer to Reichs-Uschla, 7 June 1927, BA, NS 26/ Folder 86; and Bouhler to Heinemann, 10 June 1927, ibid.

56. Heinemann to Pfeffer, 31 Mar. 1927, BA, NS 26/Folder 86.

57. Reichs-Uschla (Heinemann) to Pfeffer, 15 June 1927, BA, NS 36/Folder 8.

58. Ibid., Heinemann to Hitler, 6 July 1927.

59. See above, chapter 4.

60. Orlow, *The Nazi Party, 1919–1933,* pp. 71–72, 92–94.

61. See the excerpts from both papers, dated 4 June 1927, BDC, OPG, Folder *Joseph Goebbels.* Goebbels sent them to Hitler. Some, like Helmut Heiber (*Goebbels,* trans. John K. Dickinson [New York, 1972], p. 53), suggest that Goebbels's clashes with the police were deliberately provoked as a weapon against too much silence and a lack of attention in the bourgeois press.

62. Goebbels to Hitler, 5 June 1927, BDC, OPG, Folder *Joseph Goebbels.*

63. Ibid., "Protokoll über die Versammlung v. 10 Juni 1927"; and G. Strasser to Goebbels, 12 June 1927.

64. G. Strasser to Hess, 15 June 1927, ibid. The Strassers complained several times to Hitler about Goebbels's lack of neutrality as editor in chief of *Der Angriff*, but Hitler's only reply was: "Obviously your paper is the official party organ in Berlin . . . but I cannot stop Goebbels from running a private paper of his own." See Otto Strasser, *Hitler und Ich* (Constance, 1948), p. 123.

65. Reichs-Uschla, "Vortrag," 21 June 1927, BDG, OPG, Folder *Joseph Goebbels*.

66. "Der Wunsch ist der Vater des Gedankens," *VB*, 25 June 1927.

67. Reichs-Uschla (Heinemann) to Rudolf Rehm (member in Berlin), 17 Oct. 1927, BDC, OPG, Folder *Joseph Goebbels*.

68. Volz, *Daten der Geschichte*, p. 19.

69. Orlow, *The Nazi Party, 1919–1933*, p. 51.

70. Ibid., pp. 117–118.

71. *VB*, 4 Jan. 1928.

72. E. N. Peterson, "The Bureaucracy and the Nazi Party," *Review of Politics*, 28:173–174 (1966).

73. Heinemann to Uschla-Nuremberg, 1 Oct. 1926, BDC, OPG, Folder *Karl Holz*. His differences with Hitler were even noted by the Munich police; see "Münchener Polizeibericht N/Nr. 62 v. 8.12.1927," in Tyrell, *Führer befiehl*, p. 185.

74. "Rundschreiben an alle Landes- und selbständigen Ortsverbände und alle Einzelmitglieder," 20 May 1927, BA, NS 26/Folder 1374.

75. Frank to Hitler, 5 Mar. 1925; and the *Polizeipräsident* Berlin *(Abteilung IA)* to the Munich chief of police, 5 June 1931, BDC, PK, Folder *Hans Frank*. See also Hans Frank, *Im Angesicht des Galgens: Deutung Hitlers und seiner Zeit auf Grund eigener Erlebnisse und Erkenntnisse* (Munich, 1953), pp. 21–22.

76. *VB*, 4 Jan. 1928.

77. Tyrell, *Führer befiehl*, p. 147.

78. Concerning the "Hitler myth," see Nyomarkay, *Charisma and Factionalism*, pp. 3–5; and Orlow, *The Nazi Party, 1919–1933*, particularly pp. 4–5, 300–308.

3. THE UNHAPPY PARTY JUDGE

1. Buch to Amann, 11 May 1923, BA, NS 26/Folder 299. See also "Fragebogen [Buch]," BDC, PK, Folder *Walter Buch*; *Das Deutsche Führerlexikon, 1934/1935* (Berlin, 1935), p. 77; and *Reichstagshandbuch, 1932*, edited by the Bureau of the Reichstag (Berlin, 1933), p. 241.

2. Buch to William Fanderl (editor of the *Angriff*), 2 Nov. 1931, BDC, OPG, Folder *Walter Buch*.

3. From Buch's essay "Referent für Jugendfragen: Hitler Jugend," undated, BA, NS 26/Folder 1374.

4. Ibid., Buch to Professor Grimm (Nazi leader in Essen), 24 July 1930.

5. Ibid.; and excerpts from the League's constitution in Waite, *Vanguard of Nazism*, pp. 206–207. See also, Uwe Lohalm, *Völkischer Radikalismus: Die Geschichte des Deutschvölkischen Schutz- und Trutz-Bundes, 1919–1923* (Hamburg, 1970), pp. 327, 329.

6. The völkisch concept and the ideology of "revolutionary nationalism" (whose chief prophet was Ernst Jünger, a German poet and political writer) are defined by Kurt Sontheimer, *Antidemokratisches Denken in der Weimarer Republik: Die politischen Ideen des deutschen Nationalismus zwischen 1918 und 1933* (Munich, 1968), pp. 123–127, 130–134.

7. Quoted in Konrad Heiden, *Der Fuehrer: Hitler's Rise to Power*, trans. Ralph Manheim (Boston, 1944), p. 586.

8. Walter Buch, *Ehre und Recht* (Munich, 1932), p. 5.

9. Buch, "Niedergang und Aufstieg," p. 293.

10. Ibid.; and Buch, *Ehre und Recht*, p. 11.

11. "Referent für Jugendfragen," BA, NS 36/Folder 1374.

12. Buch, *Ehre und Recht*, p. 13.

13. Buch to Grimm, 24 July 1930, BA, NS 26/Folder 1374.

14. Buch, *Ehre und Recht,* pp. 15–16; and his article "Die Parteigerichtsbarkeit der N.S.D.A.P.," *VB* (Munich ed.), 28 Apr. 1934.

15. Buch, *Ehre und Recht*, p. 16. His attitude toward dueling changed later; see Walter Buch, *Des nationalsozialistischen Menschen Ehre und Ehrenschutz* (2d ed.; Munich, 1939).

16. Walter Buch, "Uschla," in *Nationalsozialistisches Jahrbuch, 1932*, edited by the Reichsleitung (Munich, 1932), p. 189.

17. Buch, *Ehre und Recht*, pp. 17, 19.

18. Ibid., p. 21.

19. Ernst Nolte, *Der Faschismus in seiner Epoche* (2d ed.; Munich, 1965), passim.

20. Walter Buch, "Ziel und Aufgaben der Parteigerichtsbarkeit," *Der Parteirichter: Amtliches Mitteilungsblatt des Obersten Parteigerichts,* 3:17 (1934).

21. Erich Eyck, *From the Collapse of the Empire to Hindenburg's Election,* Vol. I of *A History of the Weimar Republic,* trans. Harlan P. Hanson and Robert G. L. Waite (New York, 1970), p. 59.

22. Buch to Amann, 28 June 1923, BA, NS 26/Folder 299; Buch to Grimm, 24 July 1930, BA, NS 26/Folder 1374; and "Fragebogen," BDC, OPG, Folder *Walter Buch.*

23. Buch wrote in his letter of resignation to the *Deutscher Vaterländischer Orden* ("German Fatherland's Order"): "I have been with the N.S.D.A.P. since the year '21 and therefore count myself as one of its oldest members." See Buch to the DVO, 13 May 1927, BA, NS 26/Folder 1374. Regarding his initial meeting with Hitler, see "Walter Buch," NA, M-679 (Records of the Department of State Special Interrogation Mission to Germany, 1945–1946), 1/0215. On the founding of the Karlsruhe Ortsgruppe, note Maser, *Die Frühgeschichte,* pp. 316, 320.

24. Buch to Amann, 11 May, 17 June, and 28 June 1923, BA, NS 26/Folder 299.

25. Ibid., Buch to Amann, 28 June 1923.

26. Ibid., "Abschrift: Dienstleistungszeugnis über Major a.D. Buch," 2 June 1918, and other letters.

27. Görlitz and Quint, *Hitler,* pp. 176–177.

28. Gordon, *Hitler and the Beer Hall Putsch,* pp. 431–432; Hofmann, *Der Hitler Putsch,* pp. 157, 258; and Gerd Rühle, *Die Kampfjahre, 1918–1933,* Vol. I of *Das Dritte Reich: Dokumentarische Darstellung des Aufbaues der Nation* (Berlin, 1936), p. 106.

29. "Walter Buch," 17–18 July 1945, NA, RG 165 (War Department Historical [Schuster] Mission). See also, Buch to Hitler, 1 Oct. 1928, BA, NS 26/Folder 1375. The date of the letter and whether or not Buch actually sent it to Hitler are uncertain. The original is handwritten in dull pencil and divides itself nicely into two parts: one deals with Buch's personal relations with his chief and the other with removing misfits

(Schädlinge) from the party. Buch may have written two letters and dated only one.

30. Buch to Amann, 28 June 1923, BA, NS 26/Folder 299. Concerning Buch's experience as chairman of the DVO's court of honor, see "Erkenntnis des zur Klärung des Ehrenangelegenheit zwischen Major von Xylander und Hauptmann Weiss," 1 Mar. 1926, BA, NS 26/Folder 1374.

31. On Buch's rank in the SS, note the Reich leader of the SS (*Reichsführer SS*, RFSS), Himmler, to Buch, 2 Dec. 1933, BDC, OPG, Folder *Walter Buch*.

32. Buch to Hitler, 1 Oct. 1928, BA, NS 26/Folder 1375 (see note 29 of this chapter).

33. Gerda Bormann to Martin Bormann, 28 Nov. 1943, in H. R. Trevor-Roper, ed., *The Bormann Letters: The Private Correspondence between Martin Bormann and His Wife from January 1943 to April 1945*, trans. R. H. Stevens (London, 1954), pp. 34–35.

34. Buch to Hitler, 1 Oct. 1928, BA, NS 26/Folder 1375 (see note 29 of this chapter).

35. Krebs, *Tendenzen und Gestalten*, p. 198.

4. THE ROAD TO POWER, 1928–1933

1. *Nationalsozialistisches Jahrbuch, 1927*, edited by the Reichsleitung (Munich, 1927), p. 93; and *VB*, 25/26 May 1930.

2. *VB*, 10 Dec. 1927.

3. *NSDAP Mitgliedsbuch* (Munich, 1927), p. 4, BDC, PK, Folder *Franz von Pfeffer*.

4. "Erklärung des Parteivorsitzenden, 30.11.27," prepared by Buch, BDC, OPG, Folder *Karl Kaufmann*; and Pfeffer to Reichs-Uschla, 30 Nov. 1927, BA, NS 36/Folder 8.

5. "Munder v. Paul Essich," BDC, OPG, Folder *Eugen Munder*.

6. "Denkschrift über die Ursachen zur Gründung der Nationalsozialistischen Arbeitsgemeinschaft Gross-Breslau," undated; and Reichs-Uschla, "Beschluss," 26 Nov. 1928, BDC, OPG, Folder *Helmuth Brückner*.

7. Reichs-Uschla, "Bericht," undated; and SABE, 10 Sept. 1928, BDC, OPG, Folder *Robert Ley*.

8. Ibid., Reichs-Uschla to Adolf Trumpf (Schleb Manfort O.Gr.), 26 Nov. 1928.

9. Ibid., Buch to Butmann, 31 Dec. 1928.

10. Hitler to Ludwig Käfer (leader of the Middle Nuremberg NSDAP), 15 Dec. 1927, BA, NS 36/Folder 4.

11. Ibid., "Arbeitsplan der Opposition der O.Gr. Nürnberg," undated; and "Streicher—ein politischer Charlatan," *Deutsche Volkszeitung*, Apr. 1928.

12. Ibid., Hans Herpig (leader of Oberkotzau O.Gr.) to the RL, 27 Mar. 1928; and W. Schuberth (leader of Kulmbach O.Gr.) to Hess, 27 Apr. 1928.

13. Ibid., Buch to Streicher, 2 Feb. 1928; and Buch to Käfer, 8 Feb. 1928.

14. Ibid., Hess to Käfer, 17 Apr. 1928; and Käfer to Hess, 27 Apr. 1928.

15. From the statistics in Orlow, *The Nazi Party, 1919–1933*, pp. 129–130; and Karl Erdmann, *Die Zeit der Weltkriege*, Vol. IV of *Handbuch der deutschen Geschichte*, ed. Bruno Gebhardt (8th ed.; Stuttgart, 1959), p. 347.

16. Nuremberg O.Gr. to the RL, 27 June 1928, BA, NS 36/Folder 4.

17. "Bekanntmachung," 25 Apr. 1928, BDC, PK, Folder *Walter Buch*. The order was published in *VB*, 28 Apr. 1928: "The orders of the Investigation and Conciliation Committee, to whose presidency I have named Party Comrade Walter Buch on 2.1.28 and whose assistants are Party Comrades Lawyer Dr. Frank II and City Councilman Graf, are to be obeyed by all party members and officers inclusive of the first chairman of the party at any time. Disobedience of this order is considered a rejection of party discipline and a resignation from the movement."

18. As keenly observed by Orlow, *The Nazi Party, 1919–1933*, p. 80. As an example of how the RL attempted to foster this erroneous view of the Reichs-Uschla, see Reichs-Uschla to Josef Grohe (party member and later GL of Cologne-Aachen), 13 Aug. 1929, BDC, OPG, Folder *Josef Grohe*.

19. Precise details on this affair are missing, but see "Buch," 17–18 July 1945; and "Dr. Hans Frank," 24 Sept. 1945, NA, RG 165.

20. Strasser to the RL, 13 Oct. 1928; "Klage 'Kampfverlag' gegen Karl Siepmann und Josef Terboven," 27 July 1928; and Gregor Strasser's complaint to the RL, 20 June 1928, BDC, OPG, Folder *Otto Strasser*.

21. Ibid., Reichs-Uschla (Buch) to Strasser, 13 Oct. 1928. Although it was the aim of the RL to preserve a united press, competition among Nazi newspapers was quite prevalent during this period. Most Gauleiters (including Goebbels) gave their own Gau organs precedence over even the *VB*. See Roland Layton, Jr., "The *Völkischer Beobachter,* 1920–1933: The Nazi Party Newspaper in the Weimar Era," *Central European History,* 3:363 (1970).

22. Reichs-Uschla to Kaufmann, 24 Aug. 1928; and Kaufmann to Hitler, 29 Aug. 1928, BDC, OPG, Folder *Karl Kaufmann.*

23. Ibid., Hess to Kaufmann, 23 Feb. 1929 and 28 Feb. 1929. The official announcement of Kaufmann's appointment as Hamburg Gauleiter appeared in the *VB*, 18 Apr. 1929.

24. Buch to Hitler, 1 Oct. 1928, BA, NS 26/Folder 1375 (see above, chap. 3, note 29).

25. See "Hallermann v. Sigmund Jung," 1928, BDC, OPG, Folder *Sigmund Jung*; "Frank v. Hans Bahlke," 1930, BDC, OPG, Folder *Hans Frank*; and "Zander v. Baldur von Schirach," 1932, BDC, OPG, Folder *Elsbeth Zander.*

26. The "League of National Socialist German Lawyers," see *Nationalsozialistisches Jahrbuch, 1929,* edited by the Reichsleitung (Munich, 1929), p. 139.

27. The *VB* and its editorial staff (spearheaded by Rosenberg, Wilhelm Weiss, and Buch) were constantly in trouble with the authorities over the paper's slanderous articles. See Layton, "The *Völkischer Beobachter*," pp. 365–369.

28. Landgericht Munich I to Buch, 25 May 1932, BDC, OPG, Folder *Walter Buch*; and Wilhelm Hoegner, *Die verratene Republik: Geschichte der deutschen Gegenrevolution* (Munich, 1958), p. 230.

29. See, for example, "Geist und Kampf: Aus einer Rede vor der Hochschulgruppe Berlin des N.S.D.St.B. [*Nationalsozialistischer Deutscher Studentenbund,* or Nazi Student Association]," undated, BA, NS 26/Folder 1375.

30. *VB*, 26 Jan. 1929 and 27 Oct. 1928.

31. See "Nieland v. Josef Wagner [Westphalia-South GL]," 1932, BDC, OPG, Folder *Josef Wagner*; "Kube v. Wagner," BDC, OPG, Folder *Wilhelm Kube*; and "Meyer-Quade v. Holz," BDC, OPG, Folder *Karl Holz.* Being paid as speakers (seven marks per speech, plus free board, lodging, and travel) became

especially crucial to unemployed party members and SA men in Lower Saxony. See Noakes, *The Nazi Party*, pp. 142–143.

32. Buch to Grohe, 13 Aug. 1929, BDC, OPG, Folder *Josef Grohe*; and "Richtlinien," Aug. 1929, NA, T-81, 164/303395-303408.

33. "Richtlinien," Aug. 1929, NA, T-81, 164/303395.

34. Ibid., 303396. For instance, Reichs-Uschla to Karl Lenz (Hesse-Darmstadt GL), 7 Dec. 1931, BA, NS 22/Ordner 877.

35. As examples, see Kaufmann's removal of his Gau-Uschla chairman (Hamburg), Reichs-Uschla to Kurt Korn, 17 Feb. 1931, IfZ, F 28, p. 78 (photocopy); and ibid., 303367, the chairman of Stockelsdorf Orts-Uschla to his Kreis-Uschla in Schleswig-Holstein, 9 Nov. 1931, protesting his removal over disagreements with his Ortsgruppenleiter.

36. Ibid., 303406-303408, under "Verfahren der Uschla" and "Beschwerdeweg."

37. See the request in *VB*, 13 Aug. 1929; and "Rundschreiben: An die Gauleitungen und Untergauleitungen und Bezirksleitungen," 6 Nov. 1929, IfZ, F 28, pp. 12–13 (photocopy).

38. Reichs-Uschla to Middle Franconia GL, 12 Nov. 1930, BDC, OPG, Folder *Karl Holz*.

39. Buch to Wagner (Baden GL), 26 Nov. 1930, BDC, OPG, Folder *Peter L. Riedner*.

40. "Rundschreiben Nr. 1," 4 Feb. 1930, IfZ, F 28, p. 17 (photocopy).

41. Bracher, Sauer, and Schulz, *Die nationalsozialistische Machtergreifung*, pp. 844–848, 850–855, 880–896; Bennecke, *Hitler*, passim; and Joachim Fest, *Das Gesicht des Dritten Reiches: Profile einer totalitären Herrschaft* (Munich, 1963), pp. 193–203.

42. Hitler, *Mein Kampf*, 2:608.

43. Hitler to Osaf Pfeffer, 1 Nov. 1926, Bennecke, *Hitler*, pp. 237–238. See also Hitler's "Parteibefehl," *VB*, 5 Dec. 1928, and "Nationalsozialisten lasst Euch nicht provorzieren!" in the *VB*, 5 Aug. 1929.

44. Buch to Pfeffer, 13 Sept. 1930, BA, NS 26/Folder 1374. In the margin is the note "not sent."

45. "SABE 7," 7 Nov. 1926, p. 240, and "Grundsätzliche Anordnungen der SA [GRUSA] III," 3 June 1927, p. 248, in Bennecke, *Hitler*.

46. Reichs-Uschla (Buch) to Plauen Orts-Uschla, 3 Jan.

1930, IfZ, F 28, p. 14 (photocopy). Copies of the letter were sent to the OSAF and all Gau-Uschlas. Contrary to Noakes, *The Nazi Party*, p. 182, the SA did come within the jurisdiction of the Uschla system.

47. "GRUSA VIII," 10 May 1930, IfZ, F 28, pp. 22–24 (photocopy).

48. Ibid., "Rundschreiben Nr. 3," 18 Dec. 1930, p. 62 (photocopy).

49. When Hitler appointed Himmler RFSS on 6 Jan. 1929. See Roger Manvell and Heinrich Fraenkel, *Himmler* (New York, 1965), p. 17.

50. Reichs-Uschla to Goebbels, 8 May 1930, BDC, OPG, Folder *Otto Strasser*.

51. The only available account of this stormy discussion on 21 and 22 May is Strasser's. Apparently, Buch and Hess were with Hitler in Berlin to advise the Führer on the meeting, Strasser, *Hitler und Ich*, p. 147.

52. Strasser to the RL, 6 June 1930, BDC, OPG, Folder *Otto Strasser*; and Strasser, *Mein Kampf*, pp. 40–41.

53. Gross-Berlin Gau-Uschla, "Beschluss," 27 June 1930; and Goebbels to Reichs-Uschla, 23 June 1930, BDC, OPG, Folder *Otto Strasser*. Strasser's account of his final days in the party and of his resignation is in his *Mein Kampf*, pp. 68–69, and *Hitler und Ich*, pp. 147–149. Even though it is likely that Hitler was about to expel Strasser, there is no solid evidence to prove that he did so (as Orlow asserts that he did, *The Nazi Party, 1919–1933*, p. 211). Until evidence is produced, one can assume that Strasser did resign from the party.

54. Strasser, *Mein Kampf*, p. 69.

55. Fritz Dickmann, "Die Regierungsbildung in Thüringen als Modell der Machtergreifung: Ein Brief Hitlers aus dem Jahre 1930," *Vierteljahrshefte für Zeitgeschichte*, 14:454–464 (1966).

56. Erich Eyck, *From the Locarno Conference to Hitler's Seizure of Power*, Vol. II of *A History of the Weimar Republic*, trans. Harlan P. Hanson and Robert G. L. Waite (New York, 1970), pp. 255, 268–269, 278–280.

57. Tyrell, *Führer befiehl*, p. 352.

58. For example, "Feder v. Hinrich Lohse [Schleswig-Holstein GL]," 1930, BDC, OPG, Folder *Hinrich Lohse*.

59. "Rundschreiben Nr. 3," 18 Dec. 1930, IfZ, F 28, pp. 66–67 (photocopy).

60. *VB*, 1/2 Jan. 1931.

61. Buch to Ferdinand Hiddessen (chairman of Silesia Gau-Uschla), 27 Mar. 1931, BDC, OPG, Folder *Kurt Kremser*.

62. Erdmann, *Die Zeit der Weltkriege*, p. 352.

63. "Quartelsberichte, Januar-März, 1931," by SA colonel Messmer, and quoted in Joseph Veltjens (SA *Oberführer* or senior colonel, Brandenburg) to SA company commander Kollmorgen (Ostmark Gau), 7 Apr. 1931, BDC, OPG, Folder *Walter Stennes*.

64. *VB*, 18 Feb. 1931.

65. SS major general (East) Klege to Reichs-Uschla, 9 Sept. 1930; and Werner Markau (Nazi member in Potsdam) to Reichs-Uschla, 16 Jan. 1931, on the "friction between S.A. and S.S. in the Berlin district office," BDC, OPG, Folder *Walter Stennes*. On Hitler's visit to Berlin and Stennes's complaints, see Stennes to Röhm, 28 Feb. 1931, BA, NS 26/Folder 325; and Bracher, Sauer, and Schulz, *Die nationalsozialistische Machtergreifung*, pp. 847–848.

66. Veltjens to Kollmorgen, 7 Apr. 1931, BDC, OPG, Folder *Walter Stennes*.

67. *VB*, 4 Apr. 1931; and Heiden, *Hitler*, p. 285.

68. "Die Stennes-Revolte: Aus dem Mitteilung des Landeskriminalpolizeiamts (IA) Berlin vom 1.5.31, Nr. 9," BDC, *Slg. Schu.*, Ordner 278, p. 348 (photocopy).

69. *VB*, 4 Apr. 1931.

70. Supposedly, Strasser told Stennes: "A half revolt is a total defeat. For that reason you must pursue this to the end. You now have power in Berlin. You have the *Angriff* occupied and thereby a newspaper in your hands." See Strasser, *Mein Kampf*, p. 71. The text of Stennes's proclamation is in Deuerlein, *Der Aufstieg der NSDAP*, p. 349.

71. Strasser, *Mein Kampf*, p. 71.

72. For example, Reichs-Uschla to Berlin Gau-Uschla, 30 Mar. 1931, and the enclosed testimony, "Auszug aus einem Geheimbericht eines unbedingt zuverlässigen Vertrauensmannes," 27 Feb. 1931, BDC, OPG, Folder *Walter Stennes*.

73. *VB*, 4 Apr. 1931; Göring, "Anordnung III," 17 Apr. 1931, BA, NS 26/Folder 325; and ibid., Göring to the RL, 22

Apr. 1931, detailing the system through which SA leaders were expelled.

74. For example, Schlange (Brandenburg GL) to Göring, 7 Apr. 1931, requesting the expulsion of eight SA leaders as "continual stinkers and obstructionists" *(dauernde Stänkerer und Quertreiber)*; Silesia GL to Göring, 17 Apr. 1931; Mecklenburg-Lübeck GL to Göring, 17 Apr. 1931; "Aufstellung der durch die Stennesrevolte in Brandenburg a.H. ausgeschlossenen Pgg. und SA-Leute," 17 Apr. 1931, listing forty members expelled; Mecklenburg-Lübeck GL to Göring, 30 Apr. 1931; Pomerania GL to Göring, 2 May 1931; and "Aufstellung der ausgeschlossenen SA Führer und Männer Schlesiens," 2 June 1931, showing thirty-eight expulsions. All are in BDC, OPG, Folder *Walter Stennes.*

75. Ibid., Reichs-Uschla, "Beschluss," in the Reichs-Uschla's letter to Melitta Wiedemann (Berlin), 8 July 1931; and "Bekanntmachung," *VB*, 5/6/7 Apr. 1931. Hitler's later reflections on the revolt and Goebbels's performance are in Andreas Hillgruber, ed., *Henry Picker: Hitlers Tischgespräche im Führerhauptquartier, 1941–42* (Munich, 1968), p. 189, the entry for 24 June 1942.

76. The RL claimed that order had been recovered long before, however. See "Der 'Angriff' fest in der Hand der Reichsparteileitung," *VB*, 8 Apr. 1931. On the protest of the *Angriff* employees, see ibid.

77. Reported by the GL in "Aufstellung der durch die Stennesrevolte," 17 Apr. 1931, ibid.

78. For example, battalion commander Merker to the Oberführer, SA *Gruppe Ost*, 4 Aug. 1931; "Aussagen Standartenführer Mosdorf gegen Kreisleiter Färber," 1 July 1931; Ernst Käsmann (leader of the Gau's Factory Cells Organization, *Nationalsozialistische Betriebszellenorganisation*, or NSBO) to Kunkel (Gau-Uschla member), 9 Aug. 1931; Ulrich Jaene (Potsdam Ogrl.) to Reichs-Uschla, 20 Aug. 1931; and Brandenburg Gau-Uschla to Reichs-Uschla, 9 Aug. 1931, in BDC, OPG, Folder *Ernst Schlange.*

79. Ibid., Reichs-Uschla (Buch) to Schlange, 21 Aug. 1931.

80. Ibid., Buch to Süss and Schlange, 25 June 1931.

81. SA Lieutenant General Krüger to the OSAF, 22 Oct. 1931, BDC, OPG, Folder *Walter Stennes.*

82. OSAF to SA *Gruppe Berlin-Brandenburg* and Schlange,

29 Oct. 1931; and Reichs-Uschla to Schlange, 2 Nov. 1931, BDC, OPG, Folder *Ernst Schlange*.

83. Buch to Erich Engelbrecht (Berlin member), 12 Nov. 1931, in ibid.

84. According to a report of the Prussian police in May, "Die Stennes-Revolte," BDC, *Slg. Schu.*, Ordner 278, pp. 349, 352 (photocopy). See also the newspaper accounts in BA, NS 26/Folder 83.

85. *VB*, 4 Apr. 1931 and 5/6/7 Apr. 1931. The broader impact of the Stennes affair on the party is discussed by Orlow, *The Nazi Party, 1919–1933*, pp. 219–226.

86. Reichs-Uschla to Berlin Gau-Uschla, 8 Apr. 1931, BDC, OPG, Folder *Walter Stennes*. Hitler's authority to remove any party member without an Uschla hearing was granted him by Article 4, "Satzung," 22 May 1926, BA, NS 26/Folder 91.

87. As, for example, in the case of Goebbels. Note also, Rudolf Jordan (Halle-Merseburg GL) to Buch, 8 May 1931, remarking about such powers being telephoned him during the revolt, BDC, OPG, Folder *Walter Stennes*.

88. Articles 1, 3, 10, 11, and 12, "Richtlinien für die Untersuchungs- und Schlichtungsausschüsse der Nationalsozialistischen Deutschen Arbeiterpartei (Uschla)," 15 Apr. 1931, BA, NS 22/Ordner 380.

89. Article 10, "Richtlinien für die Untersuchungs- und Schlichtungsausschuss der Nationalsozialistischen Deutschen Arbeiterpartei (Uschla)," 1 Jan. 1933; and Röhm to Reichs-Uschla, 2 Dec. 1932, in ibid.

90. Ibid., "Richtlinien," 15 Apr. 1931, Articles 10, 19, and 20.

91. Tyrell, *Führer befiehl*, pp. 352, 383; and Orlow, *The Nazi Party, 1919–1933*, pp. 239–240.

92. Orlow, *The Nazi Party, 1919–1933*, p. 235.

93. "Rundschreiben Nr. 4," 26 Oct. 1931, BDC, *Slg. Schu.*, Ordner 267^I, pp. 86–88 (photocopy).

94. "Rundschreiben Nr. 5," 5 Dec. 1931, NA, T-81, 164/303376–303377.

95. For example, Dr. Saalfeldt (Ogrl. Eutin, Schleswig-Holstein Gau) to Eutin Orts-Uschla, 22 Aug. 1931, ibid., 303382–303383; and Orlow, *The Nazi Party, 1919–1933*, p. 228.

96. *Das Deutsche Führerlexikon*, p. 155; and *VB*, 27 Feb. 1929.

97. Orlow, *The Nazi Party, 1919–1933*, pp. 256–273.

98. Ibid., p. 257; and Holzschuher to Hitler, 2 Sept. 1932, BDC, OPG, Folder *Wilhelm von Holzschuher*.

99. Goebbels, *Vom Kaiserhof*, p. 16, the entry for 1 Jan. 1932, wrote: "The year 1932 must be the year of decision." Buch informed a close friend that any "child can see that we will take control of the [German] government in the not-too-distant future." See Buch to W. R. Köhler, 11 Nov. 1931, BDC, OPG, Folder *Walter Buch*.

100. Henry Ashby Turner, Jr., "Big Business and the Rise of Hitler," *American Historical Review*, 75:61–62, 66 (1969).

101. Orlow, *The Nazi Party, 1919–1933*, p. 282.

102. Buch, when questioned about the possibility of approaching Hitler on the subject, merely shrugged and replied that he could "accomplish nothing." See "Denkschrift Karl Horn zum Fall Danzeisen/Buch," NA, T-175 (Records of the Reich Leader of the SS and Chief of the German Police), 467/987587.

103. For example, "Hitlers Stabschef im Selbstporträt: Ein aufschlussreicher Brief Röhms," *MP*, 9 Mar. 1932; and Helmuth Klotz, *Broschuere mit Briefen Roehms aus La Paz im Jahre 1928/29 an den Arzt Dr. Heimsoth* (1932), in BDC, *Slg. Schu.*, Ordner 402, p. 29 (photocopy).

104. "Abschrift: Mord-Brief," 14 Mar. 1932, NA, T-175, 467/987561; and material relating to an investigation of the plot by the SS in October, NA, T-253 (Records of Private German Individuals), 22/473059–473063. See also, Thilo Vogelsang, *Reichswehr, Staat und NSDAP: Beiträge zur deutschen Geschichte, 1930–32* (Stuttgart, 1962), p. 308; and Heinz Höhne, *Der Orden unter dem Totenkopf: Die Geschichte der SS* (Gütersloh, 1967), pp. 71–73.

105. *MP*, 8 Apr. 1932.

106. Horn, one of the conspirators, claimed that both Buch and Schwarz were deeply involved, "Denkschrift Karl Horn," NA, T-175, 467/987572–987578, 987582. See the summaries of the trial in ibid., 6 July 1932, and the *Augsburger Postzeitung*, 7 July 1932. A somewhat biased account of the conspiracy is in Friedrich Stampfer, *Erfahrungen und Erkenntnisse: Aufzeichnungen aus meinem Leben* (Cologne, 1957), pp. 251–253.

107. Orlow, *The Nazi Party, 1919–1933*, p. 282.

108. Goebbels, *Vom Kaiserhof*, p. 87, the entry for 23 Apr. 1932; and Eyck, *From the Locarno Conference*, pp. 378–392.

109. "Gau-Verordnungsblatt [Schleswig-Holstein], Nr. 1," 25 May 1932, NA, T-81, 164/303137.

110. "Gau-Verordnungsblatt [Schleswig-Holstein], Nr. 2," 21 Sept. 1932, ibid., 303012.

111. "Rundschreiben Nr. 6," 6 Oct. 1932, BA, NS 22/ Ordner 380.

112. Buch to Wagner (Westphalia-South GL), 29 Sept. 1932, BDC, OPG, Folder *Josef Wagner*.

113. H. Haberstroh (chairman, Schleswig-Holstein Gau-Uschla) to all Ortsgruppen in the Gau, 19 Sept. 1932, NA, T-81, 164/303020.

114. Reichs-Uschla to Gau-Uschla chairmen, 10 Sept. 1932, BDC, OPG, Folder *Walter Buch*.

115. Article 1, "Richtlinien," 1 Jan. 1933, BA, NS 22/ Ordner 380.

116. Ibid., Articles 4 and 30. An early precursor of the "special court" may have been the bimonthly meetings of the RL department chiefs begun by Hitler with Buch's aid in 1929. See Buch's memo to the RL, 6 Mar. 1929, BA, NS 22/Ordner 877.

117. Ibid., Articles 4 and 7.

118. Ibid., "Rundschreiben Nr. 1 der Leiter des Personalamtes," 12 Jan. 1933.

5. THE COURTS AND THE NAZI REVOLUTION, 1933–1934

1. Goebbels, *Vom Kaiserhof*, pp. 253–254, entry for 30 Jan. 1933.

2. See Hitler's order, "Verfügung," 18 Mar. 1933, BDC, OPG, Folder *Walter Buch*, which was printed in *VB* (Berlin ed.), 23 Mar. 1933; and *VB* (Berlin ed.), 15 June 1933.

3. *VB* (Berlin ed.), 26/27 Feb. 1933.

4. Martin Broszat, *Der Staat Hitlers: Grundlegung und Entwicklung seiner inneren Verfassung* (Munich, 1969), pp. 104–108.

5. Bracher, Sauer, and Schulz, *Die nationalsozialistische Machtergreifung*, pp. 536–544; and Eric Barculo Wheaton, *The Nazi Revolution, 1933–1935: Prelude to Calamity* (New York, 1969), p. 274.

6. Goebbels, *Vom Kaiserhof*, p. 287, entry for 24 Mar. 1933.

7. Max Domarus, *Triumph: 1932–1938*, Vol. I of *Hitler: Reden und Proklamationen, 1932–1945* (Munich, 1965), p. 246.

8. Broszat, *Der Staat Hitlers*, p. 253.

9. See NSDAP, Reichsschatzmeister, *VOBl*, Nr. 45/46, 30 Apr. 1933; and *VB* (Berlin ed.), 22 Apr. 1933.

10. "Verfügung," *VB* (Berlin ed.), 8 July 1933.

11. Ibid., 9 Sept. 1933; and Buch's article "Die Parteigerichtsbarkeit," *VB* (Munich ed.), 28 Apr. 1934.

12. OPG, "Rundschreiben Nr. 12," 8 Jan. 1934, BA, NS 22/Ordner 877.

13. *VB* (Berlin ed.), 24 May 1933. The affidavit, which was standard throughout the Third Reich, is in "Anordnung Nr. 24/37," 9 Feb. 1937, by Hitler's deputy, Hess, BA, NS 26/Folder 1181b.

14. "Keine Freimaurer in der N.S.D.A.P.," *VB* (Munich ed.), 26 May 1933.

15. Wagner to the Dortmund Kreis-Uschla, 31 May 1933; and Dortmund Kreis-Uschla to Reichs-Uschla, 13 June 1933, BDC, *Slg. Schu.*, Ordner 267^I, pp. 60–61, 69 (photocopy).

16. As an example, see Terboven (GL Essen) to Buch, 20 Mar. 1934, BDC, OPG, Folder *Josef Terboven*.

17. See above, chap. 4.

18. Reichs-Uschla to Munder, 21 June 1933; and Munder to Hess, 17 July 1933, BDC, OPG, Folder *Eugen Munder*. Note also, NSDAP *Mitgliedschaftsamt* ("Membership Office") to the district treasurer of Württemberg-Hohenzollern Gau, 22 Feb. 1938, BDC, PK, Folder *Eugen Munder*.

19. Reichs-Uschla to Schwarz, 15 Mar. 1932; and East Prussia Gaugericht to the Reichs-Uschla, 19 Mar. 1936, BA, NS 36/Folder 3.

20. Peter Diehl-Thiele, *Partei und Staat im Dritten Reich: Untersuchungen zum Verhältnis von NSDAP und allgemeiner inneren Staatsverwaltung, 1933–1945* (Munich, 1969), p. 56.

21. Hubert Schorn, *Der Richter im Dritten Reich: Geschichte und Dokumente* (Frankfurt/Main, 1959), pp. 43–44.

22. See Buch's article "Ziel und Aufgaben der Parteigerichtsbarkeit," *Der Parteirichter*, 3:17 (1934). The sad plight of those members expelled from the "Thalburg" party local (or those individuals who did not become members of the NSDAP) is in William S. Allen, *The Nazi Seizure of Power: The Experi-*

ence of a Single German Town, 1930–1935 (Chicago, 1965), pp. 233–235.

23. "Verzeichnis der in Schutzhaft befindlichen SS.-Angehörigen," 4 Sept. 1933; and "Verzeichnis der in Schutzhaft befindlichen SA.-Angehörigen," 4 Sept. 1933, by the political police, BA, NS 26/Folder 221.

24. IMT, *Trial of the Major War Criminals* (Nuremberg, 1947–1949), 21:260, Document Nr. 65 (see special supplement). The author takes no credit for the poor translation.

25. Koch to Witt (the imprisoned adviser), 24 July 1933; and the Reich Office for Agrarian Policy (Darre) to Reichs-Uschla, 2 Aug. 1933, BDC, OPG, Folder *Erich Koch.* See also, Peter Hüttenberger, *Die Gauleiter: Studie zum Wandel des Machtgefüges in der NSDAP* (Stuttgart, 1969), p. 108.

26. Prussian Ministry of Agriculture, State Domains, and Forests to Reichs-Uschla, 31 July 1933, BDC, OPG, Folder *Erich Koch.*

27. Ibid., Darre to Reichs-Uschla, 2 Aug. 1933; and Koch to Witt, 24 July 1933.

28. According to Dietrich, *Zwölf Jahre*, p. 259.

29. Reichs-Uschla, "Beschluss," undated, BDC, OPG, Folder *Erich Koch.*

30. Ibid., Koch to Buch, 8 Nov. 1934.

31. Reichs-Uschla, "Rundschreiben Nr. 11," 9 Dec. 1933, BA, NS 22/Ordner 380.

32. Ibid., "Verfügung," 4 Jan. 1934, signed by Hess.

33. "Gesetz zur Sicherung der Einheit von Partei und Staat v. 1 Dezember 1933," *RGBl*, edited by the Reich Ministry of the Interior (Berlin, 1933), 1:1016.

34. Ibid. Also note his article, *VB* (Munich ed.), 29 Apr. 1934.

35. "Entwurf einer Denkschrift über die Errichtung einer Partei- und SA-Gerichtsbarkeit," signed by Hitler and sent to the Reich minister of the interior, Frick, on 19 Sept. 1933. See IfZ, MA 108 *(Reichsjustizministerium)*, Fasz. 5429, Nr. 6, 196, 198 (microfilm). Hitler's italics.

36. Ibid., 201.

37. Frick to Hess, 28 Sept. 1933, BA, NS 22/Ordner 380.

38. Ibid.

39. *RGBl*, I:1016 (1933).

40. "Text der Richtlinien für die Parteigerichte vom 17.2.

1934," C. Haidn and L. Fischer, *Das Recht der NSDAP* (3d ed.; Munich, 1938), pp. 697–699. Also useful for the purely administrative functioning of the Parteigerichte is Mason's "The Judicial System of the Nazi Party," pp. 96–103.

41. Haidn and Fischer, *Das Recht*, pp. 700–704.

42. See above, chap. 6; and Haidn and Fischer, *Das Recht*, pp. 697–699, 709.

43. Haidn and Fischer, *Das Recht*, pp. 706–718.

44. Ibid., pp. 720–722, 733.

45. See ibid., "Vorschriften über das Schnellverfahren," pp. 728–730, and "Rechtshilfe," pp. 731–732.

46. Note the decree of the Prussian Interior Ministry, *VB* (Berlin ed.), 24 Nov. 1933; and E. N. Peterson, *The Limits of Hitler's Power* (Princeton, N.J., 1969), pp. 36, 41–42, 86.

47. Haidn and Fischer, *Das Recht*, p. 703.

48. For example, the OPG was responsible for the removal (between 1934 and 1936) of the director of the Reich *Rundfunkkammer* ("radio chamber") and several staff members in Goebbels's Ministry for People's Enlightenment and Propaganda (restricted material in the BA). The OPG and Gaugerichte also investigated civil-service employees in the state governments: see the president of the Bavarian *Landesarbeitsamt* ("state labor office") to all departmental offices, 11 July 1933, BA, NS 22/ Ordner 380.

49. Deputy Führer (signed by Bormann) to all Reichsleiters and Gauleiters, 4 July 1935 (*"Betr.* Austritte von Beamten aus der NSDAP"), BA, NS 26/Folder 152.

50. Diehl-Thiele, *Partei und Staat*, p. 57; and Broszat, *Der Staat Hitlers*, p. 157.

51. As described by Martin Broszat, "Zur Perversion der Strafjustiz im Dritten Reich," *Vierteljahrshefte für Zeitgeschichte*, 6:390–442 (1958).

52. Hans Frank, *Neues deutsches Recht*, Vol. II of *Hier spricht das neue Deutschland!* (Munich, 1934), p. 10. See also, Hermann Göring, *Reden und Aufsätze* (Munich, 1938), pp. 136–155.

53. "Staatl. Konzentrationslager III Esterwegen. Liste derjenigen Schutzhäftlinge die in der SA–bezw. SS gewesen sind," undated, NA, T-175, 240/2730272–2730277.

54. "Bericht über die im Schutzhaftlager Hohnstein einsit-

zenden Angehörigen der SA, SS und des Sta. [Stahlhelm]," undated, ibid., 2730267.

55. Franken Gaugericht, "Beschluss," 25 May 1934, BA, NS 26/Folder 1883.

56. Ibid., *Polizeidirektion* ("police headquarters") Nuremberg-Fürth to the Bavarian political police (Munich), 20 June 1934.

57. Ibid., police headquarters Nuremberg-Fürth to the Reichsstatthalter Bavaria ("Betreff: Festnahme des Ingenieure Ludwig Böck in Nürnberg"), 10 July 1934; and police headquarters Nuremberg-Fürth (Abt. II) to the local *Untersuchungsgefangnises* ("prison for those under investigation"), 18 July 1934.

58. On Buch's close friendship with Strasser, see Buch to Strasser, 16 Mar. 1933, BA, NS 26/Folder 1375.

59. "Buch," 17–18 July 1945, NA, RG 165; and "Theresa Reinwald," 29 Oct. 1945, NA, RG 238 (Collection of World War II War Crimes Records, Nuremberg). Reinwald was Buch's private secretary from May 1933 to January 1944.

60. Bell to Röhm, 24 Mar. 1933, BA, NS 26/Folder 1608. Note also, Heinrich Bennecke, *Die Reichswehr und der Röhm Putsch* (Munich, 1964), p. 59; and "Buch," 17–18 July 1945, NA, RG 165.

61. Himmler, "Führer vorgetragen am 6.VI.1936," BDC, PK, Folder *Johann Lödell*; and Heiden, *Hitler*, pp. 440, 443–445. Some, like Erich Kern, *Adolf Hitler und das Dritte Reich* (Oldendorf, 1971), p. 125, claim that Buch accompanied Hitler to Bad Wiessee to arrest Röhm and Spreti. Reinwald, who appeared to be well versed on Buch's professional career, argued at Nuremberg that Buch was never involved in the purge. See "Reinwald," 29 Oct. 1945, NA, RG 238.

62. "Bemerkungen des Reichskanzlers a.D. Prof. Dr. Brüning zu den Aufzeichnungen des Generals Liebmann" (Brüning's interview with Dr. Helmut Krausnick, 2 June 1953), IfZ, ED 1/1–2 (*Aufzeichnen Gen. d. Inf. a.D. Curt Liebmann, 1922–59*), p. 357; and Heinrich Brüning, *Memoiren, 1918–1934* (Stuttgart, 1970), p. 19.

63. "Buch," 17–18 July 1945, NA, RG 165.

64. See, for example, Deputy Führer (Wagner) to Buch, 14 Dec. 1934, BDC, *Persönlicher Stab Reichsführer-SS Schriftgutverwaltung*, 10:1063. On Buch's visits with Hitler, see "Reinwald," 29 Oct. 1945, NA, RG 238.

65. T. W. Mason, "Labor in the Third Reich, 1933–1939," *Past and Present*, 33:112–142 (1966).
66. Hess to Buch, 22 Oct. 1934, BDC, PK, Folder *Robert Ley*.
67. *VB* (Berlin ed.), 13 Nov. 1934; and Hess, "Anordung," 25 Oct. 1934, NA, T-988 (World War II War Crimes Records: Prosecution Exhibits Submitted to the International Military Tribunal), 215/090692–090693.
68. "Buch," 17–18 July 1945, NA, RG 165.
69. Lohse to Hess, 7 Nov. 1934; OPG to Lohse, 12 Nov. 1934; and Hess to Lohse, 6 Dec. 1934, BDC, OPG, Folder *Hinrich Lohse*.
70. *VB* (Berlin ed.), 26 Oct. 1934. The work condemned was Engelbert Huber's *Das ist Nationalsozialismus: Organisation und Weltanschauung der NSDAP* (Stuttgart, 1934). Party proceedings were also introduced (with the result being expulsion) against a University of Berlin professor who "misinterpreted" German prehistory. See "Alfred Rosenberg," 23 July 1945, NA, RG 165.
71. See Hitler's speech closing the rally, "Die Aufgabe der N.S.D.A.P.," *VB* (Berlin ed.), 12 Sept. 1934.
72. "Die Parteigerichtsbarkeit," ibid., 10 Sept. 1934.

6. IRON CLAMPS OF THE MOVEMENT, 1935–1939

1. See Buch's foreword in *Richtlinien: Auszug aus der Satzung und Geschäftsordnung für die Parteigerichte*, edited by the Reichsleitung (Munich, 1934), p. v.
2. Buch to Wagner (Baden GL and Reichsstatthalter), 20 Feb. 1935, BDC, OPG, Folder *Peter L. Riedner*.
3. "Zweites Gesetz zur Sicherung der Einheit von Staat und Partei vom 29. März 1935," *RGBl*, 1:502 (1935).
4. "Rundschreiben Nr. 54/35 [Westfalen-Nord Gauschatzamt]," 22 Aug. 1935; and "Rundschreiben Nr. 11/35 [Westfalen-Nord Gaurechtsamt]," 13 Aug. 1935, BA, NS 26/Folder 164.
5. Ibid., "Besonderes Rundschreiben [Westfalen-Nord Gauschatzamt]," 3 Aug. 1935.
6. "Abschrift: Anordnung 214/35," 5 Nov. 1935, by Hess, BA, NS 26/Folder 152; and Dietrich, *Zwölf Jahre*, pp. 180–181.
7. "Die Richter der Partei sollen Priester am Recht sein," *VB* (Berlin ed.), 16 July 1935.

8. Or so said Arthur Kaufmann (Pomerania Deputy GL) to his district, county, and local leaders, 5 July 1935, BA, NS 26/Folder 152.

9. OPG, "Anordnung 17," 4 May 1935, *Der Parteirichter,* 11/12:59 (1935).

10. Pomerania Deputy GL to all district, county, and local leaders, 19 July, 1935, BA, NS 26/Folder 152; and OPG, "Anordnung 25/35," 6 Aug. 1935, ibid., 1/2:3 (1935).

11. The departments at the Reich level least affected by the Nazi purge were the Ministry of the Interior, Franz Seldte's Ministry of Labor, and General von Blomberg's War Ministry. Even Bormann was unable to transform these ministries into party strongholds. See Peterson, *Limits of Hitler's Power,* pp. 36, 41–42, 86.

12. "Aus der Partei ausgeschlossen," *VB* (Berlin ed.), 18 Jan. 1935.

13. Diehl-Thiele, *Partei und Staat,* p. 57.

14. Bormann to all Reichsleiters and Gauleiters, 4 July 1935, BA, NS 26/Folder 152.

15. Ibid., "Abschrift: Rundschreiben 49/36," 1 Apr. 1936 ("*Betr.* Austritt und Ausschluss vom Beamten aus der NSDAP"); and "Abschrift: Verfügung 50/36," 29 Mar. 1936, also by Hess.

16. OPG, "Anordnung 48," 25 Nov. 1936, *Der Parteirichter,* 6:27 (1936).

17. See above, chap. 5, note 48.

18. Note, for example, Goebbels's office, "Vermerk," 23 June 1939, NA, T-70 (Records of the Reich Ministry for Public Enlightenment and Propaganda), 102/3624737, discussing the punishment of Franz Martini, a long-time party member and reporter for the Stuttgart and Cologne radio stations.

19. Kreisgericht Cologne, "Beschluss," 15 July 1937; and Goebbels's office, "Vermerk," 7 Oct. 1937, NA, T-70, 101/3623469, 3623479.

20. See particularly, Dietrich Orlow, *The History of the Nazi Party: 1933–1945* (Pittsburgh, Pa., 1973), pp. 166–167; and "Reinwald," 29 Oct. 1945, NA, RG 238. Reinwald noted that Buch began seeing Hitler far less regularly after 1936.

21. *Gauschatzmeister* ("district treasurer") AO to Schwarz, 7 Oct. 1937 and 18 Apr. 1939, NA, T-81, 147/0186933, 0186939. For further discussions concerning the AO's Gaugericht, see above, pp. 158–160.

22. Gauschatzmeister AO to Schwarz, 26 Feb. 1938, NA, T-81, 146/0184715. Kurt Lüdecke's book was *I Knew Hitler: The Story of a Nazi Who Escaped the Blood Purge* (New York, 1937).

23. Schwarz to the Gauschatzmeister AO, 20 June 1938 ("Vertraulich! Streichung der Mitgliedschaft und Eintragung in die schwarze Liste, heir: ehem. Pg. Kurt G. Lüdecke."), NA, T-81, 146/0184719.

24. RFSS security service (*Sicherheitsdienst*, or SD) Ludwigshafen to *Kreisleitung* ("county leadership") Fürstenfeldbruck, 13 Apr. 1937; and Himmler to the Bavarian Minister of the Interior, 1 June 1935, NA, T-175, 491/9352655, 9352674.

25. This was even confirmed by Bormann, "Rundschreiben Nr. 4/37," 9 Jan. 1937, BA, NS 26/Folder 1181b.

26. Diehl-Thiele, *Partei und Staat*, pp. 58–59.

27. NSDAP, deputy Führer, *VOBl*, Nr. 162, Feb. 1938.

28. "Anordnung Nr. 20/37," 29 Jan. 1937, BA, NS 26/ Folder 1181b. See also his "Anordnung Nr. 185/37," 22 Dec. 1937, in the same folder.

29. "Some Berlin Jews" to Buch, 26 Apr. 1936, in Helmut Heiber, "Aus den Akten des Gauleiters Kube," *Vierteljahrshefte für Zeitgeschichte*, 4:78 (1956).

30. "Rundschreiben Nr. 99/36," undated, by Hess, in ibid., pp. 77–78. See also, James McGovern, *Martin Bormann* (New York, 1968), p. 71.

31. Schulz then became a ranking member of the Reich organization department under Gregor Strasser. See Schulz to Buch, 2 July 1929; and Buch to the Reich Minister for Occupied Areas, Gottfried Treviranus, 6 May 1930, BA, NS 26/Folder 1374.

32. Baldur von Schirach, *Ich glaubte an Hitler* (Hamburg, 1967), pp. 272–273.

33. Broszat, *Der Staat Hitlers*, pp. 262–263.

34. See, for example, Bormann to Buch, 8 Jan. 1934; and Buch to Bormann, 13 Jan. 1934, BA, NS 22/Ordner 380.

35. See above, chapter 7.

36. "Anordnung Nr. 104/38," 27 July 1938, NA, T-988, 222/095222. Concerning the amnesty, see the OPG to Willi Meiss (member in Rio de Janeiro), 16 Jan. 1940, NA, T-81, 147/0186788.

37. Ley to Hess, 25 Jan. 1937, BA, NS 26/Folder 277. Ley

contended that it was "completely impossible to subordinate one Reichsleiter [himself] to another Reichsleiter [Schwarz]."

38. "Die Parteirichter," *VB* (Berlin ed.), 18 Sept. 1935.

39. Gaugericht AO, "Beschluss," 20 Feb. 1935, NA, T-81, 146/0185569; and ibid., 27 Oct. 1935.

40. "Uschla Reichsleitung," ibid., 26 July 1933.

41. "Tarnung," ibid., 25 Aug. 1937.

42. "Anordnung 24/37," 9 Feb. 1937, BA, NS 26/Folder 1181b.

43. "Anordnung 30/35," 15 Nov. 1935, *Der Parteirichter*, 5:21 (1935).

44. Himmler to Schwarz, 22 Apr. 1941, a copy of which was sent to Buch the same day, NA, T-175, 80/2599687–2599688; and ibid., "Bekanntmachung," 12 Nov. 1935.

45. "Anordnung Nr. 108/37," 31 Aug. 1937 (*"Betrifft*: Verhängung von Geldstrafen durch Parteidienststellen."), BA, NS 22/Ordner 380.

46. OSAF to SA-Gruppe Kurpfalz (Mannheim), 17 Dec. 1938, BA, NS 26/Folder 318.

47. See "Buch," 17–18 July 1945, NA, RG 165; and Orlow's second volume on the party's history in the Third Reich, *The Nazi Party, 1933–1945*, p. 218.

48. See, for example, Bingen Kreisgericht (Hessen-Nassau Gau) to Bingen Amtsgericht, 31 Jan. 1938 ("Betr.: Überlassung der Sitzungsräume des Amtsgerichts"), NA, T-81, 166/305861; and Haidn and Fischer, *Das Recht*, p. 740.

49. As an example, see "Gaugericht Baden der NSDAP: Ersuchen um Auskunft aus dem Strafregister," 15 Oct. 1938, NA, T-81, 228/5009690–5009692.

50. Bingen Kreisgericht to München-Oberbayern Gaugericht, 8 Jan. 1938, NA, T-81, 166/305897–305899.

51. Typical problems facing the Gaugerichte can be noted in Pomerania Gaugericht to all Kreis and Orts judges, 17 Oct. 1935, BA, NS 26/Folder 152; and Westphalia-North Gaugericht, "Rundschreiben Nr. 2/36," 13 Jan. 1936, BA, NS 26/Folder 164.

52. As, for example, the Württemberg Gaugericht led by its experienced chairman, Otto Hill. See *VB* (Berlin ed.), 8 Nov. 1934.

53. An instance was a case involving the county master hunter and forester in St. Goar (Hessen-Nassau Gau), Lambert.

See Bingen Kreisgericht to St. Goar Kreisgericht, 18 July 1938, NA, T-81, 176/324557.

54. See "Bruno Albers v. Jakob Stumpf," and particularly Bingen Kreisgericht, "Aktennotiz," 20 May 1938, ibid., 324539.

55. According to the OPG, the "decision of an honor court in the economy" was not "binding," and the OPG promised the Gaugericht that it would "deal with the Reich Economic Ministry." See OPG to Westphalia-North Gaugericht, 7 Mar. 1942, NA, T-81, 152/0154974.

56. Düsseldorf Gaugericht, "Beschluss," 23 Dec. 1937; and the Deputy GL (Karl Overhues) to Maass, 16 July 1937, NA, T-81, 228/5009878, 5009884.

57. Pomerania Gaugericht to all Kreis and Orts judges, 17 Oct. 1935, BA, NS 26/Folder 152.

58. As, for example, in the resignation of Eugen Kühborth, Nieder-Ingelheim (Hessen-Nassau Gau). See Bingen Kreisgericht to Nieder-Ingelheim Orgl. (Glässel), 8 Aug. 1938; and Küborth to Glässel, 7 Nov. 1938, NA, T-81, 176/324513, 324523.

59. Bingen Kreisgericht, "Beschluss," 12 Feb. 1938, NA, T-81, 166/305879–305881.

60. The vast differences in the state bodies are discussed in *Meldungen aus dem Reich: Auswahl aus den geheimen Lageberichten des Sicherheitsdienstes der SS, 1939–1944*, ed. Heinz Boberach (Munich, 1968), pp. 375–380.

61. Pomerania Gaugericht to all Kreisgerichte and Ortsgerichte judges, 17 Oct. 1935, BA, NS 26/Folder 152.

62. See, for example, OPG, "Im Namen des Führers," 11 Nov. 1939; OPG, "Im Namen des Führers," 4 May 1939; and Gaugericht AO to *Landesgruppenleitung* ("provincial group leadership") Brazil, 9 July 1938, NA, T-81, 146/0184680–0184683, 0184675–0184679, 0185589–0185590.

63. Hans-Adolf Jacobsen, *Nationalsozialistische Aussenpolitik, 1933–1938* (Frankfurt/Main, 1968), pp. 90–160; and *The German Reich and Americans of German Origin* (New York, 1938), p. vi.

64. Gauschatzmeister AO to the Reichsschatzmeister, 14 July 1937, NA, T-81, 147/0186093, concerning the Gaugericht's refusal to admit a "provisional member" from New York City who had served six months in jail for establishing a house of prostitution. See also, "Kundgebung der Auslandsorganisation der N.S.D.A.P.," *VB* (Berlin ed.), 9 Sept. 1934.

65. See Andor Hencke's memo, "Das Auswaertige Amt und die Auslandsorganisation," NA, M-679, 2/0489; and "Einheitliche Betreuung der Reichsdeutschen im Ausland," *VB* (Berlin ed.), 3 Feb. 1937.

66. OPG to Wagner, 4 Feb. 1941, NA, T-81, 57/60195.

67. Heydrich to Gaugericht AO, 19 Mar. 1938, NA, T-175, 80/2600381–2600395. Heydrich's story was corroborated by Himmler's adjutant, Wolff, who made the same cruise earlier.

68. Ibid., 2600394; and Gaugericht AO to Wolff, 23 Aug. 1938, 2600373.

69. "Abschrift: Rundschreiben 8/35," 13 Aug. 1935, by Ley, BA, NS 26/Folder 152; and Reich Ministry of Justice to the Osaf, 24 Sept. 1935, BA, NS 26/Folder 318.

70. "Die jüdische Bluttat in Paris," *VB* (Berlin ed.), 9 Nov. 1938. See also Helmut Heiber, "Der Fall Grünspan," *Vierteljahrshefte für Zeitgeschichte,* 5:134–135 (1957).

71. Domarus, *Triumph,* pp. 970–973; and Dietrich, *Zwölf Jahre,* pp. 55–56.

72. Concerning Goebbels's motives, see Raul Hilberg, *The Destruction of the European Jews* (Chicago, 1961), pp. 22–23; and Peterson, *Limits of Hitler's Power,* pp. 57–58.

73. Hilberg, *Destruction of the European Jews,* p. 23.

74. Heydrich to the SD and state police offices, "Abschrift des Blitz-Fernschreibens aus München vom 10.11.38 1 Uhr 20," NA, T-988, 214/089501–089504. See also Martin Broszat, Hans-Adolf Jacobsen, and Helmut Krausnick, *Konzentrationslager, Kommissarbefehl, Judenverfolgung,* Vol. II of *Anatomie des SS-Staates,* ed. Hans Buchheim (Freiburg, 1965), p. 335.

75. *VB* (Berlin ed.), 11 Nov. 1938.

76. *FT,* 11 Nov. 1938; and the Nuremberg police report, "*Betreff*: Besondere Vorfälle bei der Protestaktion gegen die Juden in Nürnberg," NA, T-81, 57/60275.

77. SS-*Sturm* ("company") 10/25 (Geldern Kreis) to SS-*Sturmbann* ("battalion") III/25, 14 Nov. 1938, in Wolfgang Scheffler, *Judenverfolgung im Dritten Reich* (Berlin, 1964), p. 74; and Allen, *Nazi Seizure of Power,* p. 273.

78. The figures, which first became known at the Nuremberg Trials, were given by Heydrich to Göring. See "Stenographische Niederschrift von einem Teil der Besprechung über die Judenfrage unter Vorsitz von Feldmarschall Göring im RLM

[Reich Air Ministry] am 12. November 1938, 11 Uhr.," NA, T-988, 214/089610.
79. "Antwort auf die feige jüdische Mordtat," *VB* (Berlin ed.), 10 Nov. 1938.
80. *FT,* 11 Nov. 1938; and the OPG's report on the pogrom to Göring, "Bericht über die Vorgänge und parteigerichtlichen Verfahren, die im Zusammenhang mit den antisemitischen Kundgebungen vom 9. November 1938 stehen," NA, T-988, 216/090729.
81. IMT, *Trial of the Major War Criminals,* 21:466.
82. "Bericht über die Vorgänge," NA, T-988, 216/090730–090731.
83. OSAF (judicial and legal office) to the SA-Gruppe Kurpfalz (Mannheim), 17 Dec. 1938, BA, NS 26/Folder 318.
84. "Bericht über die Vorgänge," NA, T-988, 216/090731.
85. Ibid., 090731–090740.
86. Ibid., 090731–090732.
87. OPG, "Im Namen des Führers," 10 Jan. 1939, against Johann Hintersteiner and Friedrich Schmidinger, NA, T-81, 57/59987–59993.
88. OPG, "Im Namen des Führers," 11 Jan. 1939, ibid., 59976–59986.
89. "Bericht über die Vorgänge," NA, T-988, 216/090732.
90. OPG, "Im Namen des Führers," 20 Dec. 1938, NA, T-81, 57/60002.
91. Ibid., 60003.
92. OPG, "Im Namen des Führers," 12 Jan. 1939, against Werner Puchta, Werner Görmer, Guido Immerthal, and Kurt Müller, ibid., 60048–60051.
93. OPG, "Im Namen des Führers," 12 Jan. 1939, against Max Ulrich, Emil Schudwitz, Fritz Rückstein, Ernst Kubin, Max Tybussek, and Wilhelm Strysie, ibid., 60033.
94. OPG, "Im Namen des Führers," 9 Feb. 1939, against Hans Aichinger and Walter Kopfgartner, ibid., 60073.
95. OPG, "Im Namen des Führers," 5 Jan. 1939, also against Heinrich Gutt, ibid., 60037. See, moreover, OPG, "Im Namen des Führers," 6 Jan. 1939, against Heinrich Schmidt and Ernst Meckler, ibid., 60040–60047.
96. "Bericht über die Vorgänge," NA, T-988, 216/090737–090738.

97. Quoted in Alexander Bein, "Der jüdische Parasit," *Vierteljahrshefte für Zeitgeschichte*, 12:140 (1965).
98. "Richtlinien für das Verfahren bei der Aufnahme neuer Mitglieder in die NSDAP.," 10 July 1939, NA, T-81, 225/5006111–5006123.
99. OPG to Gaugericht AO, 11 Aug. 1939, NA, T-81, 147/0186523; and Bormann, "Anordnung Nr. 140/39," 14 July 1939, NA, T-988, 216/090820. Dual membership in the NSDAP and the Christian Science religion was also forbidden, see "Rundschreiben Nr. 122/39," 3 June 1939, by Bormann, NA, T-988, 222/095225.
100. "Richtlinien," 10 July 1939, NA, T-81, 225/5006123; and Broszat, *Der Staat Hitlers*, p. 253.

7. EPILOGUE: THE WAR YEARS

1. "Buch," 17–18 July 1945, NA, RG 165.
2. An instance was the Chancellor 1st Class in the German consulate in Valparaiso, Chile, August Knierin. See the OPG to NSDAP Mitgliedschaftsamt, 18 Mar. 1941, NA, T-81, 147/0185938.
3. As in the case of the "provisional member," Gustav Gauerke, a consulate secretary in New York who went over to the United States. See Gaugericht AO, "Ablehnungs-Beschluss," 29 May 1941, NA, T-81, 146/0184931.
4. NSDAP, Deputy Führer, *VOBl,* Nr. 210, July 1940.
5. Baden Gaugericht to the Gau personnel office, 9 Apr. 1942, NA, T-81, 229/5010546.
6. Eugene Davidson, *The Trial of the Germans: An Account of the Twenty-two Defendants before the International Military Tribunal at Nuremberg* (New York, 1966), pp. 44, 46–47; and Hüttenberger, *Die Gauleiter*, pp. 201–202.
7. Hilberg, *Destruction of the European Jews*, p. 86.
8. OPG to the Nuremberg police president (Martin), 12 Dec. 1938, NA, T-81, 57/60355.
9. See the police document "*Betreff*: Besondere Vorfälle bei der Protestaktion gegen die Juden in Nürnberg.," ibid., 60275–60283.
10. "Buch," 17–18 July 1945; and "Franz X. Schwarz," 21 July 1945, NA, RG 165.
11. "Julius Streicher," 2 Sept. 1945, ibid.

12. "Reinwald," 29 Oct. 1945, NA, RG 238.

13. Ibid.

14. Ibid.

15. "Hans Frank," NA, M-679, 1/0473.

16. "Reinwald," 3 Sept. 1945, NA, RG 238.

17. Ibid., 29 Oct. 1945.

18. "Rosenberg," 23 July 1945, NA, RG 165.

19. Dietrich, *Zwölf Jahre*, p. 171; and Helmut Heiber, ed., *Reichsführer!* . . . *Briefe an und von Himmler* (Stuttgart, 1968), p. 109.

20. Himmler to Buch, 14 Apr. 1942, NA, T-175, 125/2650077–2650079.

21. Joseph Goebbels, *The Goebbels Diaries, 1942–1943*, ed. and trans. Louis P. Lochner (New York, 1948), p. 174 (Goebbels's entry for 17 Apr. 1942).

22. Ibid., p. 229 (Goebbels's entry for 23 May 1942).

23. "Walter Buch," 31 Oct. 1945; and "Reinwald," 29 Oct. 1945, NA, RG 238.

24. Goebbels, *Diaries*, p. 229 (Goebbels's entry for 23 May 1942).

25. OPG to Wagner, 12 Oct. 1942, BDC, PK, Folder *Josef Wagner*.

26. "*Richtlinien für die Parteigerichte der NSDAP*: Verfügung des Führers V 22/42 vom 21.11.1942," BA, NS 22/Ordner 877.

27. "Buch," 17–18 July 1945, NA, RG 165.

28. Boberach, *Meldungen aus dem Reich*, pp. 285–286, 344–346.

29. See, for example, Bingen Kreisgericht to GL of Hessen-Nassau (Gaugericht), 15 July 1944, NA, T-81, 166/305914.

30. "Buch," 17–18 July 1945, NA, RG 165. To the author's knowledge, no records of proceedings have survived.

31. Adolf Hitler Schools were special schools established in 1937 for training future party leaders; see Dietrich Orlow, "Die Adolf-Hitler-Schulen," *Vierteljahrshefte für Zeitgeschichte*, 13: 272–284 (1966). The predecessor to the AHS, the *Ordensburgen* ("Castle of the Order"), formed in 1933, became subject to the control of the Parteigerichte in 1936. See OPG, "Anordnung 40/36," 1 Oct. 1936, *Der Parteirichter*, 3/4/5:15 (1937).

32. "Einstweilige Verfügung," 28 Jan. 1944, NA, T-81, 229/5010740–5010741.

33. Emscher-Lippe Kreisgericht, "Beschluss," 7 June 1944, NA, T-81, 166/305902–305908.

34. IMT, *Trial of the Major War Criminals*, 21:260, Document Nr. 8 (see special supplement).

35. The order is referred to in Wagner (GL and Reichsstaathalter of Baden) to Maass, 14 Nov. 1944, NA, T-81, 228/5009865. See also, Jakob Sprenger (Hessen-Nassau GL) to his Kreisleiters, undated, NA, T-988, 257/039888.

36. "Abschrift: Vorlage," 30 Nov. 1944 ("Betrifft: Verhalten des Gauleiters a.D. Frauenfeld, während seines Osteinsatzes als Generalkommissar auf der Krim."), NA, T-175, 125/2650547–2650553.

37. See, for example, "Reichsleiter Buch 60 Jahre Alt," *VB* (Munich ed.), 25 Oct. 1943; and Schirach, *Ich glaubte an Hitler*, p. 296.

38. Bormann to Himmler, 10 Mar. 1942, NA, T-175, 125/2650080. See also "Buch," 31 Oct. 1945, NA, RG 238. Regarding the vast expansion of Bormann's authority, see Hüttenberger, *Die Gauleiter*, pp. 195–213; and Diehl-Thiele, *Partei und Staat*, pp. 216–259.

39. Gerda Bormann to Martin Bormann, 28 Nov. 1943, Trevor-Roper, *The Bormann Letters*, pp. 34–35.

40. "Heinrich Lammers," NA, M-679, 2/0735.

41. Hoegner, *Die verratene Republik*, p. 381; and Gerald Reitlinger, *The SS: Alibi of a Nation, 1922–1945* (New York, 1968), p. 462.

42. "Walter Buch," 5 Sept. 1945, NA, RG 238.

43. Ibid., 31 Oct. 1945.

44. Ibid.

45. See the excerpt of the report of the American military governor, "Courts and Judicial Procedures: German Courts and Military Courts," U.S. Department of State, ed., *Germany, 1947–1949: The Story in Documents* (Washington, D.C., 1950), p. 177.

46. In the words of Friedrich Meinecke, *Die Deutsche Katastrophe: Betrachtungen und Erinnerungen* (Wiesbaden, 1946).

47. Note Goebbels's admission of this, Goebbels, *Diaries*, p. 174 (his entry for 17 Apr. 1942).

Bibliography

I. UNPUBLISHED SOURCES

Berlin Document Center, Berlin (BDC)
Oberstes Parteigericht (OPG)
Parteikorrespondenz (PK)
Persönlicher Stab Reichsführer-SS Schriftgutverwaltung
Sammlung Schumacher (Slg. Schu.)

Bundesarchiv, Koblenz (BA)
NS 22   Reichsorganisationsleitung der NSDAP
NS 26   NSDAP Hauptarchiv
NS 36   Untersuchungs- u. Schlichtungsausschuss, Reichsleitung

Institut für Zeitgeschichte, Munich (IfZ)
ED 1/1-2 Aufzeichnen Gen. d. Inf. a.D. Curt Liebmann, 1922–
         1959
F 28   Dr. Korn, Private Dokumente, 1927–1938
MA 108   Reichsjustizministerium

National Archives, Washington, D.C. (NA)
Microcopy M-679   Records of the Department of State Special
                   Interrogation Mission to Germany, 1945–
                   1946
Microcopy T-70   Records of the Reich Ministry for Public
                   Enlightenment and Propaganda
Microcopy T-81   Records of the National Socialist German
                   Labor Party
Microcopy T-175   Records of the Reich Leader of the SS and
                   Chief of the German Police
Microcopy T-253   Records of Private German Individuals

Microcopy T-988   World War II War Crimes Records: Prosecution Exhibits Submitted to the International Military Tribunal
Record Group 165   War Department Historical (Schuster) Mission
Record Group 238   Collection of World War II War Crimes Records (Nuremberg)

II. PUBLISHED SOURCES: NEWSPAPERS, JOURNALS, YEARBOOKS, AND BIOGRAPHICAL HANDBOOKS

Newspapers

Augsburger Postzeitung
Deutsche Volkszeitung (Nuremberg)
Fränkische Tageszeitung (Nuremberg)
Münchener Post (MP)
Münchner Neueste Nachrichten
Völkischer Beobachter (Berlin, Munich) *(VB)*

Journals

Nationalsozialistische Monatshefte: Zentrale Politische und Kulturelle Zeitschrift der NSDAP
Der Parteirichter: Amtliches Mitteilungsblatt des Obersten Parteigerichts
Der Schlesische Erzieher
Verordnungsblatt der Reichsleitung der Nationalsozialistischen Deutschen Arbeiter-Partei (VOBl)

Yearbooks

Nationalsozialistisches Jahrbuch

Biographical Handbooks

Das Deutsche Führerlexikon, 1934/1935. Berlin, 1935.
Reichstagshandbuch, 1932. Edited by the Bureau of the Reichstag. Berlin, 1933.

III. PUBLISHED SOURCES: MEMOIRS, DIARIES, PAMPHLETS, AND DOCUMENTARY COLLECTIONS

Memoirs and Diaries

Bouhler, Philip. *Kampf um Deutschland.* Berlin, 1939.
Brüning, Heinrich. *Memoiren, 1918–1934.* Stuttgart, 1970.
Dietrich, Otto. *Mit Hitler in die Macht.* 26th ed. Munich, 1938.

————. *Zwölf Jahre mit Hitler*. Cologne, n.d.

Frank, Hans. *Im Angesicht des Galgens: Deutung Hitlers und seiner Zeit auf Grund eigener Erlebnisse und Erkenntnisse.* Munich, 1953.

Goebbels, Joseph. *The Goebbels Diaries, 1942–1943.* Edited and translated by Louis P. Lochner. Garden City, N.Y., 1948.

————. "Das Tagebuch von Joseph Goebbels, 1925/26." Edited by Helmut Heiber. In *Schriftenreihe der Vierteljahrshefte für Zeitgeschichte,* 9:1–141 (1961).

————. *Vom Kaiserhof zur Reichskanzlei.* 35th ed. Munich, 1942.

Göring, Hermann. *Aufbau einer Nation.* Berlin, 1934.

Hillgruber, Andreas, ed. *Henry Picker: Hitlers Tischgespräche im Führerhauptquartier, 1941–42.* Munich, 1968.

Hitler, Adolf. *Mein Kampf.* 2 vols. 16th ed. Munich, 1933.

Hoegner, Wilhelm. *Die verratene Republik: Geschichte der deutschen Gegenrevolution.* Munich, 1958.

Krebs, Albert. *Tendenzen und Gestalten der NSDAP: Erinnerungen an die Frühzeit der Partei.* Stuttgart, 1959.

Lüdecke, Kurt. *I Knew Hitler: The Story of a Nazi Who Escaped the Blood Purge.* New York, 1937.

Rauschning, Hermann. *The Voice of Destruction.* New York, 1940.

Röhm, Ernst. *Die Geschichte eines Hochverräters.* 5th ed. Munich, 1934.

Schirach, Baldur von. *Ich glaubte an Hitler.* Hamburg, 1967.

Stampfer, Friedrich. *Erfahrungen und Erkenntnisse: Aufzeichnungen aus meinem Leben.* Cologne, 1957.

Strasser, Otto. *Hitler und Ich.* Constance, 1948.

————. *Mein Kampf: Eine Politische Autobiografie.* Frankfurt/Main, 1969.

Pamphlets

Buch, Walter. *Ehre und Recht.* Munich, 1932.

————. *Des nationalsozialistischen Menschen Ehre und Ehrenschutz.* Munich, 1939.

Frank, Hans. *Neues deutsches Recht.* Vol. 2 of *Hier spricht das neue Deutschland!* Munich, 1934.

Documentary Collections

Boberach, Heinz, ed. *Meldungen aus dem Reich: Auswahl aus*

*den geheimen Lageberichten des Sicherheitsdienstes der SS,
1939–1944.* Munich, 1968.

Deuerlein, Ernst, ed. *Der Aufstieg der NSDAP in Augenzeugenberichten, 1919–1933.* Düsseldorf, 1968.

Göring, Hermann. *Reden und Aufsätze.* Munich, 1938.

Haidn, C., and Fischer, L. *Das Recht der NSDAP.* 3d ed.
Munich, 1938.

Heiber, Helmut, ed. *Reichsführer!* ... *Briefe an und von Himmler.* Stuttgart, 1968.

Hitler, Adolf. *Hitler: Reden und Proklamationen, 1932–1945.*
Vol. 1: *Triumph: 1932–1938.* Edited by Max Domarus.
Munich, 1965.

———. *Reden des Führers: Politik und Propaganda Adolf Hitlers, 1922–1945.* Edited by Erhard Klöss. Munich, 1967.

International Military Tribunal. Vol. 21 of *Trial of the Major
War Criminals.* Nuremberg, 1947–1949.

Jochmann, Werner, ed. *Nationalsozialismus und Revolution:
Ursprung und Geschichte der NSDAP in Hamburg, 1922–
33 (Dokumente).* Frankfurt/Main, 1963.

Michaelis, H.; Schraepler, E.; and Scheel, G. *Die Weimarer Republik: Das kritische Jahr 1923.* Vol. 5 of *Ursachen und
Folgen: Vom deutschen Zusammenbruch 1918 und 1945 bis
zur staatlichen Neuordnung Deutschlands in der Gegenwart.*
Berlin, 1958.

Reichsgesetzblatt. Edited by the Reich Ministry of the Interior.
Berlin, 1933, 1935.

*Richtlinien: Auszug aus der Satzung und Geschäftsordnung für
die Parteigerichte.* Edited by the Reichsleitung. Munich,
1934.

Trevor-Roper, H. R., ed. *The Bormann Letters: The Private
Correspondence between Martin Bormann and His Wife
from January 1943 to April 1945.* Translated by R. H.
Stevens. London, 1954.

Tyrell, Albrecht, ed. *Führer befiehl: Selbstzeugnisse aus der
"Kampfzeit" der NSDAP.* Düsseldorf, 1969.

U.S. Department of State. *Germany 1947–1949: The Story in
Documents.* Washington, D.C., 1950.

IV. PUBLISHED SOURCES: SECONDARY ACCOUNTS

Abel, Theodore. *The Nazi Movement: Why Hitler Came to
Power.* New York, 1966.

Allen, William S. *The Nazi Seizure of Power: The Experience of a Single German Town, 1930–1935.* Chicago, 1965.

Arendt, Hannah. *The Origins of Totalitarianism.* 2d ed. New York, 1958.

Bein, Alexander. "Der jüdische Parasit," *Vierteljahrshefte für Zeitgeschichte,* 13:121–149 (1965).

Bennecke, Heinrich. *Hitler und die SA.* Munich, 1962.

———. *Die Reichswehr und der "Röhm-Putsch."* Munich, 1964.

Bracher, Karl. *Die deutsche Diktatur: Entstehung, Struktur, Folgen des Nationalsozialismus.* Cologne, 1969.

———; Sauer, Wolfgang; and Schulz, Gerhard. *Die nationalsozialistische Machtergreifung: Studien zur Errichtung des totalitären Herrschaftssystems in Deutschland, 1933/34.* 2d ed. Cologne, 1962.

Broszat, Martin. "Die Anfänge der Berliner NSDAP, 1926/27," *Vierteljahrshefte für Zeitgeschichte,* 8:85–118 (1960).

———. "Zur Perversion der Strafjustiz im Dritten Reich," *Vierteljahrshefte für Zeitgeschichte,* 6:390–443 (1958).

———; Jacobsen, Hans-Adolf; and Krausnick, Helmut, eds. *Konzentrationslager, Kommissarbefehl, Judenverfolgung.* Vol. 2 of *Anatomie des SS-Staates.* Edited by Hans Buchheim. Freiburg, 1965.

———. *Der Staat Hitlers: Grundlegung und Entwicklung seiner inneren Verfassung.* Munich, 1969.

Buchheim, Hans. "Die SS in der Verfassung des Dritten Reiches," *Vierteljahrshefte für Zeitgeschichte,* 3:127–157 (1955).

Bullock, Alan. *Hitler: A Study in Tyranny.* New York, 1961.

Chanady, Attila. "The Disintegration of the German National Peoples' Party, 1924–1930," *Journal of Modern History,* 39: 65–91 (1967).

Davidson, Eugene. *The Trial of the Germans: An Account of the Twenty-two Defendants before the International Military Tribunal at Nuremberg.* New York, 1966.

Dickmann, Fritz. "Die Regierungsbildung in Thüringen als Modell der Machtergreifung: Ein Brief Hitlers aus dem Jahre 1930," *Vierteljahrshefte für Zeitgeschichte,* 14:454–464 (1966).

Diehl-Thiele, Peter. *Partei und Staat im Dritten Reich: Untersuchungen zum Verhältnis von NSDAP und allgemeiner innerer Staatsverwaltung, 1933–1945.* Munich, 1969.

231

Erdmann, Karl. *Die Zeit der Weltkriege*. Vol. 4 of *Handbuch der deutschen Geschichte*. Edited by Bruno Gebhardt. 8th ed. Stuttgart, 1959.

Eyck, Erich. *From the Collapse of the Empire to Hindenburg's Election*. Vol. 1 of *A History of the Weimar Republic*. Translated by Harlan P. Hanson and Robert G. L. Waite. New York, 1970.

————. *From the Locarno Conference to Hitler's Seizure of Power*. Vol. 2 of *A History of the Weimar Republic*. Translated by Harlan P. Hanson and Robert G. L. Waite. New York, 1970.

Fabricius, Hans. *Geschichte der Nationalsozialistischen Bewegung*. 2d ed. Berlin, 1937.

Fearnside, W. Ward. "Three Innovations of National Socialist Jurisprudence," *Journal of Central European Affairs*, 16: 146–155 (1956).

Fest, Joachim. *Das Gesicht des Dritten Reiches: Profile einer totalitären Herrschaft*. Munich, 1963.

Flechtheim, Ossip K. *Die KPD in der Weimarer Republik*. Frankfurt/Main, 1969.

Franz-Willing, Georg. *Die Hitlerbewegung: Der Ursprung, 1919–1922*. Hamburg, 1962.

The German Reich and Americans of German Origin. New York, 1938.

Görlitz, Walter, and Quint, Herbert. *Adolf Hitler: Eine Biografie*. Stuttgart, 1952.

Gordon, Harold J., Jr. *Hitler and the Beer Hall Putsch*. Princeton, N.J., 1972.

Halperin, S. William. *Germany Tried Democracy: A Political History of the Reich from 1918 to 1933*. New York, 1946.

Heiber, Helmut. "Aus den Akten des Gauleiters Kube," *Vierteljahrshefte für Zeitgeschichte*, 4:67–92 (1956).

————. "Der Fall Grünspan," *Vierteljahrshefte für Zeitgeschichte*, 5:134–172 (1957).

————. *Goebbels*. Translated by John K. Dickinson. New York, 1972.

Heiden, Konrad. *Adolf Hitler: Das Zeitalter der Verantwortungslosigkeit*. Zurich, 1936.

————. *Der Fuehrer: Hitler's Rise to Power*. Translated by Ralph Manheim. Boston, 1944.

————. *A History of National Socialism*. New York, 1935.

Hilberg, Raul. *The Destruction of the European Jews.* Chicago, 1961.

Höhne, Heinz. *Der Orden unter dem Totenkopf: Die Geschichte der SS.* Gütersloh, 1967.

Hofmann, Hanns. *Der Hitlerputsch: Krisenjahre deutscher Geschichte, 1920–1924.* Munich, 1961.

Horn, Wolfgang. *Führerideologie und Parteiorganisation in der NSDAP (1919–1933).* Düsseldorf, 1972.

Huber, Englebert. *Das ist Nationalsozialismus: Organisation und Weltanschauung der NSDAP.* Stuttgart, 1934.

Hüttenberger, Peter. *Die Gauleiter: Studie zum Wandel des Machtgefüges in der NSDAP.* Stuttgart, 1969.

Jacobsen, Hans-Adolf. *Nationalsozialistische Aussenpolitik, 1933–1938.* Frankfurt/Main, 1968.

Kele, Max H. *Nazis and Workers: National Socialist Appeals to German Labor, 1919–1933.* Chapel Hill, N.C., 1972.

Kern, Erich. *Adolf Hitler und das Dritte Reich.* Oldendorf, 1971.

Kühnl, Reinhard. *Die nationalsozialistische Linke, 1925–1930.* Meisenheim/Glan, 1966.

————. "Zur Programmatik der Nationalsozialistischen Linken: Das Strasser-Programm von 1925–1926," *Vierteljahrshefte für Zeitgeschichte,* 14:317–333 (1966).

Layton, Roland V., Jr. "The *Völkischer Beobachter,* 1920–1933: The Nazi Party Newspaper in the Weimar Era," *Central European History,* 3:353–383 (1970).

Lebovics, Herman. *Social Conservatism and the Middle Classes in Germany, 1914–1933.* Princeton, N.J., 1969.

Lingg, Anton. *Die Verwaltung der Nationalsozialistischen Deutschen Arbeiterpartei.* Munich, 1939.

Lohalm, Uwe. *Völkischer Radikalismus: Die Geschichte des Deutschvölkischen Schutz- und Trutz-Bundes, 1919–1923.* Hamburg, 1970.

McGovern, James. *Martin Bormann.* New York, 1968.

Manvell, Roger, and Fraenkel, Heinrich. *Himmler.* New York, 1965.

Maser, Werner. *Die Frühgeschichte der NSDAP: Hitlers Weg bis 1924.* Frankfurt/Main, 1965.

Mason, John Brown. "The Judicial System of the Nazi Party," *American Political Science Review,* 38:96–103 (1944).

233

Mason, T. W. "Labour in the Third Reich, 1933–1939," *Past and Present*, No. 33, pp. 112–141 (Apr. 1966).

Meinecke, Friedrich. *Die Deutsche Katastrophe: Betrachtungen und Erinnerungen.* Wiesbaden, 1946.

Noakes, Jeremy. "Conflict and Development in the NSDAP 1924–1927," *Journal of Contemporary History*, 1:3–37 (Oct. 1966).

———. *The Nazi Party in Lower Saxony, 1921–1933.* London, 1971.

Nogee, Joseph L., ed. *Man, State, and Society in the Soviet Union.* New York, 1972.

Nolte, Ernst. *Der Faschismus in seiner Epoche.* 2d ed. Munich, 1965.

———. *Die Krise des liberalen Systems und die faschistischen Bewegungen.* Munich, 1968.

Nyomarkay, Joseph. *Charisma and Factionalism in the Nazi Party.* Minneapolis, Minn., 1967.

———. "Factionalism in the National Socialist German Workers' Party, 1925–26: The Myth and Reality of the 'Northern Faction,'" *Political Science Quarterly*, 80:22–47 (1965).

Olden, Rudolf. *Hitler.* Translated by Walter Ettinghausen. New York, 1936.

Orlow, Dietrich. "Die Adolf-Hitler-Schulen," *Vierteljahrshefte für Zeitgeschichte*, 13:272–284 (1965).

———. "The Conversion of Myths into Political Power: The Case of the Nazi Party, 1925–1926," *American Historical Review*, 72:906–924 (1967).

———. *The History of the Nazi Party: 1919–1933.* Pittsburgh, Pa., 1969.

———. *The History of the Nazi Party: 1933–1945.* Pittsburgh, Pa., 1973.

———. "The Organizational History and Structure of the NSDAP, 1919–23," *Journal of Modern History*, 37:208–226 (1965).

Peterson, E. N. "The Bureaucracy and the Nazi Party," *Review of Politics*, 28:172–192 (1966).

———. *The Limits of Hitler's Power*, Princeton, N.J., 1969.

Reitlinger, Gerald. *The SS: Alibi of a Nation, 1922–1945.* New York, 1968.

Rühle, Gerd. *Die Kampfjahre, 1918–1933.* Vol. 1 of *Das Dritte*

Reich: Dokumentarische Darstellung des Aufbaues der Nation. Berlin, 1936.

Scheffler, Wolfgang. *Judenverfolgung im Dritten Reich.* Berlin, 1964.

Schmidt-Pauli, Edgar von. *Die Männer um Hitler.* Berlin, 1933.

Schmiedchen, Johannes. *Führer durch den Nationalsozialismus.* Berlin, 1933.

Schoenbaum, David. *Hitler's Social Revolution: Class and Status in Nazi Germany, 1933–1939.* Garden City, N.Y., 1966.

Schorn, Hubert, *Der Richter im Dritten Reich: Geschichte und Dokumente.* Frankfurt/Main, 1959.

Scott, William G. *The Management of Conflict: Appeal Systems in Organizations.* Homewood, Ill., 1965.

Sontheimer, Kurt. *Antidemokratisches Denken in der Weimarer Republik: Die politischen Ideen des deutschen Nationalismus zwischen 1918 und 1933.* Munich, 1968.

Staff, Ilse. *Justiz im Dritten Reich: Eine Dokumentation.* Frankfurt/Main, 1964.

Turner, Henry Ashby, Jr. "Big Business and the Rise of Hitler," *American Historical Review,* 75:56–70 (1969).

Vogelsang, Thilo. *Reichswehr, Staat und NSDAP: Beiträge zur deutschen Geschichte, 1930–1932.* Stuttgart, 1962.

Volz, Hans. *Daten der Geschichte der NSDAP.* 9th ed. Berlin, 1939.

Waite, Robert G. L. *Vanguard of Nazism: The Free Corps Movement in Postwar Germany, 1918–1923.* New York, 1969.

Wheaton, Eliot Barculo. *Prelude to Calamity: The Nazi Revolution, 1933–35.* Garden City, New York, 1968.

Wheeler-Bennett, J. W. *The Nemesis of Power: The German Army in Politics, 1918–1945.* Compass ed. New York, 1967.

Index

Act for the Securing of the Unity
of Party and State: decreed,
118–119, 121; Second, 136
Adolf Hitler Schools, 225 n.31
agrarian policy, 115–116
Amann, Max: appointed party
secretary, 12; in charge of *Völkischer Beobachter*, 20; not
prosecuted, 176; mentioned, 4,
7, 59, 60, 131, 179
anti-Semitism: Buch's, 54–58, 63;
NSDAP, 111–113, 133, 139. *See
also* Jews
AO. *See* Auslands-Organisation
("Foreign Countries Organization")
Arbeiter, Bauern, Soldaten, 94
archive, party, 11
Auslands-Abteilung ("Foreign
Department"), 76
Auslands-Organisation ("Foreign
Countries Organization"): procedure and policy, 158–159;
mentioned, 142
—Gaugericht: keeps tabs on diplomats, 142–143; its relation to
OPG, 158; its use of Gestapo,
172

Baden: hostility in, 59; 1930
elections in, 86; NSDAP in,
109

Badische Wochenzeitung, 58, 59
Bahr, Paul, 155
Bavaria: and failure of 1923
Putsch, 14–15; NSDAP banned
in, 17; ban lifted, 19–20; 1932
elections in, 102; NSDAP take-
over in, 109–110
Bavarian Peoples' Party (Bay-
erische Volkspartei), 110
Bavaria-Swabia, Upper, 70
Bayerische Volkspartei ("Bavarian
Peoples' Party"), 110
Bayreuth Gaugericht, 183
BAZ. See *Berliner Arbeiterzeitung*
Behr, Karl, 182–183
Bell, Georg, 100, 128–129
Berlin: NSDAP banned in, 44–45.
See also Putsch of 8–9 November
1923; Stennes, Walter
Berliner Arbeiterzeitung:
threatened by *Der Angriff*, 46,
72, 84–85
Berliner Tageblatt, 45, 47
Berlin Gau-Uschla, 85, 95
Berlin Ortsgruppe, 33
"black list," 143
black shirts. *See* Schutzstaffeln
Böck, Ludwig, 127–128
Bohle, Ernst, 143, 158, 159
Bormann, Gerda (Buch), 61, 144–
145, 184–185
Bormann, Martin: sees Hitler,

239

establishing party order, 9; wounded, 60; and Stennes rebellion, 91; and Brandenburg dispute, 93; given authority in Prussia, 108; his role in SA purge, 129; his response to Kristallnacht, 163, 164; requested to halt state court proceedings, 168; his Luftwaffe, 171; and removal of Streicher, 173–174; mentioned, 4, 7, 94, 115, 131, 139, 160

Goss, Anton, 31–32

Grabow, Hans, 141

Gradl, Georg: and expulsion case, 127–128; mentioned, 39–40

Graf, Ulrich: appointed to Reichs-Uschla, 26, 28–29; with OPG, 118; mentioned, 67, 74, 99

Grauert, Dr. Ludwig, 139–140, 144

Greater German People's Community (Grossdeutsche Volksgemeinschaft), 18, 20, 28

Grimm, Wilhelm: appointed to Reichs-Uschla, 99; given Reichsleiter status, 108; with OPG, 118; and importance of racial purity, 133

Grossdeutsche Volksgemeinschaft ("Greater German People's Community"): develops, 18; defunct, 20; mentioned, 28

Grünspan, Herschel, 161

GRUSA. See Grundsätzliche Anordnungen der SA

Guttemplerorden ("Independent Order of Good Templars"), 148

Halle-Merseburg Gau, 33

Hallermann, Georg, 73

Hamburg: elections in, 97; NSDAP in, 109

Hanover-Brunswick, 70

Hasenörhl, Franz, 159

Heinemann, Bruno: used as troubleshooter, 9; first Reichs-Uschla chairman, 26; chairman of National Committee for Organization, 26–27; used to assert Munich supremacy, 30; role in Gaus' dissensions, 32–33; retires, 36, 50, 51; and Dinter quarrel, 37–38; and ruling on Pfeffer, 41–44; his role in Strasser-Goebbels feud, 46–47; replaced in Organisationausschuss, 50; Hitler's friction with, 61; his conflict with Pfeffer, 82; mentioned, 7, 29

Helldorf, Count Wolf von, 181

Hess, Alfred, 158

Hess, Rudolf: sees Hitler, 4–5; and Strasser-Goebbels quarrel, 46–47; and dissension in Nuremberg, 70; on effect of expulsion, 115; and Parteigerichte directive, 120–121; gathers materials against Röhm, 128–129; in competition with Ley, 131–132; instructed to enforce traffic regulations, 137; investigates party resignations of civil servants, 140; and issue of "double jeopardy," 143–144; questions Kube, 145; deals with Parteigerichte appeals, 147; command on recruitment and acceptance, 148; and Kristallnacht, 163; attends Streicher hearings, 174; flies to England, 175; mentioned, 7, 73, 113, 146, 155

Hessen, 97, 109

Heydrich, Reinhard: his role in SA purge, 129; and AO court, 159–160; and Kristallnacht, 162, 163; mentioned, 55

242

London party group, 158
Low Countries, 171
Lübeck: elections in, 86; NSDAP in, 109
Lüdecke, Kurt: his *I Knew Hitler,* 142–143
Ludendorff, Erich Friedrich Wilhelm von: in elections, 19; heads Tannenberg-Bund, 30–31; and Saxony dissension, 32
Lutze, Victor: named Osaf, 129–130; and Kristallnacht proceedings, 164

Maass, Paul, 156
Magdeburg, 125–126
Marxism: compared to Naziism, 4; as threat to Naziism, 58
Mergenthaler, Christian, 67
Meyer, Alfred, 139
Meyer-Quade, Joachim, 75
Militant Association (Kampfbund), 13, 14, 15
Ministry for People's Enlightenment and Propaganda, 140–141
Moulin-Eckart, Count du, 100, 128, 129
Müller, Hermann, 86
Munchener Post, 100
Munder, Eugen: forced to resign, 67; requests readmittance, 113
Munich: 1923 Putsch in, 14; political parties and organizations in, 194 n.26
Munich Ortsgruppe: establishing supremacy of, 19, 30
Murr, Wilhelm, 55
Mutschmann, Martin: appointed Gauleiter, 20; and dissension in Saxony, 30–33; mentioned, 7

National Committee for Organization (Organisationsausschuss), 26, 50
National Socialist Factory Cells Organization (NS-Betriebszellenorganisation), 111
National Socialist German Workers' Party. *See* Nationalsozialistische Deutsche Arbeiterpartei
National Socialist Letters (NS-Briefe), 29, 44
National Socialist Working Association (Nationalsozialistische Arbeitsgemeinschaft), 29, 44, 85
Nationalsozialistische Arbeitsgemeinschaft ("National Socialist Working Association"), 29, 44, 85
Nationalsozialistische Auskunft ("Information Department"), 103
Nationalsozialistische Deutsche Arbeiterpartei ("National Socialist German Workers' Party"): methods of handling internal strife in, 1–2, 35, 186–187, 188; statutes, 5; heterogeneity of, 6–7; predecessors of Parteigerichte in, 9–10; leadership of, 11–12; first Reichsparteitag, 13; banned after Putsch, 17; factions develop in, 18; membership of, 18, 48–49, 65–66, 87, 97, 98; function of Gauleiters in, 20–21; Uschla structure in, 22; code of honor of, 23; membership regulations, 25, 65, 71; no double memberships, 31, 98; restructuring, 34–35, 48–49; control of, and Strasser-Goebbels quarrel, 46–47; changed image of, 49–50; and role of Reichs-Uschla, 51–52; deputies and members of legislature, 66; in 1928 elections, 70–71; in 1930 elections, 86–87; and handling of Stennes revolt, 91; in Landtag elections, 97; dissension and frustration in

1932, 101–102; in 1932 elections, 101–102; its drive for power, 103; seizes power, 107; in 1933 Reichstag election, 109; flooded with membership applications, 110–114; its "racial purity," 111–113, 133, 139, 188; significance of membership in, 114; expulsion from, 114–115, 123–127; declared only legal party, 115; its relationship to state, 115, 118, 125; interferes with government and state courts, 126; after Röhm purge, 130; Parteigerichte power over, 136; civil-service members of, 139–140, 142-144; preachers in, 146; membership supervision, 147–149; embezzlement and slander quarrels in, 154–155; membership in, for foreign Germans, 158–159; its response to Kristallnacht, 163, 168–169; new membership directive for, 169–170; its agreement with Wehrmacht, 171–172; its members during war, 172–173; protection of its leaders, 175–178; condones corruption, 176–177; duties of members, 182–183; handling discord in, 186–187, 188

Nationalsozialistische Kraftfahrer-Korps ("Nazi Motorized Corps"), 122, 136, 171–172

Nazi Frauenschaft ("women's auxiliary"), 136

Nazi Motorized Corps (Nationalsozialistische Kraftfahrer-Korps), 122, 136, 171–172

Nazi party. *See* Nationalsozialistische Deutsche Arbeiterpartei

Nazi Student Association (NS-Studentenbund), 94, 136

Neue Front, 72

New York party group, 158

Nicolai, Dr. Helmut: in dispute with Loeper, 125–126; mentioned, 7

Nieland, Dr. Hans, 76

Norgall, Franz, 166

NSAG. *See* Nationalsozialistische Arbeitsgemeinschaft

NS-Arztebund (Doctor's League), 136

NS-Betriebszellenorganisation ("National Socialist Factory Cells Organization"), 111

NS-Briefe ("National Socialist Letters"), 29, 44

NS-Bund deutscher Techniker (League of German Technicians), 136

NSDAP. *See* Nationalsozialistische Deutsche Arbeiterpartei

NSDStB. *See* NS-Studentenbund

NSKK. *See* Nationalsozialistische Kraftfahrer-Korps

NS-Kriegsopferversorgung ("War Victims Society"), 136

NS-Lehrerbund ("Teachers' League"), 136

NS-Studentenbund ("Nazi Student Association"), 94, 136

NS-Volkswohlfahrt ("Welfare Association"), 136, 150

Nuremberg, 39, 173–174

Nuremberg Ortsgruppe: disorder in, 67, 69–70

Oberste SA-Führer (Osaf). *See* Lutze, Victor; Röhm, Ernst

Oberste SA-Führung (OSAF): relationship of, with Reichs-Uschla, 82–83; Brandenburg SA complains to, 93; informed of proceedings against SA, 164; mentioned, 91, 96

Oberstes Parteigericht ("Supreme party court"): Reichs-Uschla becomes, 117, 119; structure of, 118; jurisdiction of, 122–123; increasing secrecy of, 130; role

248

Rio de Janeiro party group, 158
Röhm, Ernst: and Führer's procrastination, 6; as Hitler's follower, 12; leads Freedom Party, 18; organizes Frontbann, 31; commissioned SA chief of staff, 81-82; plans new SA-Uschla directive, 87–88; demands obedience from Stennes, 89; influence of, 96; attack on, 99–100, 101, 128–129; mentioned, 7, 28, 91, 93, 122, 130, 145
Rosenberg, Alfred: as Hitler's follower, 12; and GDVG, 18, 28; in charge of *Völkischer Beobachter*, 20; and NSAG, 30; on protection of party, 178; mentioned, 7, 60, 131
Rotary Club, 148
Rote Hakenkreuz ("Red Swastika"), 50
Ruhr: French occupation of, 14
Ruhr Gau, 40–42, 73
Rust, Bernhard: in NSAG, 29; mentioned, 7, 131, 133

SA. *See* Sturmabteilung
Sachverständigenbeirat für Bevolkerungs- und Rassepolitik ("Council of Experts on Population and Race Policy"), 130
San Francisco party group, 158
Sauckel, Fritz: replaces Dinter, 36–38; mentioned, 55, 131
Saxony: revolution attempted in, 14; dissension in, 30–32; 1930 elections in, 86; NSDAP in, 109
Scandinavia, 171
Schaumburg-Lippe, 97
Schilgen, Josef, 155
Schlange, Ernst: appointed Gauleiter, 20, 33, 92, 93; replaced, 44
Schleicher, General Kurt von, 104, 128

Schleswig-Holstein, 70
Schlichtungs-Ausschuss ("Conciliation Committee"), 9–10, 21
Schneider, Ludwig: with OPG, 118; and importance of racial purity, 133; becomes head of OPG 1st chamber, 141; hears Streicher case, 174; recommends stronger punishments, 177; hears Wagner case, 178–179; ordered removed, 179; mentioned, 176
Schüler, Bruno, 113
Schulz, Paul, 100, 101, 145
Schutzstaffeln (Protection Squads): development of, 12; relationship of, with Uschlas, 21, 81, 87, 95-96; motto, 23; Buch serves in, 61; membership, 87, 111; and Stennes revolt, 89, 91; assume control of police in Prussia, 108; as Hilfspolizei, 108, 109; and Parteigerichte jurisdiction, 122–123; as vehicle of intimidation, 126; conduct SA purge, 128–129; Buch's difficulties with, 129–130; investigate Frau Buch, 145; protection for members of, 149–150; in Kristallnacht persecution, 161–167; conflicts of, with soldiers, 171; mentioned, 136
Schwarz, Franz Xavier: party treasurer, 12, 20; and GDVG, 18; audits party organizations, 34; and conspiracy against Röhm, 100, 101; works with membership applications, 111; and party's insurance program, 137; investigates Lüdecke, 142–143; Ley's criticism of, 147; his membership ceiling, 147, 169; investigates Wolff swindle, 149–150; mentioned, 7, 131, 145
SD. *See* Sicherheitsdienst
Secret State Police. *See* Geheime Staatspolizei (Gestapo)

251

Weimar Republic, 13, 14, 56–57
Welfare Association (NS-Volks-
wohlfahrt), 136, 150
Wells, Otto, 110
Welt am Abend, 45, 46, 47
Weser-Ems, 70
Westdeutscher Beobachter, 68
Wolbert, Eugen, 173
Wolff, Karl, 149–150
women's auxiliary (Nazi Frauen-
schaft), 136
Württemberg, 67, 109

Württemberg-Hohenzollern
Gaugericht, 154
Wystrack, Hans, 199 n.54

Zander, Elsbeth, 50, 73
Zech, Graf von, 139
Zehnle, Herbert, 182
Zentrum Partei ("Catholic Center
Party"): officials removed, 108;
and passage of Enabling Law,
110; mentioned, 86, 125
Ziegler, H. S., 37–38